FROM
THE
CHRIST MIND

BOOK II

FROM
THE
CHRIST MIND

BOOK II

Jesus of Nazareth

Memoir
B O O K S
Chico, CA

From the Christ Mind, Book II
Copyright © 2015 by Darrell Morley Price

ISBN: 978-1-937748-23-4
Library of Congress Control Number 2015943408
First Edition

Memoir Books
An Imprint of Heidelberg Graphics
2 Stansbury Court
Chico, California 95928

Send inquiries to
Darrell Morley Price
P.O. Box 4123
Chico, Calif. 95927

Contents

Without the Teachers of God, there would be no salvation.
They give form to the lessons the Holy Spirit teaches.
They represent the Truth in all They say, do, and think.
The way stands open before Them.
Everyone will join Them in time.
Why wait?

Foreword

This is the second book in the *From the Christ Mind* series. Together they are meant to be a later day supplement to the incomparable teaching that is *A Course in Miracles*. Like the Course, the teaching presented in these pages emanates from the Mind of Jesus of Nazareth. I have written down the teaching as I have received it; and there has been a careful process of editing and arranging the material, always guided by Jesus. Always we have tried to make the teaching as clear as possible; yet it still requires the active engagement of the mind of the reader. Communication in the world of separation always requires the joining of two or more minds.

I suggest you read the words slowly, a few sentences at a time. You need not rush; eternity is always here and now and awaits only your recognition and readiness. The words are presented in a way that will both open the mind to the Truth they are representing, and lead the mind, if you allow it, to a new way of thinking and understanding.

I pray this teaching will be of value to all who read these pages, and that it may help you on your spiritual journey through the world of dreams and back to your Creator.

Any errors of content or in the expression of this material are mine and mine only. For that, I ask the reader's forbearance and forgiveness.

May God bless you and keep you, and I pray that you may soon awaken as the Self, the Christ, that you have always been. Thank you. Thank you, Father.

Darrell Morley Price
Chico, California
May 2015

CHAPTER ONE

Salvation

Whenever is the time, and wherever you are is the place to find Truth. Truth is not somewhere else far away, a something that must be diligently sought. It is closer to you than your own heartbeat. There is no distance that separates you from the Truth at this very moment. How can there be a gap between Truth and illusion, between what exists and what does not? The ego would have you believe such a gap exists, for the ego must maintain a sense of separation in your mind, a belief that you are separate from the Truth here and now. Thus must Truth be a future goal to be reached, waiting always somewhere far ahead, never immediate or present. To live in time and bypass the present by projecting a future result, is to be an ego whose real concern is to maintain separation and postpone the realization of Truth indefinitely.

The awakening to Truth is the disappearance of the ego, the sense of a separate self. A self that is separate from the world and everything in it, seemingly complete in itself, is in fact the denial of the Self created by God, and a very effective defense against it.

Do you understand salvation, what it is and its requirements? Salvation is the freeing of your mind from the effects of its errors of thought, the correction of all false ideas and beliefs and the subsequent transformation of experience. Salvation is the process of spiritual awakening. What must you do to be saved? Do you want to be saved? Surely you realize that to attain a goal, you must desire it, have some understanding of it, and make an effective and consistent effort to reach it. Some discipline is always required to accomplish anything in the world of form.

Salvation is the purpose of *A Course in Miracles,* the goal towards which the mind training is directed. Its purpose is accomplished through the healing of the mind, the correction of all error that the mind be empty, ready, and able to receive the Truth. The mind that has accepted, has attained salvation, is free of fear and resting in the Self. Now it can offer salvation to all its brothers, for salvation is accepted for all and freely given that it may be shared.

What has as its purpose the liberation of the mind from all bondage, from the tyranny of the ego and the darkness of ignorance, cannot but succeed for its purpose is total and uncompromising. All the Power of God is contained within the desire for salvation. That is the only desire arising from the mind of separation that is whole and true, and has as its aim to leave illusion behind forever and return to what is only true. This desire, this inspiration to return to your Father, is the gift of the Holy Spirit, Who has been holding it for you since time began. He joyfully offers it to you when you are ready, and through your acceptance is salvation assured. When may be unknown, the circumstances not yet clear, yet through your sincere desire for salvation, it is given you.

What is the price to be paid for salvation? Only the giving up of what was never true. The release of all attachment to fear, sin, and guilt. The relinquishment of the need to attack and defend, to suffer and die. Can this be a sacrifice? Letting go of all limitation, of everything that ever caused you pain? Is the return to a real state of sanity, joy, happiness, freedom and Love, anything but highly desirable?

If you could truly see the state you are actually in without confusion and denial; if you could see what salvation offers you, you would not hesitate one moment and salvation would be immediate. The lack of clarity in your mind, the as yet undeveloped ability to discern truly what is in your highest interest, keeps you a prisoner to the past, to the ego, by your own choice. Whether conscious or unconscious, it is a choice that governs your life and determines its conditions. The necessity of learning to choose differently by learning to think differently, is why the process of salvation must work itself out in time.

Learning

Learning is a necessary condition of life in a world of time and separation. Learning is an ability you invented as a part of your mind's capacities. Yet when learning proceeds under the Holy Spirit's guidance, according to His purpose, it is used to undo illusions, to learn in an entirely new way; learning is used to set you free rather than to imprison. Repetition is an essential learning principle. Without it, learning cannot be achieved. However, repetition takes place in time and prolongs the need for time. The ability and necessity to learn is fundamental to the mind of perception. Without it, a world cannot be constructed and maintained. When perception took the place of knowledge, it became necessary to undergo a learning process to correct perception that knowledge may return. Although learning does not exist in the condition of knowledge, learning is needed to reduce uncertainty that you be made ready for the return of knowledge. When the Holy Spirit has guided you to learning's end, it is needed no more, and in the state of mind beyond all learning are you made ready for Truth's return.

Your mind must be taught rightly in order to go beyond all learning and perception. Your formidable ability to learn must be understood in the Light of Truth, and used for Truth's return. All that has been learned in the past, the ego's thought system and its values, all that you have taught yourself, must be recognized as false that you may let it go and leave your mind open to receive true ideas.

Real learning is a process in which the falsity of your mind is undone, and the learning of what is true takes place. Illusion cannot be long maintained when you refuse the lessons it would teach you. To choose Truth, and to devote all learning and teaching to meeting the conditions under which Truth can return, is the only use of your learning ability in this world that is truly useful, and the only learning goal that is meaningful.

Problems

What is the answer to all your apparent problems? You have no problems but one: separation from your creative source. Every problem you ever had, have now, or will ever have, arises from and is a form of this one error. In reality, you cannot be separate from God as you live, move, and have your Being in Him. Yet in dreams where you seem to be separate from all you experience, does this one error, this belief in what could never be, seem to take many forms. Each problem appears with its apparently unique characteristics, and seemingly calls for its own solution. And indeed, in a world of form, will solutions to problems be specific to each one.

Yet is the content of every problem the same, no matter how it appears. It is illusion. And the solution is always the same: a miracle offered you by the Holy Spirit in your mind to correct your wrong perception. This fact makes all problems, no matter the appearance, equally easy to resolve. The forgetting of this fact leads to belief in a hierarchy of illusions, with some more 'real' and thus more difficult to overcome. There is no order of difficulty in miracles, thus there is no hierarchy of illusions. All are healed with equal ease if they are given to the Holy Spirit to be replaced with miracles.

When miracles are all you want, all your problems will vanish, for you will no longer need them. The recurring 'problems' and conflicts of human life are but the symptoms that follow the fundamental error of misidentification. To identify with the ego and the thought system of separation, is to choose the guide to pain, suffering, and disaster. When you ask the ego to make your decisions, the state of peace that is your true home is all but forgotten. How can that which was born as a faulty response to a problem that did not exist, do anything other than create more problems that do not exist? As it was created, so it will create. It cannot do otherwise. Yet are its creations just imagination with no basis in Truth.

The Cause of Suffering

What is needed above all else is the recognition of the cause, the source of all apparent troubles that afflict you. The failure to recognize the source of pain and suffering will simply perpetuate it. Without correction, will problems continue to multiply and never will there be an end to them. They are, every one, simply the results that follow your fundamental error.

You are not an ego, a separate self confined to a body, fighting its way through a hostile world, condemned to trudge wearily across a barren landscape. You are in no danger except from your own mistaken thoughts. Your fear and guilt haunt and pursue you, seeming to threaten your peace and well being. Projected outwardly, they appear as if apart from you, malevolent forces poised always to attack. Human figures, situations, and events that seem to cause suffering and loss, simply embody your beliefs about yourself and give expression to your wishes.

Perhaps the hardest thing to understand, to accept, is your complete responsibility for what you see and experience. Nothing happens to you against your will. Nothing is forced upon you. Everything but reflects your wishes until you decide otherwise. You are the dreamer of the dream in which you find yourself. In that is your freedom and your salvation.

Forgiveness

What if what you think you did to yourself and others had no effect on anyone? In truth, nothing in the world of illusion is happening at all. The actions themselves and the effects they seem to have are but part of the dream. To forgive yourself and everyone and everything through the recognition that there is nothing to forgive in the world of dreams, is to set yourself and the world free from all thoughts of sin and guilt. Only the guiltless are forgiven for it is only they who forgive. When you are unwilling to forgive, you cannot receive. You are forgiven through the act of forgiving your brother. Through this are both forgiven, and both are set free to be themselves.

There is no time to waste for the world is tired; all who live here have grown weary, bent low under the heavy burden of sin and guilt you have laid upon them. Now is the time to forgive the world that you may be forgiven and set free at last to return to your home in Heaven. While you languish in chains, the world is not free. While the world suffers your guilt, you remain in bondage to sin, suffering, and death. You and your brothers rise or fall together; all are joined in the One Mind. No one can be free while he keeps his brother in chains.

Nothing is more important for you to do than to forgive. All else pales in comparison. The entire Plan of Atonement rests upon the willingness to forgive. Love will heal your wounds and set you free, and forgiveness is the most comprehensive form of Love in the world of separation. Through forgiveness is the edifice of sin and guilt that upholds separation undone forever, and you are set free to return to God's Kingdom. Nothing can compare to the joy you will feel on that day.

Whenever you are tempted to withhold forgiveness, remember who it is you are forgiving. Always and only are you forgiving yourself, for it is your 'sins' you see in your brother. It is your guilt for which he stands condemned. To forgive your brother is literally to forgive yourself. You cannot love your brother unless your love yourself; you cannot love yourself without loving your brother also. This circle of Love has no beginning and no end for it extends forever. All are included in its gentle and merciful embrace; no one is left outside.

Loose the world by the act of forgiveness and forgiveness will rest upon you and you will be free. Freedom is a gift from God and must be shared in order to keep it. When you are free, you will see that freedom belongs to all, and you will grant all your brothers the right to live freely. You will deny no one what rightly belongs to them, and God will give you everything that belongs to you because He gave it to you in your creation.

Whatever the cost of freedom, you will pay it. There is nothing in this world that can come between you and freedom except your refusal to meet its conditions. The condition of freedom is surrender to Truth, for freedom is not an illusion and cannot be found there. Only in your relationship to Truth can true freedom be found. What is incapable of being bound in any way is free by its very nature. In the awakening to and as the Self, is freedom revealed as the very condition of your Being.

What is most important to remember is always to include your brother's welfare in every decision you make. Remember that decisions are never made in isolation; every one affects the whole. The power of God's Son is always expressed for the Whole Sonship. If you would be aware of the power given you by God in your creation, you must recognize that it can only be used in the service of all of God's Creation.

The Center of Being

What is necessary to discover within yourself is the still, deep center of your Being where the Self abides. The Self has never left you though It disappeared from conscious awareness. Your mind, the mind you experience as you, shines by a light that is not its own, the Light of the Self. Eventually you will be able to follow that light back to Its Source. If you would do this, you must become disciplined in your mind through a mind-training such as found in *A Course in Miracles.* An untrained mind can accomplish nothing for it lives in a state of chaos, at the mercy of the many conflicting thoughts and impulses that drive it. Never will you know peace and happiness until your mind is free of the insanity that has gripped it since time began.

The Christ Light has as its purpose to illuminate all the dark places in your mind that you would keep hidden. All the secret hates, the deeply cherished grievances you hold against your brothers, the dark memories of sin you would forget yet not let go; all that you would conceal from the Holy Spirit must be exposed to the Light of forgiveness that it be healed. These sins, this proof of guilt you cling to, are like a deep sickness that poisons your mind and prevents true healing.

What you are unaware of, what resides in your mind below the threshold of conscious awareness, exerts its influence nevertheless. The energy of mind must be free to return to Light. The mind must be free of false ideas and free of the contraction imposed upon it by fear, for these obstruct the mind's natural freedom. All falsity, and in particular all grievances, hide the Light in you and act as heavy weights that tether the mind to the earth when it would soar through the heavens. The mind must be emptied of all that holds it down and prevents its freedom of movement. Whatever else you do to heal the mind, and there is much to this process, you must release the ancient, deep seated grievances and hatred that have held you a prisoner to fear for so long.

Fear and unforgiveness are always found together; where one is, there will the other be also. To forgive unconditionally is to reject fear in all its forms. To replace grievances with the expression of Love will ultimately heal all fear until only Love remains. When once again Love is all you are, will freedom be restored and the Kingdom will be yours. Do not wait on time or waste it in idle pursuits while pain and sorrow follow not far behind. Let us hasten to return to our Father, our Home. He is waiting for your return; this is what you really seek, what you desire with all your heart.

All the seeking of this world is but the misguided attempt to find, to recover what was never lost. The deep fear and emptiness within your mind is the driving force behind all your seeking; the dim recognition that something is lacking, that fulfillment is necessary, is the thought that begins the search. This thought, though barely conscious, is nonetheless what gives reason and direction to your activities. Yet is it partial and incomplete, and the effort that arises from it is misguided and ultimately leads you nowhere.

Goals

All the things you seemingly want to accomplish, the goals you find so important that dominate your life, all of these are but substitutes for what you really want. Your heart cries out for meaning, for true purpose. In a world that seems to be separate from you and unaware of, even indifferent to your existence, the frightened mind must seek shelter and purpose through its activities. By keeping active, in constant motion, it feels secure in its accomplishments and safe from the intrusion of chaos. Whatever goals you may have are highly esteemed, their nature matters not, for it is your goals you depend on to give life meaning and purpose. In truth, it is not the goals you want but the experience they bring. A state of happiness, of fulfillment and peace, is what you seek.

To feel worthy of being loved is the impetus that impels you to seek accolades and the approval and admiration of others. You believe that if others, be they many or just certain individuals, approve of and admire what you do, then is your worthiness demonstrated and proven. Thus is the recognition accorded you by others, the criterion by which your worth is established. There is no shakier or more uncertain ground upon which to rest than the fickle and constantly changing opinions of the ego. Your worth has been established by God and has nothing to do with the world of form.

Whichever goals you may seek are meaningless unless they are shared by the Holy Spirit. He alone knows if they are part of your one true goal, or if they hinder it. The true goal of every life is to awaken to the Love, freedom, and Unity, that is the Self. In your awakening is everything included, and the entire world brought closer to the end of time. True healing is never limited, it includes all.

Teaching you to change your mind about what you value and believe is the functional purpose of *A Course in Miracles*. What you value, and the beliefs that support and arise from your values, are directly responsible for the conditional circumstances and the direction of your life. Your life is a direct expression of the attempt to fulfill and attain what is valued. The line along which your life develops is established by the goals you choose, and these are determined by what you value and what you value negatively, what you wish to avoid.

Whatever the goals you choose, you will build your life on them, for goals express purpose and purpose is what holds your life together. Purpose can be expressed or unexpressed, conscious or unconscious. If you are not conscious of purpose in your life, then it is certain that you are following the ego's purpose no matter what the appearance. The ego will always choose purpose for you; it has a constant purpose and never falters in its dedication to that purpose. All thoughts, all feelings and desires, the impulses that spur you to action, all have one purpose and overriding aim: to maintain the sense of separation and the specialness that is its reward. To this end, the ego will use everything in your life for nothing escapes its notice or its need to control.

CHAPTER TWO

What You Desire

When the desire to be something other than what you are in Truth arises in your mind, you must recognize it and refuse. To follow this desire, this wish that is so deeply embedded in your mind, will always leave you alone and comfortless. There is a way to recognize when you are acting out the wish for illusion. Do you feel anything other than a state of joy, of peace? Is happiness and a sense of gratitude your experience at this moment? If not, then you have chosen wrongly and you must choose again. Do not delay, for you will only gain by returning your mind to Truth.

Whatever you desire truly in your heart, you will be given. Whether you are aware of your secret wishes and desires or not, they will bear fruit. The fruit may be bitter, tasteless, or it may be beautiful beyond imagination. The desire that gave it birth determines the nature of the fruit. When you desire the things of time, the appearances and conditions that will change and disappear, you desire nothingness. You will be disappointed. A heart set on ephemeral conditions and attainments will find what it values, but never will it find peace and freedom from fear. The desires that rule your heart will set the course of your life. Your lack of awareness of them matters not.

If you would be free to live in peace, in a state of joy and happiness, you must desire this above all else. The many conflicting wishes that lie hidden must be exposed to the Light of awareness. They do not reflect your will nor do they arise from what is true. Too long has the desire for illusion in all its forms shaped your mind and your choices. All it has ever brought you is suffering and death. They are the only reward for your faithfulness to the ego. Now is the time to turn your heart back to Truth where you belong. You never wanted the bitter fruit that grows on the barren tree of illusion. How often you have watered this tree with your tears and spilled your blood on its lifeless soil. No more, no more.

The Journey to Truth

When you begin the journey back to Truth, the road seems to stretch endlessly before you. Do not believe it. There is no distance to be covered to reach what is true, for it has never left you. Even now you live, move, and have your Being in God. You always have and you always will. Life in a dream of separation is only possible through the misuse of your Mind's creative power. Mind nonetheless remains as It is, unaffected by your hallucinatory projections. You can release them in an instant if you desire Truth and only Truth with all your heart.

However, very seldom is this the case; consequently, the journey back seems to take time because you believe you are in time. You need go nowhere to find Truth, but you must become aware of everything in your mind that denies and obstructs It. The false ideas that dominate your thinking and feeling, prevent the Truth from dawning. Just beyond your awareness, the Light awaits your invitation to return. Brightly shining, blinding in Its intensity, the Light will fill your awareness instantly if you will but open yourself to It.

The end result of all your seeking is always the same: disappointment. It cannot be otherwise. The one who seeks is himself the problem. All seeking that is initiated and directed by you, operating from a thought system based in the past, simply perpetuates the meaningless identity you have given yourself. The Truth need not be sought. It was never lost. You are. You have lost yourself in a dream in which God has been excluded, and you are playing a role as if in a play, a play in which nothing is as it seems and the ending is always the same: the hero dies.

Sooner or later everyone will tire of the repetition of what has always been meaningless. At some crucial point in the journey, recognition of the futility of what has gone before will arise in the mind of the one who has struggled for so long. The idea of continuing a meaningless journey that ends in oblivion will lose its appeal. The mind will open ever so little, and the Light will shine in. Now the real life can begin.

Real life is that which partakes of Reality, which has some relationship with It. As long as your life is just a stale repetition of what has gone before, its nature will be illusion, and all its activities meaningless. The past is over and gone; to hold it in memory and imagine that what has long since passed away is still here and now, and to respond to it as if present, is to dance with shadows. No more substance does it have than what shadows possess. Surely to act as if shadows are real, and live among them quite heedless of the nothingness surrounding you, is insanity. To see what is not there, and give it life through your perception, is to do nothing while imagining you are doing something.

To live life in this condition is a tragic waste of time and energy. Yet that is exactly what you do while you sleep yet dream that you are awake. To sleep away lifetime after lifetime, lost in the oblivion of dreams, prolongs the unnecessary suffering of God's Holy Son. To be separate from your Father and your Self is a tragedy of immense proportions. When you return to full awareness of Truth, you will forget the world of dreams and everything in it; no trace of it will remain in the mind restored to Holiness. A mind that is Whole, restored to sanity, has no room for insanity.

Whatever you do, do it with your entire being, do not hold back. Put yourself fully into what you do and your life will come alive. The resistance to being fully present prevents you from being fully alive. Resistance is but a form of fear; fear will always oppose life and inhibit its full expression.

You are responsible for your life in every way. Do not waste it. Do not live half heartedly. Do not refuse to give, to help whenever you can. You were given everything in your creation; even now is this still true. Your privilege and responsibility is to give without ceasing. By giving everything to everyone, you learn that you have a limitless store of loving gifts to give. Through the learning of this important lesson, you will realize that you are Love Itself, limitless and all encompassing.

The Ego and God's Plan

Whatever the mind wills to do, it can accomplish. This is beyond question. However, it is possible to will self destructively. You may not realize you are doing so, but if what you desire to accomplish is of this nature, that is what you will get. The question then becomes would you desire this accomplishment if you were aware of the consequences? The obvious answer is no.

The ego must conceal the consequences of following its directions or you would withdraw your allegiance. Even a mind lost in the insanity of the dream, would not march willingly to its destruction. The ego's goals are always attractively wrapped so as to divert your attention from what is really being given, which is nothingness. To use the power of your mind to chase shadows is a terrible waste. To pursue nothingness when you could have everything, is a tragedy of epic proportions.

To follow the ego's guidance is to be complicit in your own destruction. It would have you use the power of your will to defeat yourself in every way. Surely this is not what you want? Your ignorance of what you are really doing, coupled with your identification with what you are not, has cost you freedom and happiness, giving you nothing but bondage and suffering in their place. No one in their right mind would choose this.

The Holy Spirit has the task of restoring you to your right mind. His task is made much easier when you decide to cooperate with Him fully. If you will trust Him to guide you in all that you do, if you follow His guidance to the best of your ability, setting no preconditions on His answers to your requests for help, you will save yourself much time and shorten your journey home immeasurably. To trust the Holy Spirit, the Voice for God, is to trust God and God's Plan for your salvation. Only God's Plan will work. You have probably noticed by now that your plan has failed consistently. When this recognition has become clear and stable, you will see unmistakably that there is no other choice to make than to accept and follow the plan given you by God. You will thus be fulfilling your one responsibility: to accept the Atonement for yourself.

The Purpose of the World

Do all the things you value so highly, desire so avidly, and pursue with such single minded dedication, bring you happiness? Do they fill the deep sense of emptiness in your heart, or bring peace to your restless mind? Can anything that is of this world ever satisfy you wholly?

The world was not made as a place in which satisfaction and fulfillment could be found. That was never its purpose and never will be. The world was made to be the place where Love was absent, and separation from God and from the Wholeness of your Self was the condition of your being. Where fear replaced Love, and perception took the place of knowledge. Where chaos had banished the laws of God, and the dreamer was left to wander across a barren landscape littered with decaying hopes and empty promises. Where desolation is complete and relentless, leaving you to wander alone and friendless, your heart filled with despair.

Never will you find a true home in a world whose purpose is to keep you in exile, and conceal the deep longing for God that lives still in your mind and heart. The belief in the reality of separation has crippled your ability to understand who you are and what your true purpose is. The thought system of separation has taken over your mind, reinforcing and maintaining separation, limiting your perception and experience. There is nothing in your experience of yourself and others; all of it is but dream perceptions, empty and meaningless.

How long will you go on like this, pretending to be other than what you are, casting your brothers in your own illusory image? Until you have had enough of pain and sorrow, of useless journeys and empty attainments, you will continue the vain struggle to find purpose and meaning in a world devoid of both. There is a pain threshold that will be reached somewhere in your journey through time. It cannot be otherwise, for all things of this world will come to an end, even your attachment to it. The level of tolerance for pain can be very high; it can vary greatly, but it is not limitless. You will eventually tire, you will reach the end of your capacity to endure suffering.

The Restoration of Truth

No one will leave this world until they are ready. As long as a single desire for illusion in place of Truth remains, you will continue the journey that goes nowhere. While illusion still attracts you, you will remain a prisoner in this world by your own choice. When the pain of bondage to illusion is greater than your attraction to it, the journey home begins in earnest. Although the journey unfolds in time, it is already over. You are actually standing in place, observing as time passes you by, imagining a life that goes on all around you. What you are doing does not really matter, for in a dream nothing is really happening. Where you are in your mind is all important; it is in the mind that learning takes place. Real learning results in correct understanding which paves the way for the return of knowledge.

All things that seem to happen in the dream are lessons if correctly used and understood. All events, situations, experiences, and circumstances will provide you with the opportunity to learn. You are constantly given the chance to remember who you are in Truth, and respond with Love and forgiveness for all. Thus you will be led deeper and deeper into your own mind, uncovering all that must be healed, all that denies the Light, preferring to hide in darkness. Your mind will return to the Light for that is what it is. Nothing can prevent this although you may delay the inevitable as long as that is your wish. All relationships will be seen in a new Light, the Light of Holiness. They will no longer be based on the bargaining of the ego: get much and give little. Giving will replace the need to get, Love will replace fear. Every relationship will become an opportunity to give all that you are, and an acknowledgment of all that your brother is.

Whatever you do, you must do with Love for that is what you are. To act without Love is to deny your brother and yourself. If you do so, you will feel the guilt of betrayal, and fear will not be far behind. To be unaware of what you are, is to be a pale substitute that has taken the place of Truth. The pain of that lies heavily upon your mind, obstructing its natural state of joy, leaving it gray and lifeless, prone to sadness. How could you not feel a deep and profound sorrow at the loss you have suffered through your own decision?

What can you do to restore your mind to Truth? You need only decide not to decide. All your decisions made on behalf of yourself alone, are but the continuation of the original decision to turn away from Wholeness. In that did the choice to be as you are not, become your 'reality', and an entire world of separation arose to bear witness to what you wanted to believe. All your decisions since then have been attempts to confirm the reality of separation. They are the actions of a mind that has convinced itself that it is separate from its Creative Source and its Self.

The only freedom you have left in the state of illusion is the freedom to decide. Yet is this freedom lost to you while you remain unaware of what you are deciding for and what you are deciding against. Decisions made from the standpoint of the ego are but variations of the original error. This error cannot be undone while you remain committed to repeating it. That is why you must relinquish the habit of making your own decisions. All such decisions are made under the guidance of the ego, and perpetuate the ignorance that makes right decision impossible. The freedom to decide cannot be exercised while in a state of ignorance about what you are and what your choices are.

The Holy Spirit knows the right decision to be made in every circumstance and will guide you unerringly. He knows the only two choices that can ever be made no matter what the appearance. And He knows what is true and what is illusion, and the difference between them. The Holy Spirit will help you undo the confusion in your mind that makes right understanding impossible. As you learn to recognize what is the same and what is different, to recognize all that is true and all that is false under His gentle guidance, the confusion that clouds your mind will be dispelled, and its natural clarity will return. It will become increasingly evident to you that turning over decisions to Him, to make no decisions by yourself, is the only sane thing to do. Through the consistent reliance on the Holy Spirit, you will be led step by step, day by day, back to your true identity as the Christ.

The Return to Your Father

You will return to your Father when you no longer fear Him. The fear of God lies deep within every mind, waiting for the day it is uncovered, recognized as complete madness, and healed. God's Love sustains you in all you do, even now. To fear the One Who created you by giving you His Being, His Mind, His Light and Love, is an error beyond comprehension. Yet this error cannot be reasoned away. It must be faced, recognized for what it is, and dispelled with the help of the Holy Spirit. The mind created by God must return to full awareness of its Oneness with its Creator.

The only function you have was given you by God; everything you are was given in your creation. You did not create yourself. The belief that you are your own creator, and are free to choose a function not from God, is the root of ignorance, madness, and separation. To not fulfill the function given you by your Creator will give rise to guilt, thus strengthening the belief in guilt that dominates your thinking and experiencing.

Everything you have done since time began has only maintained the belief in separation. The distance that you believe exists between yourself and God, seems to be an insurmountable barrier. And it would be, if indeed there truly were a state of separation. That would mean God's Will for you has been defeated and replaced by an alien will that opposes Him; that you are not Spirit but rather are a bodily identity that is unlike God in every way. This the 'truth' the ego would have you believe, for by so doing does exile seem to be your home and the condition in which you live. The more you give credence to the ego's defense of separation, the further does the memory of God recede from conscious awareness, until driven so deeply into the unconscious, it lies beyond your ability to recover it.

Fortunately, all the help you need to remember your Father, is waiting for your willingness to use it. God does not will that His Son be not in full communication with Him, and gave answer to the perceived separation once and for all time. So is all separation over and all its seeming effects undone. Heaven merely waits for you to recognize this, that your return Home be complete. And your return waits only on your unequivocal decision to do so. Somewhere in time is the moment when you left time forever; it has already been set though you seem not to have reached it yet.

The purpose of *A Course in Miracles* and this teaching is to save you time that your salvation be hastened. Time can be shortened for you through the miracle and the blessing it brings to giver and receiver. As you learn the lessons you are given through the Holy Spirit, He collapses time for you, bringing you ever closer to the Holy Moment of release. Only your unwillingness stands in your way and only through your willingness, given to the Holy Spirit, does liberation from the bonds of illusion become possible. There is no other way, for you must be willing to give up what was never true, and surrender to the Higher Power. Freedom cannot be reached without the help that comes from beyond the prison walls.

In order to receive the gifts of God, you must first realize that you have always had them. They are what you are. In Truth, you are what you have and you have what you are. Having and Being are the same. In this world it does seem as if they are different, for you have lost the awareness of what you are, thus you are also unaware of what you have. To suddenly begin to experience something you were not aware of before, does seem as if you have been given what you previously lacked. This is just the appearance in the dream. What you are apparently given from without, actually arises from within. All that you need to know and experience is revealed when you are ready. Always has it been in your mind, waiting for you to welcome it. When you are ready to receive it into your awareness, it will become apparent.

There is no need to struggle to get something in spiritual life. All that you are looking for, the Truth that you seek, was given to you in your creation and is what you are. You have everything and you are everything. What you have and what you are has not been lost, it has simply been forgotten.

The task of spiritual life is not to seek for what was never lost, but to seek to uncover all that is in your mind that obstructs and prevents you from knowing what you are in Truth. All that is false and unnecessary must be corrected and given up, turned over to the Holy Spirit that He may replace illusion with Truth. More than this you need not do. He will do the rest, if you let Him. You need add nothing to God's Plan for salvation. To attempt to do so is to obstruct its functioning and prevent its accomplishment. This is but resistance disguised as good intentions. His Plan is perfect and the Voice for God carries it out perfectly. Surrender to God, turning your life over to the Holy Spirit, is the necessary condition for salvation.

When you reach the point in your journey where God is all you want, you will be knocking on Heaven's door and it will swing open to greet you. Your Father will not make you wait very long before He takes the last step Himself. All troubles, all possible problems, will vanish along with the world of separation. And you will dwell in your Father's House forever.

The Holy Spirit

What must be known and understood that salvation be within easy reach? Just this: that you must remember constantly who you are in Truth. If what you are is Spirit, and I assure you that is true, then to let this thought be present in your mind constantly as fact will bring conviction and understanding, and in time will open your mind to receive the direct experience of your spiritual reality. More than that you do not need, but also not less. Do not wait for that day but hasten its coming through your constant dedication and surrender. Your Father and all the Host of Heaven await your glad return.

Do you really want everything that has gone before to remain the same? Do all the activities and accomplishments of your life add up to a state of peace, of deep fulfillment? Have you found the answer to all problems that appear in your life, the one Answer that solves them all? To attempt to find different answers to all the apparently different problems is an endless task. The purpose of an endless task is to make sure that it is never completed. Completion would mean the end of conflict which is freedom, and this the ego would never permit.

There is one answer to every seeming problem or conflict that appears in your life: the Holy Spirit. He is God's Answer to the only problem you have or ever will have: separation from God. Through God's Answer was separation over and gone for all time. Yet in your mind does separation live on, held in memory and experienced as if here and now. This one problem is the source, content, and form of all problems you seem to have. In this world do problems appear as if many and varied. Different situations and circumstances present themselves, seeming to require different solutions. Conflict appears in endless variations, yet are all but empty form. The content is the same, and it is to content you must respond if you would have all problems resolved for all time. The end of conflict is the end of time; when conflict and fear have gone, time is no more. Love has no need of time, being eternal and forever beyond change of any kind.

If you allow the Holy Spirit to give answer to all that troubles you, life will become a happy dream, an effortless journey. You will become a conduit for God's Grace, giving what you have been given to all. The Gifts of God are apparent and ever present to those who want them above all else. To truly desire only what is of God, is to welcome the return of Holiness. As you realize the Holiness that resides within you, you will see only Holiness in your brother.

The Holy Spirit will respond immediately to the least invitation. This is what He has been waiting for since time began. You need only call and He will answer, and His answer is the one you need. You have listened to the voice of insanity, the ego, and it has never brought you anything but misery in one form or another. There have been periods of respite, and even a seeming happiness from time to time. But never have you found a lasting peace, a happiness that stays with you. The ego's gifts are ephemeral, fleeting, devoid of real substance. All satisfactions found in this world are hollow, empty shells whose content is nothingness. And that is all you will ever find in this dream of a world until you learn to look beyond all appearances, all seeming.

What is real, lasting, and of immeasurable value will not be found where dreaming rules. Yet it is right here and always with you. In your mind is all that is true and worth having, given you by God in your creation. How could it be otherwise, for God gives His creation all that is His. Even now, although you are unaware, you rest in God, forever safe and at peace. You must and will return to the home you once knew; there is nowhere else to go. Although you will not find Truth in the dream, you can bring the dream to Truth and see Truth reflected even here. The real world is but the reflection of Truth in the dream, yet it is a giant step in the journey, the one that will take you to the gates of Heaven.

The world you see around you is the projection of your errors of thought, the beliefs you prefer over reality. It is the out-picturing of the way you want reality to be. The world is in your mind, nowhere else. As it simply reflects back to you your thoughts, what you want to see, you can decide to see differently, to see the thoughts you share with God. The world will change accordingly, reflecting the Light and Unity of God in place of fear and sorrow. Your mind is the source of the world you see; it is in your mind that the world is healed of all suffering.

Never through the long, dark time of separation from God and your true home, have you been left abandoned and alone though that was your wish. In your confusion, driven mad by fear, you abandoned God and all that is true. Projecting the act of abandonment onto God rather than recognizing what you had done, you took refuge by projecting a world to take the place of what you thought you had lost. Yet deep in your mind the awareness remained that you had separated yourself from your Creator, and from that belief arose the sense of guilt and the fear of God. Guilt calls for punishment; the guilty always project their sins. You fear that God will attack you in retribution for your 'attack' on Him.

God does not know of attack nor can He be attacked. Your guilt, your beliefs, and fear are nothing but the imaginings of a mind lost in the confusion of separation. God has been calling you since time began, but you have not been listening. He gave answer to separation, and so it is over and gone though you hold it still in your memory. Accept His Answer to all your problems whatever their form. His one Answer is the solution to all because all problems are but different forms of the one and only problem you have: separation from God.

Do not be afraid of anything in this world. You cannot be attacked or threatened in any way. Nothing can hurt you but your own thoughts. Let the Holy Spirit teach you how to change your thinking and perception. Let Him lead you back to where you belong, to your home in God. Trust Him with your life for His Love and care for you are limitless. Let Him take you in a new direction. The old direction in which you have been traveling for so long has taken you away from Truth. You have been going round and round in a circle, repeating this meaningless journey again and again, going nowhere.

CHAPTER THREE

The Gifts of God

Holiness, like Light, extends Itself everywhere, joining with Itself unceasingly. The Holiness of the Father and the Son is the condition of all that is real. All that God created shares His Holiness. There is nothing real that does not shine in its kindly Light. Your Holiness guarantees that you will rest forever in deepest peace, undisturbed tranquility, and Love without limit.

The Gifts of God are given always to those who ask, for by asking do you receive what you already have. By giving do you accept what you have received. To ask and then to give what you receive, is the way of Love. Love only gives. Love wills only to give Itself, to extend Itself without ceasing. Among the Gifts of God is Love the highest, for all of God's Gifts are contained within It. If you have Love, you have everything and God too, for God is Love as has been often said. All Love comes from God and is God. When Love is all you have, you will know God and His Son.

The Grace of God is given freely to all but you must be ready to receive It. Our Father's Grace brings the Kingdom and the Glory to your experience in the dream. The world becomes a gentler place, a kinder place, shining with a different Light when you live in a state of Grace. When Grace envelops you, you will feel the Love of God and know you are safe. All of your cares will seem like nothing then. God's Grace rests always on those who live in service to the Great Plan of Atonement. When your only concern is to fulfill the part assigned to you, Grace will follow you everywhere and nothing will be lacking.

Fear and Ignorance

There is nothing to fear ever. All fear is misguided belief in what is not true. To believe in what will not happen to what does not exist makes no sense. There is a constant movement of mind to conceal fear or avoid it through various activities that actually strengthen it, and thus allow fear to dominate your mind unchallenged. The strange distortion of thinking that is the fear of experiencing fear prevents a rational and sane response to the presence of fear in your mind. Instead of responding directly to fear itself, you are reacting to an automatic and unconscious response to fear which is fear of fear. This convoluted and indirect response leads to avoidance, and allows the continuance of fear itself as well as the fear of experiencing it. Thus fear remains a strong influence in your mind, and a powerful motivator that drives behavior.

Few realize the role played by fear in human life. In fact, the denial and dissociation that characterize ego consciousness, make accurate perception impossible. Without perceiving the condition of your mind as it is, there is no chance to actually introduce correction, that the dark shadow of fear be lifted and freedom restored.

The first requirement for healing your mind is to become aware of what is in it. The unawareness of the content of mind, and how it affects and controls behavior, protects and maintains the ego's control and domination. You do not realize that your thinking, motivation, and behavior, arise from a part of your mind that is simply an error, a mistake made long ago and kept alive through memory and projection. The misidentification this fosters has caused untold misery, and has cost you the awareness of your true identity in God. Without the awareness of what you truly are, you will continue to be what you are not, and pay a heavy price for your ignorance.

The Power of Thought

There is no way to avoid the effects of your thinking. Cause and effect are never separate. Right thinking, thinking guided by the Holy Spirit, will have positive and helpful results. All thinking that originates with the ego, will be self defeating and will only perpetuate suffering. By the conditions of your life and the state of your mind is it apparent whose thoughts have your allegiance.

Never underestimate the power of thought. Your thought has made a world, a universe of separation ruled by chaos. The creative power of thought given you by God in your creation, has been misused to make a world that stands in opposition to God, to Love. This world does not exist in Truth, yet does the power of belief give it apparent existence in your mind. Illusions are as strong in their effects as is the Truth in your experience, until you withdraw the power you gave them and they collapse into nothingness. As long as you wish them to be true, so long will they define your life and control your mind.

The power of mind is unrecognized in the ego's world, for it is perceived as a threat. The ego does everything possible to channelize and control the use of mind, that it be used in ways that confirm and strengthen separation. The illusion of using mind to accomplish things in this world has the ego's support and approval. While you are busy pursuing worldly goals, your mind is too busy to perceive where all such goals are leading you. No matter how lofty or stimulating, all roads in this world end in death.

Do not forget your Father needs you as much as you need Him. Without your Father are you bereft of Being. His Being is yours, your Mind is His. You live and move in God; the Love in your heart is God's Love. The strength that carries you back to Truth is His. There is nothing that is truly yours that is not of God. All that you have comes from Him forever.

The Price of Freedom

What is the price of freedom? Only your self, the self that is not free. You must give up the self you made to take the place of Reality. Freedom has not gone; it has been eclipsed by the choice of illusion. You cannot have freedom and illusion; one or the other will be your state of mind, but not both. Freedom as an illusory, separate self is not possible. The self lives in bondage to fear, limited to a body, surrounded by that which is beyond its control, subject to threat from many different forces. Constant struggle and continuous defense against enemies from within and without characterize its little life.

The body can never be free; it was made as a defense against freedom, to limit and imprison the mind. Identify with the body and you have voluntarily entered the cage in which freedom cannot be found. Seek freedom as a bodily identity, and you will find but illusions of what you seek. Nothing of value, not safety, not security, not freedom, can be found in a dream in which you imagine you are what you are not. Only chaos and the repetition of a meaningless journey over and over, will be your reward for the choice of illusion over Truth.

If you would be free once again, you must return to God, for only by being as you were created, by being what you are still, can your natural state of freedom be restored. The Self is freedom, joy, bliss; It is unlimited, unbound, beyond containment of any kind. God created you as freedom itself; only your decision keeps you in chains.

Whenever you choose to be what you are not, you have decided against your freedom. Do not make the mistake of seeking freedom within the conditions of this world. You will not find it here. True freedom is unbound and unaffected by appearances, by situations and circumstances that are unstable and constantly changing. Freedom is of the Spirit, of Mind, not of the body. The body may go on as before, playing out its assigned role in the dream, yet is the Self unaffected, forever free. It is not the body that separates you from the state of freedom, it is your mind.

Now is the only time you can be free. In the present moment freedom awaits you, waiting for your choice to be as you are and leave the past behind. The past need not hold you down. Your mind will yet leave the earth and soar through the heavens on the wings of Love. Nothing will keep you a prisoner in a world of separation when you hear your Father calling, and you will only to answer Him.

Choices

Whenever you make a decision not based on Truth, you will suffer. Every decision has the power to bring you Heaven or hell. No choice is too trivial to have consequences. You will know what you have chosen by how you feel and the results it brings. Unless you are paying close attention to how you are feeling, you will not be able to associate your decisions with your state of mind. Cause and effect are never separate, and it is very important to recognize consistently the direct link between how you feel and the choices you are making.

What basis do you have to evaluate your choices except by their effects? Your unawareness of the power of your thinking and deciding, and of their effects on your mind and your life, leaves you with no consistent way to evaluate your decisions. How you use your mind is all important, for your life is the expression of the choices you are making, and your choices are the results of your beliefs.

Do you like the way you are feeling? Are you happy with the life you are leading? These questions are not about goals or achievements, but about how you feel in your mind and heart, and whether your life is an expression of Love and happiness. Is a life of unawareness about who you are and what your purpose is, worth living? Is a life not infused with Love and joy meaningful? Does it profit you to gain the whole world and yet lose the awareness of your soul? These are the questions the world never asks, for these are the questions that will place your feet on the road to freedom.

The mind of separation is limited by fear and blinded by desire. In such a condition, it cannot perceive or think clearly. The questions needing to be asked are not allowed to enter awareness. Such questions are left to the philosophers to be endlessly examined conceptually, obscured by verbal complexity, and never answered with certainty. The ego is fond of endlessly debating ideas without ever reaching resolution. As the ego understands nothing, it is not to the ego you must look for the answers you need.

Your Reality

Through the Holy Spirit in your mind, you are guided to right understanding of yourself and your part in the Great Plan of Atonement. Understanding, though it begins with verbal comprehension, must go beyond the intellect to be real understanding. What you are must be directly experienced beyond thinking, beyond concepts, for understanding to be complete. Spiritual life and its conditions and requirements cannot be understood by the intellect no matter how brilliant. The Reality of what you are is beyond body and mind, beyond feelings and concepts. Reality cannot be reached by the mind, by any egoically motivated seeking.

The Self waits for you beyond all thought and belief, all ideas of what you are and what you are not, beyond what you think you know. It waits for you in stillness and deepest silence. The Self is not known through perception. Perception leads to indirect knowing but never to knowledge. Perception is always symbolic, be it inner or outer; it can never find the Self for the Self is beyond perception. The Self can only be known by you as you without the separation that perception brings. You have never been other than the Christ and you never will be. The belief that it is possible to be something else is your only problem. This error has cost you everything and given you nothing in return.

Perception and knowledge never meet, yet can wholly unified perception approach knowledge and draw near to it, for it does not oppose knowledge in any way. Through the Vision of Christ is perception brought so close to knowledge that knowledge can flow across the little gap and restore you to the Kingdom. When you draw close enough to your Father through your Love for Him, He will reach down and lift you up.

Learning and Purpose

While you find yourself in a world of separation, in apparent association with bodily form, there is still learning to be done. Learning is a skill you invented after knowledge was lost through the separation. It became necessary for learning to take place in order to correct error in your mind and bring your mind back into alignment with Truth. While your thinking is in a state of opposition to Truth, illusion will rule your mind and maintain the imprisonment from which you suffer.

Learning, like all that you have invented, can be used by the Holy Spirit Who gives it another purpose. You have used learning to support and confirm separation, to deepen your commitment to identify yourself as a body. You have filled your mind with meaningless 'facts', and established thereby a basis from which to judge and evaluate. Through a process of constant judgment, you confirm the rightness of your perceptions, and establish your beliefs about yourself and the world as true.

Yet is perception a variable process, affected and shaped by the mind's preestablished belief system, and by what you desire to be true. Nothing in the world of perception can be trusted. Variable, constantly changing, shifting first one way then the other, perception always involves selection and interpretation. It cannot be otherwise, for the mind is always trying to find meaning and purpose under the unstable conditions and chaos of the world of separation. The mind of perception has lost the condition of knowledge; it does not know anything. Consequently, meaning and true purpose have also been lost.

Life without a sense of purpose is impossible. If the awareness of real purpose has vanished from the mind, you will find a substitute. This does not mean that what you have chosen to take the place of real purpose is real or meaningful, but you will believe in it, cherish and protect it, because you have chosen it.

By the power of belief does it become real to you. Whatever you do, you will be acting in the light of what you value as the central purpose of your life. It matters not if that purpose be conscious or unconscious. It will infuse your actions and determine your life's direction.

CHAPTER FOUR

Decision Making

Who is the one who makes decisions for you? Is it the ego, the illusory voice of separation, or is it the Holy Spirit Who speaks for God and Truth? Decisions are never made alone. They are always made in collaboration with the voice you are listening to; they always proceed from and uphold the thought system your guide represents. Your decisions stem from the belief in separation and all that entails, or they rest on Truth and move you in Its direction.

Decisions are always made with the guide you have chosen. Each decision is a choice for the ego or the Voice for God. Certainly it does not seem as if you are choosing life or death with every decision you make, yet that is exactly what you are doing. Your unawareness of this fact affects it not at all. Decisions arise from the necessity of choosing between alternatives presented you by constantly changing circumstances and events. They are at once both a response and an attempt to control the chaos of life and make it manageable. Decisions made with the ego's help are themselves an expression of chaos. They are an attempt to manage chaos by introducing more chaos. This will obviously lead to the continuation of chaos and strengthen the need to manage and control it. Chaos does not need to be controlled; it needs to be recognized as nothingness.

If you turn over decision making to the Holy Spirit, He will guide you out of chaos. You need not live in that condition though your feet still walk the earth. Through the recognition of Truth and the undoing of false mind, you may transcend its effects and live in a state of Grace where that which lies beyond illusion becomes available to you. How do you live surrounded by the chaos of separation, yet be unaffected by it? Live in a state of true consciousness with Love as your guiding Light, and all darkness will be shined away until you see the Truth reflected everywhere.

What You Have

If the good you do lives on, do you not want to do good always? By the good we mean that which helps, supports, heals, and inspires in the most positive way. By doing good always, by helping everyone everywhere, you are helping yourself in the best possible way. Everything you give to your brothers is also your gift to yourself. This is the real meaning of the expression "Virtue is its own reward." To do good, to act rightly, to be virtuous, is always in your own best interest. You only gain thereby and never do you lose.

The ego would have you believe that your interest and that of your brothers is not the same, that what is gained by one is lost to the other. The ego believes in a world of scarcity where there is never enough for everyone. Competition is the law and you must struggle to get what you need, wresting it from another if necessary. This view, if accepted, leaves you no choice but to operate in a climate of fear and suspicion where conflict is the rule and safety is found only through isolation. The world you see around you is the result of the identification with the ego's perspective. Only suffering will follow those who live from this lack of understanding.

The Holy Spirit teaches that you already have everything you need because you are everything. In Truth, having and being are the same. You have what you are and you are what you have. In the world of separation, He translates this Law of God into the forms that meet the needs you perceive. You believe your needs are many and different, so God's one Answer appears to take many forms to fulfill them. All is but illusion, yet as long as God's Son believes illusions real, He must be provided help in a form He can recognize.

If you remember your Father, and devote your life to realizing your true purpose, you will never suffer from lack. What is needed will be provided. This does not mean however, you will always have what you want. The egoically identified mind is habitually preoccupied with getting and achieving. Much if not most of what it desires is not needed in any real sense. What is not necessary for life or helpful to your real purpose, will not be provided by the Holy Spirit. All that is merely distraction or self destructive can only hurt you and delay fulfillment. Yet can you succeed in obtaining what you desire strongly enough through the misuse of your energy and intent, but you will never gain by doing so.

Mind and Time

You do not recognize what will help and what will hurt you because you do not know the difference between Truth and illusion. This <u>will</u> be learned of the Holy Spirit if you are willing to be shown the extent of your ignorance, that your mind be purified of what is false to make room for what is true. Illusion will always hurt you whether recognized or not. Being the replacement for Truth, it can only bring disaster. To lose the awareness of Truth is disaster, for all your problems arise from it.

When the wish to be what you are not replaced the knowledge of what you are, suffering became possible in your experience though not in Truth. Existence became a dream, a projection of separation from all that is real. To be separate from Reality Itself is suffering, though that fact goes unrecognized. The mind asleep and dreaming a world of form and activity does not realize the condition it is in; the deep pain of separation from God has been banished from awareness. All things of which the mind is afraid have been dissociated from conscious awareness, all memories of suffering hidden deep in the unconscious mind.

You cannot escape from what has been allowed to enter your mind by pretending it is not there. Only the decision to heal, to release it, will free you from the past you carry still. The past is always with you, although it is over. Held in memory by the refusal to let it go, it affects you still. Everything that enters the mind remains, for it is there by your invitation and decision until you decide again. To free the mind of the entire past in every sense of the word, is the purpose of the mind training.

To free yourself of the past you carry still, you must be willing to let it go. This seems like an obvious statement, too self-evident to need repeating, yet the past has a much greater hold on you than you realize. The self image, the identity you have given yourself, is an artifact of the past. It lives only in the past and seems to be who you are now only through memory, through reliving the moment of separation every moment of every day. To successfully release the past is to lose the self you have believed in for so long. To the mind long accustomed to identifying with the body and the sense of separation that is the ego, this seems to be annihilation. You fear this more than death. Yet is death only of the self. Give up the self and death will vanish from your mind forever. The old must pass away, must be expelled from present awareness through the relinquishment of the past. Only then can you be reborn as the Christ, the Holy Son of God.

Only the Christ in you is real, just as the present is the only moment of time that is real. Time and eternity intersect in the present, and the Christ waits for you there. He is always with you, waiting for your willingness to let Him back into the mind that is His. Never has He left; He cannot, for your mind and being are part of His. If that were not so, you would not exist.

The Nature of the Ego

The nature of the ego is to keep everything it finds valuable or useful for itself. It shares grudgingly and gives only to get. The ego sees the world from a position of scarcity; it believes that everything it wants, it must fight for. Conflict and competition are its approach to life, and never is sharing regarded as gain. For the ego to gain, must another lose. If you follow the ego's thought system, you are opposing God's laws with everything you do. Thus are you guaranteed suffering and loss; and conflict and sorrow will be the conditions under which you live. No other outcome is possible if you choose to follow the guide who leads you into fear and pain.

What if you were to throw caution to the winds? To be cautious means to proceed slowly, examining things very closely and carefully before making a decision. This is the essence of the human condition, is it not? To judge, to weigh, to consider, to analyze, is how human life proceeds. Or to react, to act blindly, following impulses arising from habit, from addictions, from whatever particular distortions animate the mind. Human life fluctuates between these extremes, varying according to the individual's disposition and changing events and circumstances.

The ego is itself a chaotic arrangement, feeling itself under constant threat, unaware of where it came from or where it is going. To try to control what happens to assure a favorable outcome makes perfect sense to the ego. By so doing it believes it can keep away what threatens it and assure its safety. The ego also tries to maximize what pleases it and avoid entirely or minimize what it does not like. And it will always try to avoid pain and discomfort and escape from fear.

If you do the ego's bidding; if you identify yourself as a body in separation and accept the thought system that underlies this error, you will be subject to the constant movement of fear. Where fear rules the mind, peace is absent. Fear will always bring conflict in its wake; attack and defense will characterize your life and guide your decisions. The ego is fearful of everyone and everything. It carries the memory of that fearful moment when it arose as your response to what you did not understand. The state of separation is inherently fearful because what is separate from you, you do not understand. And what you do not understand, you fear. That which you do not understand must be defended against, for it is untrustworthy. All things that appear separate are regarded with suspicion.

Trust is impossible to find in such a world, reserved for those who have 'proved' themselves worthy; even then it can be withdrawn if you feel your trust has been betrayed. The ego's trust is always given conditionally and jealously guarded that it may withdrawn at any time. No one can be trusted completely in the ego's view, for the trusted one may suddenly turn and attack. The ego cannot but project its own untrustworthiness and ever-readiness to attack onto others, for what is believed inwardly is always projected and perceived as if outside of you.

Trust

Trust can only be given to what is true and unchanging. You can trust God and His Creation which is what you are. Nothing else is worthy of your trust though you need not fear it. Would you place your trust in the shifting sands of appearances, in circumstances that are inherently unstable? Nothing in the world of appearances can be trusted. That is not where you should place your trust. Trust in God and His Answer to the separation, and the circumstances of physical life will be adjusted accordingly. The biblical injunction to seek first the Kingdom of God and all these things shall be added unto you, is true in the literal sense. Put your trust in God, allow the healing of your mind, give up the denial of and defense against the Truth, and God's Blessings will rain upon you. God's Gifts, which are not of this world, will be translated by the Holy Spirit into the physical conditions necessary for human life. Do not interfere with your Father's giving and you will receive what you need.

To receive what you need is to recognize what you already have and to accept it. Your Father gave you everything in your creation. You lack nothing, yet you believe in a world of scarcity and so is lack then a part of your experience. To recognize that all you have comes from God and to accept that fact, frees your mind and allows the Holy Spirit to provide what you need at all times and in all circumstances. Nothing else need be done, for there is indeed nothing to be done other than to recognize your complete dependence on God and surrender to that Truth.

Truth

The recognition of Truth and your relationship to It, even in a world of separation, will set your mind on the path to freedom and true Self fulfillment. Life must take place in the context of right relationship to what is true and what is false to be meaningful. The great problem of this world, to find meaning amid meaninglessness, purpose among the purposeless, fulfillment in the midst of the unfulfilled, can only be solved through commitment to living a life of service to Truth. To serve the Truth is to accept your part in the Great Plan of Atonement, and do your best to complete it. By doing this, you become a source of Light and blessing in a world badly in need of both. We stand together, all who have made that commitment, in the Light and Love of God, as one endless chain of Grace and healing that circles the entire world and reaches all the way back to Heaven. There is no place where God's Grace is not for those whose hearts are open to receive It, and by this receiving to share It with their brothers.

What is given to one is given to all, and what truly belongs to one heart extends to all hearts. How can that which is One be contained? All are included within Its beneficence. Limitless and forever extending, God's Love is always available. There is nowhere It cannot be found. Yet you must meet Its conditions, for in a world of separate bodies, Love has been replaced by fear.

Peace

Fear maintains a stranglehold on the mind that has identified itself with a body, with separation. Life as a bodily identity sees threats everywhere it looks. Surrounded by enemies waiting for the opportune moment to strike, it cannot but be fearful in the face of constant danger. If you identify with the body, with the sense of separation that is the ego's partial and distorted perception, fear will be your chosen companion and never will you find peace. The presence of fear will always engender conflict and drive peace from your mind.

Peace need not be absent from your awareness and will not be unless you value what has taken its place. The world offers you many gifts whose purpose is to take the place of peace. Do not accept the worthless offerings of the ego whose only goal is conflict. The ego does not know peace and will never accept it.

To commit yourself to peace is to turn your back on the ego in every way. You cannot identify yourself with the ego without choosing conflict as a way of life however that may be disguised. Let conflict go, banish it from your mind, and peace will prevail. Choose conflict, cherish attack in any form, and the chaos of war will obscure your natural state and peace will vanish.

There is no need to strive for peace. Like Love, it will be there when you have allowed all that obstructs your awareness of it to be healed. When the mind has been cleared of all attachment to conflict, of all need to defend and attack, peace will shine forth as your natural state. If you do not resist the Holy Spirit in His work of correcting and healing your mind, you will be speedily returned to the condition in which God is remembered.

Understanding Mind

Resistance to the Holy Spirit in the form of refusing to turn over decision making to the One Who knows, is why the transformation of mind seems to take forever. The mind is split. It contains conflicting and contradictory desires that literally obstruct and make impossible a return to Wholeness. Integration precedes Wholeness and makes it possible for the mind to recover its natural state. Integration of the mind replaces the conflicting desires and cross purposes with a single purpose, one that is true and capable of accomplishment. For those who seriously want to realize the Wholeness of Mind, the process starts with the practice of integration. To become aware of desire in all its forms that drive the mind, is the first step you must take. Without being aware of how and why the mind is as it is, you cannot begin to correct it. Present awareness, moment by moment, is the way to see your mind in action, to directly experience and become aware of the dynamics and movement of mind in your day to day life. Mind must be understood as it is, in its activity. It cannot be reduced to theory or description. Mind is alive and always active.

Through becoming aware of your mind in action, you can choose where you want it to go. You can direct it towards Truth, towards liberation, or you can continue to let the past play out its stale repetition of nothingness until you tire of it or death intervenes. As you become more and more aware of the activity of your mind, you will begin to understand how your thinking and your reactions, which are determined by your thinking, are responsible for the conditions and circumstances of your life. You will see how you are choosing happiness or conflict, Love or fear, with every decision you are making. When this becomes so consistently clear that it can no longer be denied; when you can no longer hide from what is in your mind and your responsibility for it; when self awareness becomes the way you live, then choosing begins to become consistent, for only what is true will attract you.

His Gifts

Whatever you need will be given you when you turn your life over to the higher purpose. By accepting God's purpose as your own, you stop obstructing the flow of His Gifts into your life. When your will is not exercised in opposition to His, the way is open to receive His Gifts rather than deny Them. They are always available to His children but they must be accepted first. The mind focused on the shabby offerings of the ego, on the hollow honors and attainments the world bestows, is not open to receive. "Seek ye first the Kingdom" is the admonition to direct your mind and efforts towards that which is truly valuable and worthy of having. When you do so, what you need in the worldly sense will also be given. The Holy Spirit knows what you need and will provide it if you do your part to make yourself available to receive.

The great error that prevents this availability is the belief that you need to decide by yourself. Thereby do you impose another will between yourself and God, and while you believe such a thing is possible, your opposition to your Father will effectively exclude His help. God does not and has not abandoned His children; His children have abandoned Him. You cannot receive that which you are actively opposing. Refusal will always prevent reception.

The Defense Against God

The need to defend yourself against the return of God's Presence to your awareness, is the reason behind the endless 'busyness' of the human mind. If you were to let go of all defenses against Him, your Father would reach down and lift you up. He cannot do so however, while you are actively resisting and denying Him. God remains with His Creation, it cannot be otherwise. Yet can the Son of God lose communication with his Father through the belief in an alien will. You cannot hold in your awareness what you fear and oppose. You will dissociate yourself from it, driving it from your mind and replacing it with what is an effective defense against its return.

There never will be a violation of your free will, for it was given you by God in your creation. God does not contradict Himself or violate His own Laws. Neither can anyone or anything else. His Laws were established for your protection and upheld by His Will which never changes. The responsibility for the condition of your mind, for what it includes and what it excludes, is yours and yours only. Your decisions, your choices, determine what lives in your awareness or slumbers in the depths of the unconscious. Once a decision has been made, it remains in effect until you revisit it and choose again. It matters not whether the decision was made long ago or yesterday. All of the mind's decisions are final until changed or corrected.

Whatever you truly desire with all your heart and mind will be given you without delay. "Love the Lord thy God with all thy heart and all thy mind and all thy soul," was the great law I expressed as reported in the Bible. This was the admonition to turn completely towards your Father without ambivalence, to desire only what is true, eternal, unchanging, and completely valuable. The vacillation between desiring only Truth or being attracted to illusion, prevents the acceptance of Truth now in Its completeness. A partial and erratic commitment will bring about inconsistent results.

What Limits Mind

The mind of separation, the perceptual mind, suffers from a split identity. This divides the energy of mind, weakening it, and destroys clarity. The motivation of such a mind is ambivalent and contradictory. Confusion prevails as long as conflicting desires, impulses, and goals dominate thinking and behavior. The mind is pulled in different directions, first this way and then that way. Each desire or impulse that arises takes the place of the one that preceded it. Thus is the mind in a state of constant agitation, chasing the shadows that flit across its surface, taking them to be real. While all your energy is used to perpetuate illusion, your mind will remain in bondage to what it made so long ago. The self made chains that bind you will not fall away while you are continually reinforcing them. Reinforcing faulty learning will not correct it. Faulty learning will not leave the mind that welcomed and cherished it as long as you are satisfied with the results of your thinking.

Until you recognize the cause of your suffering, you will not be willing to change your mind, to alter your thinking. To do so requires an honesty and a clarity you do not as of yet possess. It can be and must be developed however, if you would be free of suffering. The Holy Spirit will gently show you the true condition of your mind, of your life, if you will trust Him. He will help you become aware of all that you hide from yourself that you may see your mind as it is, not as you imagine it to be.

Whenever you choose what you do not realize will hurt you, you are being complicit in your own destruction. Suffering is not possible without your consent and active compliance with its conditions. Your lack of awareness of the part you play in bringing about the suffering in your life, keeps you prisoner to what you would escape. To be unaware of what shapes your life and determines its course and conditions, is to be as a leaf blown about by the shifting winds, landing for a moment it knows not where, then off again with every passing breeze. You are helpless in the face of what you do not know or understand.

The mind functions in a consistent way; this is determined by habits of thought and feeling and the beliefs that underlie them. Many beliefs are unconscious. You are unaware of them and the role they play in driving your thinking and controlling your behavior. They are not open to question or correction yet play an important role in your decisions.

The falsity in your mind cripples your understanding and limits your happiness. Everything that you believe is based on the past and does not serve you now. Unless you raise to question all that you believe, it cannot be corrected and replaced by true ideas. All that is false, untrue, yet living in your mind, must be undone to make room for Truth. There is nothing that cannot be done when the mind has been returned to Truth.

The mind in its natural state understands what is needed and what is unnecessary. What is true and what is false is easily recognized when you have allowed the Holy Spirit to guide you through the process of learning the difference between them. Your mind carries much within it in the form of old ideas, beliefs, values, and judgments. This past baggage will gradually be lifted from your mind, leaving it clean and empty, a fit vessel to receive the Truth.

There is a way to tell always what is needed and helpful and what must be discarded and left behind. That which leaves you in a state of peace, of love, of happiness, is to be accepted into your mind and cherished. All thoughts and feelings, all reactions that pull you away from the natural state of freedom, are to be corrected. Thus is your mind returned to Truth and Truth only. When only Love remains, God will return to your awareness.

Maintain Separation

Without constant and consistent effort, separation cannot be maintained for it is an unnatural state and therefore inherently unstable. Although separation is all you know, that does not mean it is your natural condition. You have forgotten who you are long ago and its memory is now beyond your reach. What is completely unnatural and unthinkable in your true state, has now become 'normal' and beyond question. The ego cannot allow you to question the reality of your experience under its guidance, for its carefully constructed picture of reality cannot stand up to careful scrutiny.

Without your consent, the picture of reality in separation will crumble into the nothingness it has always been. Only the abdication of responsibility for what you see and experience allows the ego to maintain the fiction that you are the effect of the world and not its cause. Thus are you the victim of what seems to happen to you and are not responsible for it. There are two 'logical' conclusions that arise from this view. First is the belief you are helpless in the face of what occurs, and thus you must protect yourself from the world. This perspective makes certain that fear is maintained in your mind which justifies the need to defend and attack. And you are thereby relieved of responsibility for your attacks on your brothers and unaffected by what you do to them.

The whole edifice of guilt, sin and attack, rests on the belief that you are not responsible for what happens in your life. This unquestioned assumption enables the entire belief system of separation to be maintained, and ensures the continuation of the ego's role as your guide to decision making. It is vitally important to take back the responsibility for your life in every detail. In this decision is the invitation given to the Holy Spirit to offer you an alternative to the ego's thought system.

The guide you choose to follow in your decision making determines the kind of life you will have. The ego's guidance will lead you down many different paths, each with its own experiences and goals, for this is a world of apparent differences and varying outcomes. Yet are they all the same in one important way: no matter what happens, none of it is real. To chase illusions, to choose illusory goals, is to go nowhere; and to go nowhere is to waste the precious gift of life.

Unfulfillment

There is no condition in this world that is wholly satisfying and complete. All conditions and circumstances here are temporary, incomplete, and incapable of bringing you real fulfillment. How can that which is partial and changeable, as are all experiences of this world, ever bring lasting or deep satisfaction to the one who is whole, complete, and changeless? Nothing less than the return to Wholeness will ever satisfy you wholly.

The partial and limited nature of the ego self is a self-imposed limitation on your experience of yourself. To deny your Wholeness, which is the purpose of the worldly identity, will only bring you unhappiness and suffering. Your identity in separation is the root cause of all your suffering for it is the fact of separation from God that is fear and suffering itself. This fact is simply replicated in many different forms, yet is every form of suffering simply an expression of the condition of separation. Separation from God, from your Creator, is your one and only problem, the root cause and source of all perceived suffering, lack, and limitation.

When the egoic identity fails to satisfy you; when you began to recognize the inherent futility of being a body in ceaseless pursuit of satisfaction, the mind will began to open in a new direction. The honest recognition of the lack of meaning and fulfillment in your life, will inspire you to question deeply how you live and why. If you seize this moment, this opportunity, refusing to go back to sleep, the possibility will open before you to find another way to live, a way that is meaningful and true. This is the beginning of the journey back to your real home in God.

The Desire for Truth

What can bring you lasting peace and hope of healing all that brings you pain and suffering but yourself? There is no cause of pain and suffering outside your mind, and the solution must be where the cause is. You are both the problem and the solution. Nowhere else can they be found. The world is but your attempt to obscure this fact, and keep the idea of sin and guilt alive that they be seen as if outside of you. If you realize no one but you can affect you in any way, the appearances of guilt and sin you see all around you collapse into the nothingness they have always been. Only your mind can affect you and determine the condition you are in, even in this world. All power is given unto you but you have misused it to miscreate hell and turn you back on Heaven. However, you can turn your back on hell and return to Heaven anytime you choose. Everyone will make this choice in time so why wait? To wait is to prolong the time of needless suffering. You can begin the journey home right now in this present moment. All that is required is the sincere desire to do so. The Holy Spirit will respond to all sincere aspirations for Truth.

The only requirement for Truth is a sincere desire to attain it. Given this desire, willingness will develop over time. The willingness to heal the mind of all that obstructs Truth, the willingness to meet Its conditions, will grow and strengthen and carry you home. Your home has been waiting for your return since time began, and it will wait until time is no more and all waiting ended. There is no waiting in Heaven for waiting is of time and Truth knows only the eternal now.

While you dream of time and change and things not yet come, your true home will be unknown to you; waiting for a future still to come will seem to be a fact of your experience. Your return does not wait on time but on your readiness. In any one moment you can be lifted up, and time will be left behind forever. What is left behind is only what is no longer needed. You must learn to travel light, to lay down the heavy burden of unnecessary thought, of limiting and false beliefs. These serve only to weigh the mind down and obscure its natural freedom. There is no way to fly if you are weighed down by the heavy burden you have carried for so long. The mind's natural inclination is to soar through the Heavens, yet it cannot unless the chains that bind it to the earth are broken.

Loose your mind from all it ever believed; let everything go that you have taught yourself, all your beliefs, conclusions, and assumptions. Nothing that you have been taught is true or useful on the spiritual journey. All is illusion, folly, false and limiting. You must let it go that your mind may become able to receive the Truth.

Holiness and Action

Will what you do help you or hurt you? Does what you do to others help or hurt? Do you act with Love, from Love, or from fear? Do your relations with your brothers take place in the Light of the Self or in the ignorance of the self? All selfish action will hurt you no matter what the apparent motivation. To act from the position of ego identification is to deny yourself the help you really need.

To function from the understanding that comes from trusting the Holy Spirit, is to assure yourself of real benefit that will result from your actions; all who are affected in any way by your decisions will also benefit. There is nothing that you do, think, or say that does not affect everyone and everything. To be aware of that fact is wisdom; and to live, to act, for the benefit of all is to bring Holiness Itself into all you do.

Holiness is what you are, the nature of your Being. You cannot be other than what you are. Dissociation from your real nature is the human condition, but this condition is not natural. Sure it is that in the world of seeming separation, Holiness is not apparent, being covered over by the refusal to love. Its absence is sorely felt for when Holiness is lacking, suffering will take its place. In fact, the absence of Holiness is suffering. When what is most holy marks your life through its influence, no real suffering is possible. In the presence of what is sacred, illusion loses its hold, allowing Truth to prevail.

Only the Self

Only the Self is real; all else that appears before your eyes is but the projections of mind: empty imagery without reality or substance. It is the taking of the world of appearance as real that lies behind all problems. What appears as an image in a dream cannot affect you in any way unless you forget that you are dreaming. The dream is very convincing in its effects, yet it is you who give it the power to deceive. If you remember that all life in separation is but a dream, that only God and His Creation are real, you are on your way to freedom. To recognize the bars that hold you prisoner are of your own making is the first step towards freedom. You need not break through the walls that seem to confine you; you need only recognize their unreality and you are free to go. The jailer guarding the walls all along was only your own mind. Only your thoughts keep you a prisoner to what does not exist, and only your thoughts will set you free.

Whenever the temptation to be as you are not arises in your mind, remember this: to be something other than what you are in Truth, will always lead to fear, pain, and suffering, and a deep sense of emptiness and despair. Only by being your Self can you find real fulfillment and return to freedom.

To live life as a body, an exile in a strange land, is the fate of those who refuse to question what they have been taught as reality. So long as willful ignorance blankets the mind, shutting out the Light, so long will you languish in a place that is not your home. While you refuse to raise to question the nature of the world you see, you remain its willing prisoner and will suffer at your own hand. It is your hand alone that is raised to strike, no matter from where the attack may seem to come. Forgive your brothers your sins and take back from them your demand they strike you down to punish you for what you have done. You have done nothing that calls for punishment. Only in dreams of madness could you believe such a thing. Lay down your weapons, end the war against yourself once and for all time. As you lay down all of your defenses, you will discover that nothing can threaten or disturb you in any way.

CHAPTER FIVE

Love and Peace

Love's call will reach you if you let it. This call has gone on unceasingly since time began. Yet you have not heard it because you have not been listening. The din arising from the battlefield that is worldly life has drowned out every call for Truth. The sounds of conflict will always obscure the still, small voice of Spirit. Peace is more than the absence of strife. True peace is a condition in which the thought of conflict cannot arise for its cause has been healed.

All conflict has its origin in the state of mind where fear prevails and your brother is seen as separate and unrelated to you. Fear leads easily to hatred and anger. Anger is always the desire to attack, and what you fear you will hate. Hate perpetuates fear and attack, and the cycle continues without end as long as fear and separation rule your mind.

Peace begins with the recognition that my brother is myself, that only one of us is here. With that understanding, I begin to see that all conflict starts and ends with myself. Always and only it is myself I attack and nothing is gained thereby, for only loss results. What I do to my brother, I do to myself. I can never escape the effects of what I do for cause and effect are never separated.

The mind devoted to peace as its goal becomes a beacon, set on a hill, high above the battlefield. From there, it shines upon its brothers, helping them to lay down their arms and return to peace. Peace is the home of those who love God and would extend that Love to their brothers. Love follows peace as surely as fear follows conflict. When peace fills your heart, there is room for Love only; conflict will not find a home there.

All that will happen when you renounce conflict completely is that you will leave this world forever. The dream cannot hold you captive if you refuse to live by its terms. Belief in guilt and sin and therefore the continuance of fear and the attack that follows, are the conditions set by the ego for life in a world of apparent separation.

Give All You Have

Do not believe what you see: a play of shadows appearing as if substantial, flickering images appearing on the screen of your mind. Do not be the willing victim of a trick you are playing on yourself any longer. You never really wanted to live in separation from your Father and your Self. It was all a mistake, an error, nothing more. An error that took hold of your mind and seemed to make a world of fear, suffering and death. You can leave this world at any time by changing your mind about its purpose. Let it be for you not your home but a way station, a place you are passing through, giving aid to other weary travelers before you leave it behind forever.

What would you do if I told you to give away all you have to the poor and follow me? Would you understand what I mean? To give all you have is to give only what is real, for that is what you have and that is all you have. You do not truly have what is not real; its possession is just a dream. What is real is only what comes from God, what was given in your creation. That you must give away for therein is its nature and meaning. By giving it to your brothers, you are able to keep it for yourself; your store of God's treasures only increases.

Those who lack the awareness of what they are, are poor indeed in the only real sense. To give to them all you have, is to share the peace and the Love of God. To see the Light in your brothers is to recognize them as they are in Truth. In so doing, you are following in my footsteps, doing what I have done. I will never ask you to do anything I have not done. What I did can you do also. In fact, you must do it also for therein lies your salvation. Through my example, through what I learned, can anyone find salvation through forgiveness. I call upon my brothers to forgive as I have forgiven, for in that lies your escape from pain, sorrow, and death. My life was not for me alone; its lessons were learned for the benefit of everyone. My gift to my brothers was the way I lived and the triumph over death. I proved that death is not real, that you cannot be killed. My example removed all reasons to fear and hate, leaving only love and forgiveness as the response to everyone at all times and in all circumstances.

Never True

What was never true is not true now nor will ever be. The Truth has not left your mind. The Truth is your Mind, your Being, and your life. It has always been so and always will be. Do not let belief in the projected illusion take the place of Truth any longer. It is time to return to the home that has always been yours, that awaits your decision to be as you are truly.

This decision, despite all the apparent complexity and confusion that surrounds and obscures it, is actually quite simple. You need only be willing to recognize that you are not a body; you are not all the beliefs you hold about yourself. In that recognition lies your release from every form of bondage, from all pain and suffering. This willingness, rightly exercised, will develop and grow until you are reunited with your Self. The decision that permits the return of Truth is quite simple, straight forward, and consistent in its application. Unless it remains so throughout the duration of your return journey, you will suffer needless delay.

The journey home need not take a long time. It can happen instantly if you would so choose. At any stage, at any moment on the path of return, you can let go all apparent obstructions, all experience of illusion, and disappear into the Self. Yet is this seldom the case. Why? The mind vacillates in its willingness, it commitment, its purpose. Old tendencies and habits die hard.

The human mind is a battleground, a place of warring tendencies and desires. Impulses come and go, and thoughts arise in a constant stream that demands your attention. Reactions to outside events and the emotions that arise within pull you first one way and then another. Emotions arouse thoughts, thoughts oppose or judge emotions. A swirling maelstrom of activity is the mind of separation. This constant distraction, this constant battle for your affections and allegiance, drains your energy and weakens your purpose.

The calming of the mind to bring it to a state of peace and quietness is thus essential. A quiet mind has been made ready to receive the Truth which will not wait long to enter. Truth's return is assured once the obstacles to its coming have been removed. You need only meet its conditions and you will be free once again.

Be Present

What needs to be done in every situation and circumstance no matter the conditions, is to be present wholly with whatever occurs without judgment or reaction. You can only respond fully each moment if you are not limited by or trapped by the past. If the past is operating in your mind and dominating the present, you will project onto and interpret what is happening; never will you meet the situation as it is. Only with a clear and open mind can freedom be found no matter what the circumstances, and this freedom is offered to all through the Holy Spirit.

Freedom is the gift of being present without the past, being free to act from a state of Love and Presence. To bring to the now only Love and openness is to offer healing to everyone and everything. Only by giving healing to all will you receive it. No one can be excluded from receiving the gifts you offer if you would keep them for yourself. No matter what you would do, do it with Love and you will be blessed. Happiness will always accompany Love just as sorrow will always follow fear.

The Ego's Goal

Whenever there is any doubt as to who you are and Who your Father is, stop and ask yourself this question. Who is it that doubts? What is it that does not know what it is? The ego is ignorant of the Truth of what you are for the ego knows nothing. The ego was born as a response to the terror of separation, as the identity that took the place of your true identity. Meant to be the denial of what you are in Truth and the defense against it, the ego will only tell you that you are what you are not. Do not look to the ego for validation or clarification. It will always tell you that you are a body, destined to sicken and die, for this is what it believes.

The Holy Spirit alone knows your true identity and holds that knowledge for you until you are ready to accept it. Nothing prevents you from remembering who you are except your refusal to do so. The fear engendered by the ego in your mind prevents the willingness to remember from arising to awareness to set you free. The defense against the return of the Self is so strong, well established, and consistent, that you need help to free yourself.

Although the defenses that keep you prisoner are of your own making, you have forgotten that fact and so have lost control of them. They operate below the threshold of conscious awareness; thus are they virtually autonomous and completely effective at keeping the Truth away. Truth does not oppose and cannot enter a mind where It is actively resisted. As conscious mind, caught in a dream you do not realize you are dreaming, you go about your life completely oblivious to the Truth that is in you and all around you. I once said, "You shall know the Truth and the Truth shall set you free." The Truth is freedom itself. It then follows that not to know Truth is a state without freedom, a condition of imprisonment.

The ego's goal is to keep you ignorant of who you are. Only by so doing can it keep the walls that contain your mind intact. To identify with the ego, the sense of being a separate identity, is to live in a state of ignorance. Such a state is literally harmful to your well being for the state of illusion is both the cause and the condition of suffering.

Yet is there always a solution to suffering of any kind and the ignorance that is its cause. Truth, born of right understanding and correctly applied, will remove the cause and with the disappearance of the cause do the effects vanish also. The solution to illusion, which is always a state of willful, albeit unconscious ignorance of Truth, is the choosing against illusion and the return of Truth. Light will always shine away darkness, not by attacking or opposing it, but by simply being what It is. Darkness, illusion, cannot exist in the Presence of Truth. The awareness of Truth is the answer to separation and all apparent problems that arise therefrom. Awareness of Truth is not a mental construct, a concept, for Truth cannot be made an object of thought. It cannot be experienced within the context of subject/object perception. Truth must be directly experienced in Mind Itself as what you are. There is no other way to find It and no other place It can be found.

What Is Truth

Whatever can be seen, heard, or perceived in any way is not real. Whatever can be thought of or about is not Truth. Truth cannot be captured by word, thought, or concept. It lies forever beyond the reach of the mind of separation and its activities, for Truth is One. In It is everything that is real; all of God's Creation is part of It, and nothing that was not created by God is real or true. Only the Truth is true, and what is not the Truth is not true.

Nothing that is made by the ego as part of separation and upholding the belief in separation, has anything to do with Truth. All projections of mind are illusions meant to conceal Truth, to obscure It and shatter It into many discontinuous pieces with no relationship to one another. Do not be fooled by color and form, by differences great and small. They do not matter. They are not there.

The purpose of the world you see is to blind you to Truth, to cover It up with names and labels, categories and descriptions. What is One always and only, appears as many, separated by time, space, and difference. Only thus is the fiction of the ego's existence maintained. The ego cannot survive where separation has been replaced by Unity, for the ego is the belief in separation, the thought system that arises from this belief, and the fictitious person to whom these thoughts and the body seem to belong.

The personal identity is a phantom, the ghost in the machine that isn't there. When you look for it as if it were something substantial, you cannot find it. The body is a wholly neutral thing and has no volition of itself. It simply responds to the mind's commands. There is no entity in mind. The mind is just a collection of thoughts, feelings, and impulses that was set in motion a long time ago. The sense of the 'I', of me, is just another thought although it is the most basic thought as it arose from the idea of separation, and in its arising, seemed to make separation possible by providing a central thought or axis around which the experience of separation could be constructed, and from which separation could be projected in an almost endless series of divisions.

What you are in truth is not a physical or mental or emotional quantity. What you are is completely unknown to the senses or to the thinking mind. Spirit is beyond all measurement, all conceptualization, all perception. It can only be known directly by Mind as Itself. This knowledge is not of this world for it does not lie within the limits of time and space. You cannot reach such knowledge through your efforts; the 'you' must disappear so that the Self can reveal Itself in your mind as what you truly are, beyond all thought and all sense of a separate identity.

If what you truly are has no basis in separation, and is in fact the demonstration that separation is impossible, then the separate identity that seems to be you cannot exist. In order for a thing to exist, its existence must be possible. Nothing whose existence is impossible can exist at all. Yet you find yourself an apparent bodily identity, separate from everything you see, and nowhere in the world around you is the Unity of all even remotely suggested by your experience. How can that be?

You are dreaming a dream, an impossible dream. Yet like all dreams, does the impossible and improbable seem to be true, and the conditions of your dreaming seem to determine your life and its purpose. The dreamer has forgotten the Reality from which he comes although he has never left it. Dreaming can seem to last a long, long time, yet when it is over you will see it lasted but an instant. That is all the time it took for an entire universe of dreams to arise, play out its drama, and disappear again. What else could a world made of nothingness do but vanish from the mind that gave it birth when that mind grew tired of dreaming, of its childish play, and let the memory of Truth return. And the Truth will set you free from your own nightmares. Nothing has imprisoned you in a dream of death but your decision to be what you are not, and nothing can return you to the freedom you have always known but your willingness to know your Self again. Whatever the cost of freedom, you will pay it gladly if you could but remember, even for a moment, the freedom you have always known in God.

Freedom

In this world freedom must be earned for it has been thrown away and replaced with what denies and devalues it; fear has taken its place. Fear and freedom are incompatible; freedom is a state in which fear is absent. Fear denies freedom just as freedom demonstrates that fear cannot exist. The absence of fear is Love and freedom. They are never apart and they remain with you forever. If you are to realize freedom however, you must renounce fear in all its forms and lay down all desire to attack. It is fear and only fear that robs you of freedom. In fact, when you invented fear, you turned your back on the freedom in which you were created and chose slavery instead.

Whatever you may do with your mind, you are expressing freedom or you are giving form to fear. These are the only two possibilities. Sure it is the many different responses that seem to be required in your life do not appear to be limited to these two, yet that is all you are ever called upon to choose between. One choice leads you back towards Heaven, the other maintains your place in hell. You cannot return to Heaven unless you are free to do so. To let fear rule your mind is to imprison yourself and lose sight of your true home.

Freedom begins with the recognition that fear and fear only is the obstacle to freedom. Fear weakens you, leaving you cowering behind thick walls whose purpose is to protect you from what threatens you. Yet what threatens you is a fearful projection of your own mind. When you take back your projections, ceasing to give them an autonomy they do not possess, they will lose their hold over you and you will be free.

Nothing can limit your freedom but your own thoughts. They are used to construct your prison or they are used to set you free; the choice of how they are used is yours and yours alone. It is not necessary to think according to what you have been taught by the ego. That is merely habit and is valueless in itself. The ego would have you believe that what is true is false, and what is false is true. What it teaches is always the opposite of Truth; the ego cannot survive in the Presence of Truth so it must always obscure, avoid, deny, or contradict what is true. Everything the ego has ever taught you is false and will only hurt you.

Freedom is the return to Reality. Only there will it be found. The ego is the denial of Reality; it does not know freedom for it cannot know that in whose presence it will disappear. You need not ask the ego about freedom nor accept its ideas about anything. All ideas that arise from ego consciousness make no sense and will only mislead you. What else can you expect from a mistake made so long ago and then forgotten, though it lives on in your mind as if the past were present still? Lay it down my brother, lay your burden down and return to life.

Needs

The needs you perceive are not real. They are part of the dream, and the belief that you are in need of anything is itself a fundamental delusion that upholds the foundation of the false identity. For what but a body, seemingly fragile and requiring constant care and attention, would have needs that must be constantly attended to? The illusory needs whose fulfillment takes so much of your time and energy, have but one purpose: to distract you from recognizing the one and only need you have in the world of separation.

The return of the memory of God to your awareness is the only need that is real. To heal the separation is the purpose of life, the only purpose that is meaningful and capable of accomplishment. If you devote your life to awakening from the dream, to fulfilling your only need, all your other 'needs' will be met. Your Father gave answer to all problems and needs His Son experienced in the dream projection once and for all through the creation of the Holy Spirit. The Holy Spirit takes God's one Answer and translates It into forms you recognize that meet your needs as you perceive them.

Do not forget that you are not a body. Nothing else will free your mind. Only the recognition of what you are not will open the way to experiencing what you are in Truth. You are not confined by a physical form unless you choose to be. This choice can be undone by choosing once again.

Love

Whatever occupies your mind that is not Love, be it thoughts, feelings, beliefs, or memories, must be relinquished to make room for Love. All that is not Love must be healed that Love may return and claim its own. Love belongs to you and you belong to Love. As *A Course in Miracles* states so simply and eloquently, "Teach only Love for that is what you are." If Love is what you are and you do not experience Love as it is, then you are not experiencing yourself as you are. To be the Self, the Christ, is to be Love only. If you are not being Love only, then you are being something other than what you are in Truth. This substitute identity has robbed you of your true identity by taking its place. However, this was not foisted upon you; it was a decision you made long ago, and it remains in effect until you change your mind and choose again.

What if you let go all fear, renounced fear forever, recognized it for the nothingness it is, and decided to feel only the emotion that is real, Love? What if you decided to love only, only to love? What would happen? You would be free and joy would flood your mind and carry you to God. God is Love and you are a part of His Love, a creation of His Love, and you are Love. As a channel of His Love and mercy, you have the privilege of bringing Love to a world that has denied itself what it needs most. You bring a Love that shines into all the dark and secret places hidden in the human mind. Love will illuminate all fear, all grievances. It will expose the deep sorrow, and the twisted hates that cast their dark shadow across the mind of separation. Love sees all and shines away all darkness, all that denies Love, through its beneficent gaze.

Whenever you are tempted to choose fear over Love, remember what that choice has cost you in pain and suffering. It has cost you the Peace of God and the knowledge of your true relationship with Him. Would you perpetuate this separation or would you repair it? Every choice for fear and attack in any form continues the rejection of your Creator and the deep loneliness that has marked your life ever since. Do not forget what you are choosing with each decision you make: life or death.

Love will always lead you back to life eternal. It shines away death in all its disguises leaving only the One Light. The Love and Light of Your Father is what you are. By offering only That and nothing else, you will find there is nothing else. God is your Being, your Mind, your Love, and your Life. Never forget this for your Father never forgets you.

Do not underestimate your resistance to Love, for it plays a major role in keeping the separation in place. If you would drop all defenses and simply love, this world would fall away and you would find yourself in the Presence of your Creator. Unfortunately, it is this you fear more than anything in this world although this is your only need.

When you are called upon to love, the ego offers you a distorted version of love to take Love's rightful place. The ego teaches that you are unworthy of real Love because of your sinful nature. It then teaches you that your brothers are likewise guilty. Thus the only basis you share on which Love can be established between you is your mutual unworthiness. You and your brother agree that since you are both guilty and unworthy of being loved, your relationship will maintain this guilt by never bringing it to conscious awareness. Instead, you take turns projecting onto each other in an attempt to keep guilt alive without taking responsibility for it. What results is a love/hate dynamic that characterizes to some extent most human relationships. If you honestly search your mind, you will find that you have grievances towards everyone no matter how much you think you love them.

Such relationships offer you but a parody of what Love is. Yet is there still, though masked by the ego's distortions, a kernel of Love's meaning to be found. In the honest sharing, the recognition of a true common interest, and the human attempt to forgive in good faith, Love is faintly reflected but that is enough. All your relationships have the potential to be holy relationships, and that is what they must become if you are to know Love again. Through your relationships with your brothers, you have the chance to learn forgiveness and true giving.

Giving

Whenever the opportunity arises to give, you must respond for you are always giving but to yourself. Every chance to help another by giving is a chance to share the gifts of God you have received and thus increase what you have. All that is real will only be increased by giving it away; that is why it is given you. Do not underestimate the power of your giving. Giving will set you free. It is Love that gives; and when your giving has become total, Love will return.

The ego gives always to get, but the Christ in you gives because it is His nature and brings Him joy. You cannot lose by giving truly, by giving from your heart. Whatever is given will return to you, albeit in a different form. Your store of divine gifts increases with every act of giving. Your Father only gives, He never takes. If you would be like Him, and you are like Him, you must give everything to everyone. By so doing, you are set free from the ego's thought system of fear and sacrifice. To give cannot be a sacrifice if you only gain thereby.

What the ego would have you do is limit giving to only a few and exclude all others. Even with these few however, giving is too often a kind of exchange where each gives to get. Giving that you may receive something in return is not true giving; it is rather a thinly disguised attempt to manipulate each other. Love does not manipulate, and all real giving is an expression of Love. Every gift truly given always arises from Love and includes Love no matter the form or circumstance.

Whether you should give or not is never the question. Always it is only the opportunity to give that is important. You have innumerable occasions every day to give to your brothers. A smile, a kind word, a chance to help, the form of the gift matters not. You must give and give freely, and you will always receive. As you give all you truly have freely to all your brothers, you will receive freely from your Father. He is always giving you everything as He did in your Creation, but unless you give to all as He does, you cannot accept His gifts.

CHAPTER SIX

Remember Your Father

The only way to accept your Father's Love is to love your brothers as He does. Your brothers are a part of God; they share His Being as do you. To Love God is to Love His children. It cannot be otherwise. Unless you love as He does, you will not know God. The quickest way back to your Father is to abandon yourself to Love, for God is Love.

When the time comes to leave this world, will you be ready? I am not speaking of death. You cannot leave the world through dying, but through awakening to the Truth. The time will come for everyone who walks the dusty roads of this world when the recognition arises that it is time to go; time to lay down your burdens and give up your attachment to pain and sorrow. This recognition may come as a shock or as a relief. If you are not ready to face this realization, you will simply suppress it, and it will vanish from your awareness. A chance to begin the journey back will be lost until, at some future time, the idea will rise again and take root in your mind where it will grow into a mighty force for change.

What is the best thing you can do anywhere, at anytime? Remember your Father. If you are constantly remembering your Father's Love for you, you will discover your great Love for Him, and this Love will clear all obstacles between God and your awareness of Him. Only the blocks to the awareness of God's Presence within you keep you a prisoner in a world of separation. Remove them and you would immediately find yourself in Heaven and realize you never left.

If you could instantly withdraw all investment in the illusions which so fascinate your mind, they would disappear forever, leaving you in a state of Grace. The withdrawal of allegiance must be total for one illusion contains all illusions. Heaven cannot be reached while one illusion remains to limit your mind, for Heaven is a state of limitlessness and Unity. There is no compromise between Truth and illusion. Where one is, the other is not. No matter what the cost of Truth, you will gladly pay it when once you realize its inestimable value.

All you are asked to do is to give up what is valueless and has only hurt you, causing untold pain and suffering, for what has total value and will set you free. Can the motivation for such an exchange be difficult to arouse if you see it for what it is? The problem is really this: you refuse to recognize the absolute worthlessness of everything the world holds out to you; you still think there is something to be gained, something valuable or desirable that will bring happiness or fulfillment. This split in loyalty, a lack of fidelity to a single purpose, prevents illusion from vanishing from your holy mind. A process of gradual relinquishment of the falsity that characterizes your split mind then becomes necessary and this takes time, even a long time.

The goal of *A Course in Miracles* is to bring you to a single dedication, a single purpose. This will unify your mind over time until the requisite wholeness is attained, and the mind made ready for God to take the last step. He cannot enter a mind that is not ready to welcome Him wholly.

Freedom and the Body

What can be achieved must be achieved. What cannot be accomplished must be recognized as such. You will never make illusion real no matter what you do. Give up the attempt for it will never succeed. Turn your mind back toward Truth once and for all time. Let Truth back into your life and It will set you free.

Truth and illusion cannot coexist in your mind. The presence of one denies the other. One makes up the prison in which you live, and the other is the freedom that waits for you just beyond the prison walls. If you would be free, you must stop defending yourself and welcome freedom with open arms.

Freedom threatens all the careful plans you have made, the meticulous defenses you have erected. Its only concern is to return you to the Self you left but in dreams. You cannot rediscover the Self unless you are free of the fear that makes you deny It. The ego seeks security and safety always, for it perceives a world that threatens and denies it at every turn. Surrounded by hostile forces, or so it believes, the ego obsessively seeks to insure its safety through its plans and defenses. The ego thinks its present defenses and careful plans against future uncertainties will insure the survival and continuation of its chosen home, the body.

So long as you identify with the body, you will not be free. The body itself is wholly neutral. It can be used to imprison the mind or to help you learn the lessons that set the mind free. Your decision determines how it is used and the consequences that follow. Identify with the body as the ego would have you do, and the mind has become its own jailor. Recognize that the body's usefulness is its function as a learning aid and not as a home, and you have opened the door to freedom.

When you are willing to accept the idea of the body as simply a means to communicate the Truth, which is how the Holy Spirit regards it, you will be free of the need to overemphasize its importance. When the body is seen in proper perspective, its role as means by which to limit and imprison your mind is renounced, and the body is then free to serve the Holy Spirit's purpose. Its safety and health are thus assured as long as you have need of it.

That the body is a part of your experience is undeniable. There is no need to escape from the body while it is needed as a learning and teaching aid. While you have need of it, while your learning is not complete, it can be used and used well to serve the purpose the Holy Spirit gives it. But you must see that it serves His purpose and not the ego's. The body is the ego's chosen home; to identify with the body is to accept the ego's thought system of separation, and the body will then be used to defend and maintain separation.

Accept the Holy Spirit's interpretation of the body's function and it will be used to go beyond itself. The body does not separate you from your brothers unless you assign it that purpose. As your chosen identity, your home, the body symbolizes safety through separation. All the belief in the need for defense and attack thus arises. The body is not the citadel of safety you imagine it to be, it is your prison. By your own hand, you have closed the prison doors and condemned yourself to captivity.

Peace and Sin

What is meant by the belief in sin? To believe in sin is to believe it is possible to act unlovingly, and that such acts call for punishment or vengeance. And some acts must remain forever unforgiveable. Such beliefs imprison the mind, locking it into a position where fear and conflict are inevitable and peace cannot be found. Peace is impossible for a mind committed to belief in sin. The belief in sin is the belief that God's Son can be other than what He was created to be; that God's Holy Creation can separate Itself from Its Creator and take on qualities It was not given by God; and that a separate will opposed to God's Will is possible and capable of having real effects. All this is included in the belief in the reality of sin.

Peace is impossible to attain while the mind is committed to find and defend that which denies peace in every way. Those who believe in sin are committed to conflict, and will never be free of it until they renounce the belief which gives conflict and guilt their existence. To have peace, you must give up what opposes it and makes its presence in your life impossible. Peace is God's gift to His guiltless Son. Being part of Love, peace does not exclude or oppose for any reason. Peace, like Love, is for all, and will return to any mind that sincerely desires it and is willing to meet the conditions for its return.

The Voice for God

Let no one tell you what to do or guide your actions but the Holy Spirit. No one else is capable of guiding you truly. The ego has been your guide for too long, and the road it has placed you on leads nowhere. To go nowhere over and over while believing you are going somewhere is beyond futility, it is meaningless.

There is nowhere to go but back to God; all other roads lead to oblivion. If you are tired of useless journeys that lead to imagined goals that do not exist, let go your reliance on the guide who knows nothing and turn to the One Who will lead you to the one goal that has meaning and is capable of accomplishment. Let all the goals you have pursued or will pursue be replaced by the one goal you truly desire above all others. In truth, there are no other goals, only temporary substitutes that obscure your heart's desire for a little while. If you will let yourself be led in the direction that you truly want to go, your mind will, little by little, become clear and capable of recognizing your true destination. Once this understanding is established, the illusory pursuits of this world will no longer attract you. With the mind fixed on the eternal and meaningful as the only goal worth striving for, nothing will be able to delay your homecoming, and your return to your Father's House will be met with joy and celebration. On that day you will know again who you are in Truth, and you will know your Father as He wills to be known.

In the world of perception, your Father is unknown to you for knowledge has vanished from your awareness. Yet has God not forgotten you; He calls to you unceasingly and you <u>will</u> hear His call. The constant activity of mind and body, and the ego's shrill voice, prevent His call from reaching your awareness. His call will continue until you are ready to hear it, be it sooner or later. Do not delay that time unnecessarily. Only your willingness is needed; everything else will be given when you are ready to receive.

The ego's strategy is to keep you too busy, too occupied with the activities of this world to hear any voice but its own. Yet you will hear God's call for you have been waiting for it since time began. You cannot not hear your Father calling to you for it is His Will that you return to Him, and what He wills waits not on time, being already perfectly accomplished. You can but delay your awareness of what is always and already true, and while you do, it will be lost to you.

The loss of awareness of the Truth that waits for recognition in your mind, is the root cause of all your suffering. The darkness of ignorance is drawn like a veil across the face of Christ, and so long as you desire not to lift it, it will remain. It matters not the many forms that ignorance may take, all are the same in content: the wish to be as you are not, to be separate.

The Dream of Separation

Separation was once a tiny, mad idea that mistakenly became capable of accomplishment, not in reality but in dreams, and you have been dreaming ever since. A choice was made and then multiplied many times over; the world you see is the result. The choice was not real nor did its consequences have any real effects, yet the mind believes in what it makes and gives power to its miscreations just as to its real creations. The effects of illusion are as strong in the mind that made them as are the effects of Truth, but there is one important difference. The Truth can be truly shared and illusions cannot be.

In the dream of separation do illusions seem to be shared, for only that which is shared can be experienced as real. Yet it is but a sharing of nothingness, and nothingness is shared only by those lost in the darkness of illusion. In the absence of Light, the darkness appears as if real, and all kinds of fantastic shapes are seen and believed. Witnessing to one another the reality of the shadows that appear and disappear, convinces the mind that would believe in separation that it has been accomplished. Believing that you are where you are not, has hidden your true home from your awareness and left you adrift, at the mercy of a decision made long ago that was but an error in identification.

To correct this error that lives on in your mind is the function of the Holy Spirit. The process of correction and undoing is the Atonement. When the Atonement is complete in your mind, having been fully accepted, there will be no more need for learning and perception. The mind freed of all its errors and guided in its perception by Christ's vision, will not stay long where it is not at home. Unburdened by the heavy weight of constant judgment and the belief in sin and guilt, filled with Love and Light, it will rise to Heaven for there is nothing to hold it back. When the earthly bonds are loosed, you will leave this world as it vanishes from your mind never to return.

Love and Transformation

If you were to love your brothers totally, asking nothing in return, all your relationships would be transformed. Holy relationships contain only Love and follow no laws but God's. The real purpose of all relationships is to bring you closer to God through the opportunity they provide to love and forgive. If you use them for this purpose, they become holy and lead you back to the holiness that lives within you as you.

Only through the total transformation of all your relationships, will your life be transformed into the expression of Love. Love is expressed in many ways, through thought, word, and action. It is the action of Love that heals and helps those in need. When Love rules your mind, you will be helpful and kind at all times and in all circumstances to everyone. No child of Love will ever be forsaken by His Father or by his brothers, for it is Love's function to join with and include always. Only that which has its origin in Love is truly helpful. All else is but fear and will only weaken you. Do not be afraid of Love. Love will set you free while fear will perpetuate your imprisonment.

If Love is what you are, and you do not experience yourself as loving, then you do not experience yourself as you are. How can that be? Ask yourself this question. Would I be as God created me, as I am in Truth, or would I be the self that I have made, that I have imagined myself to be? Your answer to this question determines how you experience yourself. One answer is made with the help of the Holy Spirit, the other is made on behalf of the ego, the belief in separation.

Would you be separate and fearful or would you be Love and fearless? These are always the only choices that can be made. If you see this clearly at all times and in all situations, the correct choice would be obvious. Because of the confusion that clouds your mind, you cannot tell the difference between Love and fear, and indeed are very likely to confuse the two. This is not readily apparent however, as long as you think that Love and fear can coexist as in the special relationship.

If you would free yourself of fear and return to Love, you must learn to recognize fear in all its forms and renounce them. When the obstacles to Love's Presence are removed, It will return of Itself. You need do nothing but choose against fear without exception by becoming aware of all the disguises it wears and refusing to countenance fear in any form. This will free your mind to love.

The Motivation for Action

Whatever the reasons for your refusal to do God's Will, underneath them all despite their differences, lies the same root: fear. All actions arise from one of two sources, Love or fear. If your motivation comes through the ego, it is the action of fear. When it arises through the inspiration of the Holy Spirit, the result will be Love. To be aware of what you do and why you do it is therefore very important. All action resulting from fear will have limited results, but Love's results are always limitless.

You are called upon to offer the world, to offer your brothers always and only what is highest and most beneficial. To act from fear is to offer death; to act from Love is to give eternal life. When you realize that whatever you give, regardless of the nature of the gift, you give yourself, the importance of what you give others becomes apparent for its effect on you is inescapable. We have said before that you should give others only what you would yourself receive because you <u>are</u> receiving it. The ignorance of this fact allows you to give and do unto others what you would not want given or done to you, for you literally know not what you do.

The consequences of your actions may not be associated with their cause, but this does not prevent their effects from appearing in your life. What you give, you will get always. This is another way of saying what you teach, you will learn. Remember always that you are giving only to yourself, forgiving only yourself, hating or loving only yourself, and all your thoughts and actions will come into sharp focus. In that awareness, you will be able to choose consciously what you would give and receive and what you would teach and learn.

There is no better way to assure a future unlike the past than to be aware of what you are doing in the present, and how that will determine the future. If you are choosing as the ego would have you do, you are perpetuating the past and losing the opportunity the present holds out to you. If you decide with the Holy Spirit, you are breaking with the past, utilizing the present, and freeing the future. Only the repetition of the past keeps you in bondage and drives freedom from your mind.

The Use of Time

What you do with time is all important for time is yours to use as you desire. Time itself is neutral and serves the purpose you give it. Which purpose you assign depends on the guide you choose to follow. As always there are only two: the Holy Spirit or the ego, and they use time to accomplish exactly opposite purposes.

The ego uses time to keep the past alive and assure a future that is a continuation of the past. The present is thus effectively covered over and bypassed. If you accept the ego's use of time, you will live in bondage to the past and in fear of the future. The present will evade you, and thus any hope of real change, of freedom, will be lost. Only in the present can change take place as the present is the only part of time that is real. If you were truly present, you would see the ego as the nothingness it is, and you would realize that the past is over and the future can be determined not by the past but by present decisions. Until you understand this, the present will be lost to you.

The Holy Spirit uses time in a very different way. He sees the purpose of time is to use time to go beyond time. Time is something you have invented, and like everything else you have made, it can be given another purpose. The Holy Spirit will help you bring your mind into the present, and will help you learn how to use time wisely. To use time wisely is to abide in present awareness and thus be conscious of the constant activity of your mind. Through moment to moment awareness, you begin to understand your mind as it is and become aware of the choices you are constantly making. Through awareness and understanding of this whole process of constant mind activity, you become capable of changing your mind, of making conscious choices for Truth on an ongoing basis.

The Correction of Error

Whenever you act from self will, which is to act from the belief in separation, you are moving away from God and rejecting Love. To do so is an error, and errors need correction;

correction requires willingness and surrender. All errors can and must be corrected and their consequences undone if you are to know God again, and you <u>will</u> know Him again. He wills that His Son return to full communication with Him, and so it is done. In time, this appears to be somewhere in the future, yet is time but illusion. You must choose when you will leave time forever; it can be done now or postponed till some later date. To wait is to perpetuate fear and suffering unnecessarily. To move away from God is to turn your back on Love and freedom; where God and Love are absent, fear will rule. The kingdom of fear is a barren land where suffering is never far away and joy cannot be found. This land is not your home and never will be, though you have long walked its dusty roads with bowed head and a heavy heart.

Now is the time to give up the attachment to all that you do not truly want. You never really wanted all the things you seek, all the experiences you seem to value. You came to them honestly, believing that was where your safely and fulfillment would be found. Due to the confusion in your mind, the appearances presented to you seemed to be real and capable of making you happy. Yet all you ever found was temporary relief of a kind that was never wholly satisfying. A state of confusion in the mind as the origin of all action will never bring lasting or consistent results. All action originates in the mind, for it is the mind that provides the motivation and the impulse to act. Your state of mind is therefore very important for the results you want to achieve. Both the goal and the means by which it is reached are determined by your thinking.

Thinking that arises from the belief in the reality of separation, from the thought system of separation, is by nature chaotic, confused, and inconsistent. It will never have results that do not reflect its essential characteristics. There will be no peace in the mind given to the perpetuation of confused thinking. This need not be. Only the unconscious habits of a mind misidentified as a body, prevent clarity from returning to your awareness. Therefore it is of utmost importance to become aware of all that passes through awareness and its effects on your state of mind. To do otherwise is to lose the chance to direct your mind as you would have it be. Without clarity of purpose, you will accept a thousand different goals, all of which have one thing in common: they are meaningless and lead nowhere. The preoccupation with goals that offer nothing of real value serves only to keep you distracted from life's true purpose. This is characteristic of a mind that has chosen the ego as its guide. The ego itself knows nothing and understands nothing. It can lead you nowhere but round and round in an endless circle that goes nowhere until you become so exhausted that death is welcomed as a relief. Yet death itself has no meaning and will not bring your suffering to an end.

It is life you seek, not death, and what is part of life shares its meaning. To turn away from the ego's direction is to reject confusion, pain, fear, and death, choosing Love and life in their place. You choose always between what is nothing and what is everything. To see this choice clearly as it is, is to recognize that no choice is actually possible. Recognition and remembrance of the Truth will remove all confusion and doubt from your mind, leaving it clear and empty. A mind that is clear and empty is a quiet mind, and to such a mind Truth will return.

Choice and Content

Whatever the choices that confront you seem to be, whatever the appearance, remember always that you choose content not form. The form serves to mask or to represent the content it serves. You must learn to look beyond form to the underlying content if you would choose truly. Form is multiple but content is only two. Countless forms and situations mask the content of illusion they represent. The ego would have you choose form over content, for it must always hide from you the truth of what it offers: pain, suffering and death. Nothingness is still meaningless no matter how attractive the wrapping. Do not allow yourself to be fooled any longer into choosing what you do not truly want. The confusion in your mind and the momentum of tendencies long established, prevent you from perceiving truly.

Either you want what you are deciding for or you do not. Nothing could be simpler than this. What basis for choice could be clearer than to choose what you want and choose against what you do not want? In order for this clarity to be present however, you must be truly aware of whether what you are choosing is desirable. If fact, you have been consistently confused about the nature of what attracts you and impels your choice. This has led to choosing what has hurt you and complete unawareness of what would only help. Only that which is beneficial in every sense of the word can be said to be desirable and thus worthy of your choosing.

To choose consistently that which is only helpful and supportive of your goal, requires the establishment in your mind of accurate perception of what your choices are in each and every situation. You must learn to look past all forms and see the real content of each situation and possibility. If you would choose Truth over illusion, Love over fear, you must recognize the difference between them, and see the content before you for what it is. Without this understanding, you will choose blindly and will take alternating steps forward and backward. Do not waste time vacillating between what you truly want and what you think you want. Let the Holy Spirit teach you to recognize the only choice to be made in every situation without exception.

In order to be free of all that holds you back, all attachment to what is not true must be given up. The desire for illusion, for separation, and what you think it offers, has blinded you to what is truly helpful. There is no other way back to Truth than to cut directly through the obstacles to Truth in your mind that have taken Its place. As has been so often stated, Truth has never been lost. Even now It remains as the reality by which and in which you live. Yet has the awareness of Truth as your life and Being, been lost through your decision to replace It with your own mistaken ideas. Illusions long cherished in place of Truth do not yield their hold on your mind easily. They hold you in bondage only through your consent. Withdraw your consent, your support, and they will collapse like a house of cards, returning to the nothingness from which they came. However, you cannot withdraw consent from what you are unaware of, for decisions once made no matter how long ago, remain in effect until revisited at which time they can be corrected.

Continuity and Consent

Within the context in which your life takes place, there is a seeming continuity. This continuity convinces you that what you experience is real and lasting despite the fact that it is constantly changing. You do not regard its constantly changing nature as unnatural or as possible proof of its unreality. Yet you will find, if you pay careful attention, that all things, circumstances, and situations are unstable and do not last. How can what is changeable, unstable, and untrustworthy, be real? Can certainty be found under such conditions? Reality is not something one day, and the next day changed into something else. Reality is wholly unchanged and unchanging, now and forever. Nowhere else can certainty be found. To put your faith in what is constantly changing and unreal, is to invite fear, uncertainty, and suffering. And your invitation will be accepted as your tears flow unceasingly.

Without your consent, nothing can be done. Only your consent enables the Holy Spirit to do what must be done. He needs your willingness every step of the way if He is to set you free. Your willingness, consistently exercised, allows your mind to be undone and the Truth to be revealed as you. Do not underestimate the importance of your little willingness. It was your choice made long ago and endlessly repeated since, that made the world in which you find yourself, and it is your willingness to choose again that is used to undo the world and restore you to the Kingdom.

Do not make the mistake of thinking that you can be free without letting go what is responsible for your imprisonment in the world of separation: the self you have made. What has taken the place of what God created as you, has been accepted as your identity. This acceptance has resulted in your experience of yourself as a body, separate from other bodies and objects that seem to surround you, and your mind seeming to be limited to the little space the body occupies. From this little space, you reach out to others who are also limited by the body's dimensions, and each, from their little space, attempts to communicate with others through movement and sound.

Communication

Communication is always partial and limited; never is it complete while the belief in separation rules your mind. Minds in separation can never communicate fully, for the decision to be separate is the decision to withhold communication. To communicate wholly is to give yourself entirely, to join without reservation, without fear. This cannot be done while the ego rules your mind. The need to defend and attack makes real communication impossible. To overcome separation, you must be willing to recognize your brother as part of yourself. Thereby do you choose against limitation, and choose instead to remember your Unity which is all-embracing and unlimited. This will open the door in time through which you will walk into the sunshine of God's eternal Love. Love Itself is communication, and Light also. Although the perception of bodies will remain, the mind restored to Love and shining brightly again as the One Light, is not prevented by this perception from experiencing its true dimensions. Mind is not confined to a body. It extends everywhere without limit, and in It are all things included, part of It, and in full communication forever.

Need and Meaning

When the time comes to put away what has never been needed, will you be able to do so? Your willingness is all that is required, but first you must recognize the impossibility of sacrifice. The belief in sacrifice lies beneath all sense of loss, of deprivation. So long as the idea of sacrifice attracts you and influences your thinking, so long will you struggle mightily to hold on to the past and resist the changes that are needed. In Reality, is sacrifice impossible, for what must be given up and left behind has no value. Your failure to recognize this gives rise to the resistance you feel at letting go what holds you back.

What would be the point, the reason, to gather the things of this world; to surround yourself with what has no meaning? Why would a human mind decide that its security lay in the possession of physical objects? How can concrete things provide satisfaction to something as non-concrete as a mind? Only a mind misidentified as a body could possibly make such an erroneous assumption. Once the mind has decided it is what it is not, this error begins to multiply, to build on itself. What follows is a proliferation of errors that take the mind further and further from Truth, from its original state of knowledge. Lost in the increasing complexity that surrounds, penetrates, and confuses it, the mind does not know where to turn, leaving it vulnerable to fear, confusion, and further misunderstanding.

The original error has been forgotten, buried so deep that memory cannot reach it. No longer aware of what you are, and seeming to be something else entirely, you can only respond to the 'reality' that seems to contain you and surround you. This 'reality' imposes certain conditions and limitations on your life and these in turn determine your needs. As Mind, you had no needs, only the privilege to create unceasingly by extending your Self, the Light and Love that is you. How can that which was created by God to have and be everything eternally, need anything?

Fear and Freedom

The Truth that you are has not deserted you. The awareness of It has been lost through a process of forgetting and substitution. This loss has left you with a sense of emptiness within that is so deep you cannot face it. And this too has been buried deep in your mind and covered over by the sleep of forgetfulness. What could ever take the place of what you have lost? Nothing in this world could ever fill that deep sense of emptiness, the void that lies deeply buried where your heart used to be. Your true heart has been left behind, for the heart is Love, and the world was made to be a place where Love could not enter and be Itself. The Source of love, the Creator of all that is, is feared and denied, and likewise refused entry to what you have made to take Love's place.

Your Father has not forgotten you. He calls to you unceasingly; and you will, somewhere in time, answer His call. When in time you decide to listen can be sooner or later, for it is your decision. No one can make this decision for you; the Holy Spirit waits for your willingness to turn towards Truth. He will respond to every thought, to every movement in that direction, adding His willingness to yours. When in time you remember your Father has already been determined. You need not wait however, for you can shorten time immeasurably by what you do now. There is no good reason to delay though you will invent many, and then many more. The reasons to delay your homecoming are simply your substitutions for the Love of God. If you could see them as the shabby, pale, meaningless forms they are, you would choose again. Your belief in your replacements for the Love of God is what keeps you here, lingering in a place of empty hopes and unfulfilling dreams. And stay you will until the Light dawns in your mind, showing you the futility of what you do and what you believe.

To begin again to live truly is a decision that must be made. Life in separation is not real life, but an empty imitation. The mind dulled by fear, perceiving guilt, sin, and attack all around it, is incapable of loving itself or anyone else. Love is displaced onto objects, be they bodies or things desired, and always is it limited and conditioned. Life is not possible unless your mind is free to love. Even in this world, the freedom to love can be given you but you must be willing to accept it. Freedom and Love go together as do Love and Life. Life without Love is no life at all; and where Love is, there is freedom also.

The mind must be free in order to be a fit vessel for Love's return. Fear must be uncovered, understood, recognized in all its forms, and healed that Love may reclaim Its own. To be free is to be free of fear, for it is only fear that limits and imprisons the mind. You must learn to see the role played by fear in your life, how it restricts and binds you, preventing happiness and peace from establishing themselves. When this fact is deeply recognized and understood, you will be ready to reject fear in all its forms. Unrecognized, fear will continue to affect your life in every way as your invisible companion, the stranger who has taken over your home and made you a stranger to yourself.

This great tragedy need not be. You invited fear into your home and gave it power over you. You can as well withdraw the invitation and recognize that fear has only the power you gave it. Withdraw you allegiance, your commitment to honor it; realize its nothingness as the invention of your mind, a mistake made long ago. Fear will lose its hold over your mind to the degree you refuse to believe in it, to the degree you refuse to act it out. Let not fear influence and drive your decisions or determine your state of mind. Decide resolutely to free yourself from its influence by asking the Holy Spirit to guide you in all things. He will always guide you to your strength and thus away from fear and pain.

There is never any reason to be afraid of anything at anytime. You are never in danger except from your own thoughts. Even then the danger is not real though you will experience the effect of your beliefs. Fear is kept alive in your mind by the misidentification with the body and the sense of being a separate person or entity different from other persons. As long as this error dominates your thinking and experience, fear will be your constant companion. The belief in a separate identity is the basis of fear in this world. Never will you be free of fear as long as you persist in being that whose core is fear.

Come to Your Senses

Whatever the cost of escaping from Reality, you have paid it gladly, and will continue to pay it until you realize your error.

The cost of escaping from what you truly are to be what you are not except in dreams, is pain, fear, suffering, and death. How could it be otherwise? To leave behind your true state of eternal peace and Love will only lead to a dream of madness in which chaos rules, for madness is chaos. There is no safety to be found in a world ruled by the laws of chaos. Such a world is indeed untrustworthy, and will be home to fear, and all suffering will follow.

Coming to your senses in the spiritual sense means to wake up. To look around you and realize this world is not your home; it is but a temporary resting place through which you travel. To return to sanity is to recover the capacity to make sense out of nothingness. The only sensible thing to do regarding nothingness is to recognize it for what it is and cease to think of it as what it is not. The whole problem with separation begins with believing that what was not created by God could nonetheless have real existence. Letting the mind then turn this mad idea into something that could be experienced as if real, launched the entire projection of the world of separation and everything that came with it. What left your awareness, replaced by the fantasy you had made, was the knowledge of Truth and the ability to recognize error.

No one who has forgotten the one distinction that can be made in truth, has any basis whatsoever by which to recognize error. Lost in the one big error you had made and the subsequent ones that followed, all ability to discriminate accurately between Truth and illusion was also lost. The only thing left to you was the power of decision. This cannot be taken from you although you may use it rightly or wrongly as you wish. To use the power of decision rightly, to choose Truth, you must be able to recognize Truth and error for what they are, as they are. In this, you need help from beyond the territory of the original error. Truth was lost so long ago that you cannot reach It unaided. The Holy Spirit has the task to bring you back to the Truth you left behind.

The Development of Trust

To return to Truth requires the development of trust on your part; without trust, nothing can be done. The Holy Spirit must begin by reinforcing every little movement or inclination towards Truth, thus teaching you to begin to move in Its direction. This part of the journey back can take a long time as the mind begins dimly to realize there is another purpose to life. What it thought before is now recognized as incomplete at best. At this stage, your allegiance is still divided and progress proceeds by fits and starts. If you persist, you will slowly gain momentum as the attraction of Truth will begin to draw you towards Itself. Sooner or later the recognition will dawn in your mind that you are being helped, and that this help is your way out of ignorance into the Light of Truth.

The active recognition of the Holy Spirit and the importance of the role He plays, is extremely helpful in developing trust and willingness. Willingness and trust go together; the more you learn to trust the Holy Spirit, the more willing you are to ask for and accept the help He offers. He cannot help you if you are unwilling to accept His help. All you need give Him is your little willingness to work with Him; to ask for help and act on the guidance you receive. He will do the rest. God's plan for your release is perfect and the Holy Spirit fulfills His role perfectly. You must accept and complete your part of the Great Plan, nothing more and nothing less.

What is very important to realize is that you do not know your part in the Great Plan. The Holy Spirit, Who has assigned you your part, knows it perfectly and will help you complete it if you let Him. You need not figure it out yourself. Indeed, to attempt to do so is to add the ego to your part. This will result in the failure to do what is needed, for you will be doing something else in place of what has been assigned. To try to add to what is already perfect, is to deny and obstruct.

Your role is to listen and learn. Listen to what the Holy Spirit is teaching you, learn what you are to do each day, and do it. Of yourself, you need do nothing. You cannot come to understanding by yourself. To try to understand from the perspective of the self you have made and act from that understanding, is to choose the ego as your guide. The ego's purpose is to keep separation real in your mind, and not allow you to do anything that would thwart its purpose.

The only way out of the endless maze of separation will not be shown to you by the one who guards its twisted corridors and bars the exit. Accepting salvation and the plan by which it is accomplished, must be recognized for what it is: surrender of the belief you know what must be done, and accepting that the Holy Spirit does know. In fact, you know nothing. It is extremely important to remember this always; thereby do you become willing to let yourself be guided in all things, at all times.

Never should you rely on your understanding alone for you are never alone; your decisions are made always with a guide. The Holy Spirit or the ego guide your learning, your understanding, and your actions. And which guide you choose will determine the course of your life, its conditions, its purpose, its goal, and its results.

If your goal is salvation, the escape from separation, suffering, and death, you must choose the right guide. The Holy Spirit will not fail you if you will trust Him and give Him your cooperation. The way home is sure if you allow Him to guide your footsteps and direct your mind. Do not waste time following the time worn paths that lead nowhere. Do not grasp at shadows. Turn over your mind to the One Who knows the way.

Life and Death

What is the worst thing that can happen to you in this life? What do you fear more than anything? The thought of death haunts your mind and casts its shadow across your life day and night. There is no fear that does not have its origin in the thought of death. Death represents to you the worst that could happen. Human life is lived always with the awareness that it will end someday. All your hopes, dreams, and ambitions, are a vain attempt to deny its coming, to occupy the mind with activities and give life seeming meaning and purpose in the face of death. You cannot live each day, taking yourself and your life seriously, unless you somehow blot out this awful fact from your consciousness.

Yet is death always with you. The evidence of impermanence surrounds you on all sides. Plants, animals, and people are born, arise, flourish for a while, then through change and decay they come to an end. All that is born will die. All that begins will have an end. Such is life in separation, a mad parody, a distorted reflection of life as it truly is.

Life itself is of God. All of Creation shares one life with its Creator. Life is of Spirit, of Mind. It does not come and go; It is not born to die. Life has not its origin in the birth of form nor an ending in form's dissolution. Life is eternal and beyond change of any kind. It is not life that dies as a body; the body never lived and it never dies. The body is an idea in your mind that reflects your wishes. It is wholly neutral, having no volition of its own. Death is an idea in your mind that is visited upon the body. You have never died and you never will.

Let us consider what is true. Life was given you by God in your Creation. It does not come and go nor change itself into something unrecognizable. Life is existence and existence does not end. You are a whole part of Life and Life is part of you.

Creation is Life and Life is Creation. Life and Love extend themselves as One, endlessly creating, endlessly increasing.

Death and Life appear to be opposites because the state of separation is a state of opposites. They are not opposites; they are not in opposition. Life is real and One while death is simply the sign of mind asleep and dreaming what could never be. Even in the dream however, you need not experience death as an ending, but rather as the final act in a dream of awakening. The door opens and all is Love and Light as the world and all its memories disappear and only Truth remains.

Duty and Trust

Your duty as a Teacher of God is to represent Truth in all your relationships, in all your actions in the world. To do so requires a single minded dedication to a single purpose. Your only purpose is to awaken completely as the Christ, the Self of all, and thereby to help all of life awaken with you. You want only to help in any way you can, and to offer Love to everyone in all circumstances. The Teacher of God will always strive to see the Christ in all, the Presence of the Holy Spirit in all situations. Love is what you are and Love is all you want to see. When all the world reflects only Love back to you, you will be free. To be Love Itself is to be free in every sense of the word; to be truly free is to be Love and only Love. In the state of freedom, only Love remains.

What is to be done in every situation no matter the circumstances? Give Love, see the Christ in everyone, let your words and actions be guided, and give the help that is needed in every way you can. To do this is to give your brothers everything that can be given. Your task will always be to remember that the interest of your brothers and yourself are one and the same. What is helpful to one is helpful to all. In any situation into which the Holy Spirit is invited, there will be only gain for all. He, and He only, has the vision, understanding, and the power to do this.

If you let the Holy Spirit into your life, you will be taking a big step towards peace and happiness. He knows the way, knowledge given Him by God, and He has the responsibility to introduce you to it and guide your footsteps along the path if you will let Him. The Holy Spirit assigns your part in the Great Plan of Atonement, and He helps you complete it. There is no need you have that He does not know about; He has a miracle solution for every problem you may perceive. All problems disappear with equal ease if you turn them over to Him.

The problem you still have is the lack of trust in the Holy Spirit's answers to your request for help. All too often do you have limits in your mind that you would impose on His answer. The answer He gives must fall within those limits to be acceptable to you. In such a case, you are not really asking for His answer, but rather for confirmation of your own ideas which are usually inadequate or incomplete. You do not have the knowledge or the overview to respond to the problems that seem to confront you in a way that truly solves them. Your solutions are partial, fragmentary, and result in a temporary fix that postpones the real solution.

CHAPTER SEVEN

Purpose and the Ego

The ego's purpose is always to keep you busy trying to solve problems that have no solution on the level in which they appear. Its service as a guide to action will bring about predictable results no matter what your problems appear to be. No problem will be truly solved; it will simply appear again in a different form. The form changes, shifting first one way then another, but the content never changes, being always the same regardless of form. Illusion is the content and the form of every problem, every lack, every conflict or threat. Nothing you see before you is real, nor can the problems of this world be resolved on the level of illusion.

All the seeming problems of the world you see before you simply mask the one and only problem you have: separation from God. All others are but different forms of this one problem. You have been learning to look past form that you may see content. Be willing to have the Holy Spirit show you the content behind the form every time you must make a choice. Only then can you be sure of choosing rightly.

Your Father knows what you need at all times and in all places, and His one Answer suffices. You must use His Answer, staying in touch with It throughout the day. You cannot go wrong if you will turn over decision making to the One Whose function it is. Your decisions have not saved you from misery and suffering no matter how hard you have tried to avoid them.

To do what must be done to bring you beyond the suffering inherent in separation, requires the help that is given from beyond separation. It cannot be given however, unless you choose to ask for it and receive it. Your active willingness is required, for you do not need help once or twice a day or occasionally but constantly. Your mind is always active and always choosing illusion or Truth with everything you think, say, or do. Decision making must become consistent, choosing Truth over illusion repeatedly as you go through your day, if you are to escape the madness of the world you have made. To respond effectively to the challenges and conditions you face, requires clarity of perception and understanding, and commitment to your single purpose. And you must surrender, ask for help, receive it as it comes, and act upon it.

Your life can be dedicated to one of two purposes: to live out an existence based on separation or to awaken to the Self and leave separation behind. If you choose to follow the way of separation, to live identified as a body in a world of many separate bodies, you will be the slave of time and human destiny. There is no way to realize freedom or to find lasting happiness while you are choosing a life of slavery to habit, tendencies, fear, and ignorance. A willing slave is not free nor does he want freedom.

Freedom requires that you take responsibility for your life in every way. In order to attain the state of freedom, you must recognize that you are in a state of self-imposed bondage. You, and only you, are responsible for the state you are in and the conditions under which you live, however that looks. Through your past decisions, you have put yourself there, and only you can decide to change your life. If you would go in a new direction, you must be willing to honestly examine where you are, and open your mind to a new possibility.

The Way Back

Now is the time to begin anew. Now is the time, only now. You never wanted what the world seems to offer. Its meaningless rewards and empty experiences have attracted you for a little while but now you see them for what they really are. Their meaningless wrappings disguise their content. Death is all you have ever found here. Every experience has been but the prelude to death. Can anything, no matter how attractive the wrappings, mask the death it offers you unless you wish it so?

You have been complicit in your own destruction, and now the time for healing is here. Do not hesitate. Your brother holds out his hand for he too needs the healing you will both give and receive. Now is the time to decide for Truth. Do not wait any longer. The world is suffering from the heavy burden of guilt you have laid upon it. Your brothers are waiting for you to lead them out of hell for you cannot leave here alone. You take them with you or you stay in hell together.

The way back seems to be long and arduous with obstacles on every side. Yet are the obstacles in your mind only. They will be resolved one by one or all at once as you choose. Your Friend goes with you every step of the way, sent by God to smooth the way and help you remove everything that obstructs your path. Your Friend will never desert you; see that you do not desert Him. If you do, He will merely wait until you come to your senses. He has always been with you, waiting for you to turn to Him, to ask for His help. There is nothing you do but will benefit by including Him. Every decision you make without the Holy Spirit will postpone your homecoming. Do not delay. This is all you need do: ask for help, receive the answer, accept the help, and do what you are asked. Nothing more and nothing less.

Whenever you think there is nothing more to do, think again. As long as you are in the world, the realm of perception, the journey is not over, the task is not completed. While you are here, you must always aim for the stars; the world is not your home. Never forget from where you come. Your responsibility is to bring the Light of Heaven and the Love of God into the darkness of this world. The healing you receive, you will bring to all your brothers, for you are never healed alone. Healing is for all; each healed mind will offer what it has been given to all. Thus is a chain of Atonement forged link by link until all who live in darkness have been reunited with the Christ within. Nothing else that you do even remotely compares with returning to Truth and bringing your brothers with you. All Creation rejoices every time God's Holy Son returns to Heaven.

No Reason to Fear

There is no price to pay for salvation. Salvation is not something that is bargained for in the manner of the ego, with you deciding its worth and what you are willing to give in return. Salvation's worth cannot be measured from the standpoint of fear and separation, for it comes from beyond the mind of illusion. Its purpose is to free you from the grip of fear and the ignorance of your true nature that have dominated your mind for so long.

The Holy Spirit brings the gift of salvation, given Him by God, and helps you receive and accept it that you may then offer this gift to your brothers. Like all of God's gifts, salvation is for all; therein is its meaning. When you accept it for yourself, you are accepting it for all. Its meaning then becomes your meaning as you realize that everyone is you. Whatever you do, wherever you go, you are always and only meeting yourself.

There is never any reason to complain or be afraid. You cannot be unfairly treated or threatened in any way. To believe you can is to live in fear and a constant sense of grievance. Let the Holy Spirit teach you there is no reason to fear; no one is attacking you. Your belief in the reality of attack is the source of the fear and guilt that dominates your mind. The Holy Spirit will teach you that you are not guilty and fear is never justified. And He will demonstrate, if you follow His guidance, that you can live from the perspective of Love and forgiveness which will heal the guilt in your mind and free you from fear. Do not let unconscious resistance prevent you from asking for help and gladly receiving it that you may be free.

Whenever you think you are alone and in danger, remember Who walks with you. The only limits on the help He can give are established by you. The Holy Spirit's ability to help is unlimited and available for the asking. You must ask and listen with an open mind, receive what is given, and respond as guided. His help is given always but unless you do your part, you cannot use it. Salvation requires your cooperation without which very little can be done. As God's gift, it does not require your efforts to be what it is, yet does it require your effort to be received. Salvation is freely given and must be freely received.

The reason life as a human being seems so difficult is because of the belief in, and the perception that follows, of a world in which you are alone and separate from everything you see. To walk alone and friendless through an uncaring wasteland seems to be your life. Friends you may have, but never can you trust them wholly, for each has his own interest which he will pursue at the expense of all others. In such a world there is nothing to do but protect yourself from the dangers that press in on you from every side, and build a life for yourself by seizing what you need, even if you must tear it from the grasp of your brother.

How can such a life be anything other than difficult, sad, and lonely, marked by suffering and loss, haunted by fear? You do not realize it is your mind that has made the apparent world you see and given it its characteristics. Through your lack of understanding, your confusion of cause and effect, the world seems to have power over you. Thus is life seemingly lived at the mercy of forces and events that are beyond your control and indifferent to your fate. Yet nothing is further from the Truth.

Meaning and Purpose

You have given everything you see the meaning it has for you. The meaning you give determines your response to it and its effect on you. Behind the appearance of separation is your desire to have it so; therein arises its seeming effect on you. The world you see has the power over you that you gave it, nothing more. Withdraw the desire to believe it real, and its power will vanish. Your eyes will continue to see the forms of separation, but your mind will see the Light and Love just beyond form. Through that perception, you are restored to the Unity beyond all form. Abide in that wholly purified perception, and the world will affect you not.

Now you can see the real purpose of the world: to keep God away. It was made as a place where God is absent; where you could hide from Him forever. It is not your Father's Will that you be separate from Him, and His Will is already perfectly accomplished. The journey you seem to make back to God is just your dream that you are separate still. With the help of the Holy Spirit, it becomes a happy dream, a dream of remembering, a dream of awakening. You need not suffer, though a suffering world appears all around you, if you abide in the heart of Love. Rest in the Self, give all to all, and you will be free.

To all who are sent to you, offer help. Give them what you have been given. There are no random occurrences in God's plan of salvation. Each Teacher of God helps those who come seeking healing. Those who come need your help, the help you alone can give them. The Holy Spirit uses the Teachers of God to deliver His message to those yet unable to receive it from Him. They in turn become ready and willing to work with Him, and join their efforts with those of their brothers. The ranks of God's Teachers continue to grow as long as time exists. When all have heard God's Call and responded, time will be over, quietly disappearing into eternity.

While you are here, you must continue to help the brothers who need you as much as you can. All that you give to them, you will also receive. Heaven is for all; you do not enter its gates alone. Everyone goes with you; that is what Heaven is: a state of Unity absolute in which all are included. To recognize your brother as yourself is the condition that leads back to the Kingdom. When this realization becomes well established in your mind, you will know your Father again and Love will take you home.

The purpose of all you see is to remind you of God. If you see everything with a unified mind, with the vision of Christ, you will realize that all is Light, all is Love. In that you are included, leaving you no choice but to embrace what is. To embrace what truly is means to let go all else, all that does not reflect or represent Truth. In so doing, you will learn that nothing else exists except as a dreamlike appearance that is not really there. Do not doubt the truth of what you see directly with the vision of Christ. That alone is true seeing.

The Vision of Christ

The body's eyes will always show you the witnesses to separation. That is their purpose, given them by the mind that wished separation real. Perception was made to be the means of proving your substitute for Reality is real and capable of taking its place. This could not happen in truth, but in dreams it seems possible to accomplish the impossible. The Holy Spirit will show you that what has been your reality for so long is simply a case of mistaken identity. You have taken yourself to be a body, subject to pain and death, and have believed what is not true, now or ever. You can just as easily believe what is true, but first you must be willing to accept that you have been mistaken about the nature of Reality. This acceptance, in practice, is the letting go of everything you thought you knew. You know nothing. Remember this constantly; it will serve you well.

All that you are required to do is to let go the investment in what is not real, that the Truth it obscures may return to awareness and become your experience. The effective undoing of your mind is an emptying of what now fills it so that perception may be purified. Perception, cleansed of its unconscious, fragmentary way of seeing, becomes capable of a wholly unified vision. This vision will show you the Light in your brothers, and the Love and beauty that surrounds you.

Christ's vision makes no use of the body's eyes whose purpose is to confirm separation, but proceeds directly from the mind guided by the Holy Spirit. True vision must come from a state of mind in which Truth is not excluded but welcomed. There is ultimately nothing that needs be done but to make the mind ready to receive the Truth from which the mind arises. The Truth will return when you truly desire It, and cease all activity that obstructs Its coming. Do not let what you do not know escape your notice. Your only task is to let your mind be made ready to recognize and welcome Truth when It comes. When is known only by the Holy Spirit; He will not hesitate to return you to the awareness of Truth when you are ready. Till then, wait patiently, secure in the certainty that God's Will is done.

To your mind and heart will come the knowledge that you forgot so long ago. It has been waiting, kept for you by your Guide and Teacher. Never has it left you nor have you forgotten entirely who you are. The memory awaits, hidden deep in your mind, for the readiness to let knowledge return. Awakening is the return, the remembering of the full consciousness of the Self you are now and have always been. In Truth, awakening is not a change at all. Yet in dreams is it experienced as the transformation of your mind, of your experience of yourself and the world.

The Great Plan

To all who come to you, you must give everything that you may receive everything. This receiving is actually a remembering, a revealing of what is already yours. Never have you had less than everything; you are everything. The purpose of your giving is twofold. By giving everything to your brother, you are acknowledging your brother's interest and yours are the same. This is an active recognition of Oneness. And by so giving, the memory of God's gifts returns to awareness. By your giving them away you accept His gifts as yours, and in the giving you accept their purpose. The purpose of all that God has given you is to be shared. God's gifts are for all, given to everything created in its creation. Through giving is it revealed that you have everything and you are everything. What you are, you have, and what you have is what you are.

To serve the Great Plan, you must serve all those for whom It is intended. To love God is to love His Creation. Love naturally gives Itself to all; that is how It returns to every mind. Each mind in which the flame of Love is burning brightly, leans close to another and helps kindle a new flame. Love, like fear, is contagious, and the presence of Love will grow; in Its kindly light all darkness and fear will disappear forever. You are meant to be the embodiment of Love, that you may bring Love to all who inhabit the world meant to be the place where fear rules and Love is denied. Who else but you can be the Savior of the world? Who else is there? Until you accept your part in the Great Plan of Salvation, It is not complete.

Would you serve your Father, the Creator of all that truly is, or would you serve the ego, the harsh ruler of an imaginary land where pitiful creatures come to die? If you could but see what you have lost, what you are choosing in its place and the consequences of that fateful decision, you would waste no more time wandering about in dreams, imagining you are what you are not. You would turn to your Creator, embrace His plan for salvation, and become once again what you have always been, the Christ. Because your mind lacks the clarity to perceive so clearly, it is necessary to teach you the difference between where you think and experience yourself to be, and where you truly are and will be again when the mind has been made ready to let the memory of God return to awareness.

Willingness

What is needed always is the willingness to act in the moment, to do what needs be done. In order for this willingness to be meaningfully exercised, you must be aware of the activity of your mind, that you may clearly perceive the choice presented you. Willingness goes hand in hand with the practicing of self awareness, the remembering to be present as you go about your day. It is extremely important to be conscious of the activity of your mind as it takes place in your life in the form of a continuous or near continuous stream of thoughts, images, feelings, emotions, and responses to outward conditions. Without this awareness, the willingness to choose Truth over illusion cannot be brought into play consistently. Through the consistent choice of Truth, the mind is quickly and skillfully undone. In fact, the willingness to be vigilant even every moment, to be constantly present in your mind, is necessary for your willingness to choose Truth to have a chance to do so.

Willingness itself will grow under the Holy Spirit's tutelage until it includes your entire life and all that you think, feel, and do. Willingness is the single requirement you must supply to the undertaking of the process of awakening to and as the Self. The Holy Spirit will provide everything else that is needed, and will supplement your little willingness with His.

You must learn to accept willingness in all its forms: the willingness to surrender, to turn it over, the willingness to let go all you thought you knew. Thus do you let you mind be undone. You must be willing to be continuously vigilant for Truth and against the ego. And you must be willing to let go all investment in the world of separation and all it seems to offer. Ultimately you must be willing to let go all fear and give welcome to Love that it may return and transform your life. In all these ways, these aspects of your life and mind, must willingness be brought to bear until all of your mind is healed, and all of its hidden, dark corners opened to the Light. Nothing must remain to mar the purity of your holy mind. The constant action of willingness in concert with the help given by the Holy Spirit, is the key that unlocks the door to Heaven. You cannot take Heaven by storm. The attempt to do so will drive It from your awareness. Only willingness, directed by the Voice for God will win the day.

Freedom and the Now

Now is the only time there is, the intersection of time and eternity. You must learn to rest in the now, the timeless present, in stillness and peace. To such a mind does Truth return. The present holds out to you all that you need: Love, freedom, peace and the experience of what you are. Nowhere else will you find the Self, for It does not dwell in the memories of the past nor can It be captured by future imaginings. Always and only is eternity the home of the Self, and eternity is found only in the present.

The now is the abode of freedom. To be surrendered, given over to the timeless present, is freedom. To be the Self is freedom. To be Love is to be forever free. Only when Love has reclaimed your heart and mind will you return to the state of freedom you once knew and will know again. Do not tarry here, wasting time in idle dreams, but rise and hurry to your Father's House. He is waiting to welcome you Home.

Do you know your Self? Do you remember the glorious Reality that is you? The Christ within is waiting in deepest peace, in the eternal silence that nothing can ever disturb. All the chaos and vain imaginings, the sounds of conflict and the screams of the dying, cannot reach that depth nor disturb Its stillness. The many dreams of a world of bodies, of fear and attack, are but the thinnest of veils floating on the surface of a great ocean of immeasurable vastness and depth. Leave the surface, the superficiality of form and separation; journey deep within where the Light always shines and darkness does not exist.

To Receive God's Help

Do the necessities of a world of form weigh you down? The experience of separation produces 'needs' that must be satisfied:

food, clothing, and shelter. Satisfying these needs preoccupies the human mind which seemingly must often struggle just to maintain its bodily existence. And yet, as stated in the bible, your Father knows what you need and will provide it if you let Him. You will lack nothing unless that is your choice. In the dream, conditions change and circumstances alter, but the Holy Spirit's concern and care for you is limitless and unchangeable.

To receive His help, you must be willing to accept it, and give up your need to control the conditions of your life. The attempt to control life according to your liking makes impossible the receiving of the help you need. When you are actively deciding what to do and what not to do. When it is your judgment you trust and use. When likes, dislikes, and fear determine the decisions you make, you are actively denying the Holy Spirit's help. To receive the help that is needed and always available, you must make room for it, and a sincere desire to accept what He offers must be present in your mind. As has been so often stated, no help, not even salvation itself, will be forced upon you. Your right to decide will never be infringed upon. You are totally responsible for all choices, all decisions you make. Yet is it impossible to decide alone. All decisions are made in the context of the thought system you trust. Always you choose the guide to whom you turn for help in decision making. And always there are only two guides to choose from: the ego or the Holy Spirit.

Forget not the results you get from following the dictates of the guide you choose. They are different in every way, in every respect. The Holy Spirit will lead you back to God; the ego leads you around in circles that are nowhere and go nowhere. It knows nothing but senses threat everywhere, continually defending and maintaining separation and the sense of specialness that is its chosen refuge. A refuge that reinforces fear and a sense of weakness, is no refuge at all.

God is your strength and refuge. In Him you can trust. He will never let you down; through His Voice you are led safely back to where you are and where you have always been. All danger is recognized as nothing more than foolish imagining; the goal rises constantly before you if you let Him guide your vision. Like a shining city on a hill, your Home calls to you. The Voice for God will never let you down. See that you do not let yourself down by refusing to listen to the voice of reason. It is yourself you betray when you choose the guide who takes you nowhere but to your death. Trust is needed; your life is based on it. Place that trust only where it is warranted. Give it to the One Whose Love for you is unending, the One Whose function it is to deliver you from all fear, pain, and suffering. He will guide you safely through the chaotic maze that is the world you have made, to peace and safety, to your Home in God.

The Ego as Guide

Would you have your cake and eat it too? This is exactly the ego's position on everything. The ego wants to keep guilt alive, justifying its attack and condemnation, and yet believes guilt can be seen in others and punished without effect on itself. Would you have your brother guilty and escape the effect of your own attack? That is what the ego would have you believe, for it realizes the terrible pressure of guilt in your mind must be relieved. Thus is your guilt projected onto your brother, while you are innocent. To release guilt entirely would deprive the ego of the foundation stone of its thought system and lead to its demise. Without guilt and sin, the entire thought system of separation would collapse, for its justification would vanish.

So is guilt seen everywhere and your attack justified; specialness is defended and upheld. And while you continue this mad strategy of defending yourself by attacking your brother, guilt continues to find its home in your mind, strengthening itself with every attack thought, driving Love and mercy from your awareness. What you need more than anything, you deny yourself, for you cannot deny your brother without depriving yourself. The defense of specialness is always a veiled attack on yourself. This hurts and weakens you; while your remain unaware of what you do and its consequences, you will continue to injure yourself and reinforce the belief in attack as the way to be safe.

Within the great walls you have erected, the ego rules supreme. The walls would keep out danger, keeping you safe from a hostile world. Yet their real purpose is to keep away Love, your only refuge. Love is where your safety lies; the ego will not allow this understanding to reach your mind for it does not know Love, but does recognize threat and protects itself with unceasing vigilance. What the ego would maintain, would continue, is the state of bondage in which you live and the identification with what you are not. When you withdraw this mistaken identification with a body and the sense of being a separate mind or person occupying it, freedom and Love will return and end the ego's harsh reign.

Nowhere is there safety in this world but in the warm embrace of all encompassing Love. In Love, as Love, you will give unceasingly and thus will you receive unceasingly. To those who give to all without thought of themselves, all is given. Your Father's Love surrounds you, keeping you safe forever. Let His limitless Love and care operate in your life through the acceptance of the Answer He has given you. The responsibility of the Holy Spirit is to help you in every way needed. He cannot do this if you do not accept his help. This habit, the need to do it 'your way', effectively blocks true help from being recognized and received.

Too long have you trusted the ego as your guide though it has led you nowhere. The seeming gifts and pleasures, the shiny trinkets the ego offers, fascinate and hypnotize your mind, completely obscuring the real nature of its gifts. The ego offers you nothingness disguised as somethingness, covered in shiny wrappings that appeal to the eye, to the desire for stimulation. Keeping yourself busy pursuing these attractive phantoms, you fail to notice their insubstantial nature, here one moment, gone the next. Self deception is the fuel that feeds desire. Without the need to pursue what is constantly changing and unreliable, busying yourself with non-essentials, you would quickly see through the facade of appearances and realize the emptiness behind them all.

While the ego is your chosen guide, you will never be free of delusion. The choice to give up self deception is the choice to look elsewhere for guidance. The ego has thrived on the decision to be separate, and has been your identity ever since. Until you decide against separation, you will continue to make this mistake for that is all you know. Now is the time to begin life anew by withdrawing allegiance from what has only hurt you and perpetuated your imprisonment. Turn to the One who teaches the way of freedom and Love, and guides your every step. There is no failure with the Holy Spirit as your guide; no constant search for a fulfillment that is never found. With His help you will recognize your errors, letting them be undone and replaced with true ideas and a unified perception. Your life has been filled with regret; you will not regret placing your mind and life under the Holy Spirit's care and guidance.

Wherever you go, there is work to be done. Your brothers who languish still in separation need your help; you need them as much as they need you, for you must give in order to receive. Thus does your brother offer you the gift you are looking for.

CHAPTER EIGHT

The Holy Instant

What if I were to tell you your homecoming, the full reestablishment of Truth in your consciousness, is but a moment away. In time, it seems like an almost mythical state, a goal so difficult to reach it lies somewhere in the future, attainable only after a long period of struggle. As long as you believe in sequential time will this be true for you, yet is that only a belief. It cannot be true that the Self, what you are and have always been, cannot be realized here and now. Only the false ideas that fill your mind, limiting it and distorting your perception, stand between your present state and the unified awareness of the Self. While it is true that for most who are lost in space and time, the process of undoing the false mind appears to be a lengthy one, this need not be.

At any moment, the Truth can shine into your mind and lift you above the illusion, if that is what you want and you are willing to meet Its conditions. The holy instant is waiting for you to let Truth into your awareness at any moment. Never is it far away, requiring a lengthy period of preparation to make your mind available to its coming. The Holy Spirit's gifts to you require only that you be willing to receive them without trying to control the conditions under which they are given. For that reason, they are always available, independent of the apparent conditions of time. The Holy Spirit works in time but is not limited by it; His gifts are constantly given, coming from God Who knows not time.

The insistence that you must be prepared to receive what the Holy Spirit would give, prevents the reception of what you desperately need. This is simply a delaying tactic, an expression of unconscious resistance. What could be easier than to simply accept what is so freely given and obviously valuable? The constant need to control circumstances and conditions, very effectively keeps God away. To do this is to identify with the ego's obsessive need to control, for it believes its safety depends on it. Believing itself to be constantly under threat, the conditions of life must be maintained according to the ego's liking. What can only be experienced in the present is very threatening to the ego, which always tries to limit the present by using it to reinforce the past and thus control the future.

What is important to the Holy Spirit's purpose is unknown to the ego. What the ego judges as important is overlooked by the Holy Spirit, for He recognizes all things of the ego are meaningless. What is meaningless does not exist. You must learn to overlook the ego's expression and its values if you are to replace illusion with Truth. Be aware of the movement of illusion in your mind, recognize it for what it is and choose again. Do this again and again and again, each moment and each minute and each hour until the momentum of illusion is reversed. Truth will take its place in your affections, loosening the shackles that have bound you for so long.

Only your willing cooperation with the ego's plan to maintain separation, keeps you a prisoner to what you do not truly want. You are complicit in your own destruction. The ego has only the hold over your mind that you have given it. As you become aware of this fact and of the ego's goal, the insanity of your choice of the ego as your guide becomes obvious and cannot be denied. The reluctance to accept this recognition, to choose again, will delay your homecoming. The life of separation is all you know; allegiance to the ego has been unquestioned for so long that you have forgotten your real Self.

The Christ has not forgotten you. He is waiting for the invitation to reveal His Presence in your mind, and will do so just as soon as you are ready. Do not delay this homecoming. Let the Holy Spirit teach you to recognize the errors you are making, the false beliefs in your mind and the actions that follow. Let Him correct your thoughts and return your mind to the ways of Truth. There is nothing else to be done; all else is just the perpetuation of the past with all its confusion, pain and suffering. Return to the present, the only moment there is, and discover where you are and what you have forgotten. Let the Holy Spirit reveal the place whereon you stand, the depth from which you come.

Not a moment will He waste; no effort on your part will not be rewarded and strengthened through His constant help and Presence. To your little willingness is added His own, making it a mighty force for change. You need do nothing by yourself, for He is always there, giving you what you need, telling you what you need to know, furthering your understanding. Now is the time to begin in earnest. Do not wait. Procrastination accomplishes nothing and merely prolongs the time of ignorance of your true purpose. If suffering has lost its appeal, and pleasure and pain seen as they are, you will not hesitate to consecrate your life to a higher purpose.

To delay the inevitable will bring no benefit, being the dedication to preserve separation and find safety and satisfaction in a world where they are absent. Happiness cannot be found while you build your house on shifting sands. There is no reason to pursue goals whose purpose is to conceal their meaninglessness. Your life lacks meaning while you seek for it where it cannot be found; meaning, like Truth, is within. It lies not outside of you, hidden among the shadows that seemingly surround you. Life's purpose is revealed to you when you desire this above all else. Do not give purpose to what is purposeless, to that which conceals real purpose and meaning through its frantic activity and constant diversions. You were not meant to wander distractedly across a barren landscape occupied by phantoms that seem to come and go. Your Father has created you for a purpose; let the Holy Spirit teach you where purpose can be found.

Let Go the False

Now is the opportunity to leave behind all that you do not need. To reach the heights, the gates of Heaven, you must lighten your load by throwing out what is false and unnecessary. The constant exercise of judgment, a function that is not yours, is exhausting you and sapping your strength. Do not continue the same mistakes over and over and reap the same undesirable consequences. All the suffering in your life is the result of the belief in judgment, sin, and guilt. Lay down this sword you hold against your own throat to keep Love away. Only the constant and chaotic activity of your mind denies the Truth and keeps Love from your awareness.

Allow the Holy Spirit to train your mind to let go the false and make room for the true. Let Him teach you the difference between Truth and illusion, and learn to become aware of the constant choices you are making. Learn to become consistent in your choosing of Truth over illusion. Turn decision making over to the One Whose function it is. Give Him your willingness that He may augment it with His own. The purified mind is empty, quiet, ready to welcome Truth as It comes. Be willing and welcoming; that is enough. Do not set your sights low, aim high. Your goal is far above this world and beyond it.

What you choose is up to you, the consequences will always follow. Choose Truth and Heaven Itself will bend to help. Choose illusion and you will prolong your unnecessary suffering. Thank the Holy Spirit and the Christ within you. Never forget them, the Truth of what you are, and the help that is always given. Make yourself available to receive help, and develop the clarity to use it effectively.

All Is Done

Do you know what is truly needed in every situation, what words will help, what action is called for? In all honesty you must admit you do not. Your ideas about what to do and what to say are too often determined by the past. Seldom are your truly present, without preconceived ideas that limit your understanding and shape your response. There is One however, Who knows always what help is needed, what can be given and received by everyone, with only good resulting for all. Do let Him guide your thoughts, words, and actions, your perceptions and understanding. His is the help you need. His is the help you want. Let this be the guiding principle of your life: He knows and I do not. Do not let your ignorance and the unconscious conceit that you know what you do not, cripple your mind and distort your responses.

Each day, every day, is given over to the Holy Spirit and dedicated to learning the lessons presented, thus fulfilling your responsibility. Nothing else need be done but do not forget to do nothing less. Whatever you are asked to do, do it cheerfully, with abundant willingness. All tasks assigned are for your highest good; you will only gain thereby. It may not be clear to you always that this is true, for the idea of sacrifice and the belief you must understand what you do before you do it, has been well established in your mind for a very long time. You must remember always you know nothing. This consistent remembrance frees your mind to allow the Holy Spirit to direct your life. In this way you can be consistently helpful to yourself and your brothers.

All that needs be done is done, all lessons assigned are learned; nothing is left undone or unlearned. The Holy Spirit holds the plan for the day for each one and all the people you will meet. He guides you throughout the day, helping you learn what is to be learned, inspiring your words and actions. His Love and strength are available for you to use; He is holding them for you until you are ready to accept them for yourself. The Love of God and the strength of God were given in your creation. They are your birthright. You cannot lose what was given by God although you can refuse to hold it in your awareness. The Holy Spirit holds everything that is yours, all that you have forgotten, until you are ready to allow its memory to return.

Ignorance and Wisdom

The admission of ignorance is the beginning of wisdom. A very unfortunate characteristic of those blinded by their own ignorance is that they do not realize the state they are in. They do not realize they know nothing. Until this is recognized, your ignorance will be taken for understanding, and only the perpetuation of illusion and the suffering it brings will result. To know that you do not know is the awareness that makes room for true learning to occur. Full of its own ideas and beliefs, the mind cannot receive what is true and greatly needed. An undoing of the mind is absolutely necessary; all belief in illusion must be relinquished, all ideas that lead nowhere given up. Confidence in your ability to understand on your own, to figure things out, must be replaced by trust in the Holy Spirit and the willingness to learn what He teaches. Your understanding is always based on the thought system to which you adhere. You never learn on your own just as no decisions are made in isolation. You learn and you decide with the help of one of two possible teachers: the Holy Spirit or the ego. There are no others.

What is necessary always is to be aware of which teacher you are listening to at all times. From the teacher you choose, comes the lessons you learn. You never learn alone; you always teach those who share a lesson with you what you are learning. Teach fear and separation and you will suffer. Teach only Love and Unity and all are blessed together. There is nothing you cannot do when joined with your brothers through the power of Love and forgiveness. Your lessons in forgiveness are learned for all; that learning will spread till it covers the earth.

To do that which must be done requires a sorting out of what is necessary from what is not. Giving much time and energy to what is not needed is characteristic of the sleeping mind. By so doing, the mind is kept in a constant state of confusion about what is valuable and helpful and what is valueless. Under these conditions, reaching a state of clarity is impossible. You must be willing to let the Holy Spirit guide the process of sorting out what must be done from what must be discarded. Until this sorting out is accomplished to a meaningful degree, consistent decision making is not possible.

To do what is asked of you, what is required of you, is the way to happiness and salvation. This includes not only your actions and the words you speak, but also your thoughts, feelings, and attitudes. Everything in your mind and life, all the various parts of you, must be brought into alignment with a single purpose. There is no need to do anything on your own.

To relinquish control of decision making, to turn it over, is a necessary condition for salvation to be given you. The need to control life, to control the present and plan for the future based on what was learned in the past, is the ego's response to its own uncertainty. To know nothing is to be uncertain, and the ego knows nothing.

You have one responsibility: to accept the Atonement for yourself. This is very simple in principle, yet in practice it may take a long time before its simplicity is apparent. Your mind is very complicated, being composed of different levels of awareness, many different thoughts and beliefs that often conflict, various impulses, tendencies, moods, feelings, emotions and attitudes. Thoughts and feelings chase each other across the surface of your awareness like clouds across the sky, driven by the wind. Constantly changing, giving you no rest, this confusing and apparently complex activity must be skillfully undone.

Complexity cannot be met with more complexity; this merely confuses the mind even more. The great complexity of mind is itself a condition of confusion and contradiction. You cannot undo confusion by increasing it. Confusion is undone by the application of clarity which must come from beyond the mind lost in its own complexity. The Holy Spirit teaches you the only meaningful distinction that can be made regarding the content and activity of your mind. Everything that arises in your awareness, all that you experience within or without, is either true or not true. No other distinction can be made that is meaningful or helpful. Truth or illusion are all that you can ever choose between.

Let this simple understanding be the basis from which you approach the chaotic maelstrom that is the ego mind. Its simplicity will cut through the layers of complexity and confusion that blind you to the Truth within. As you learn to distinguish the true from the false consistently, clarity and peace will return to your mind, replacing its frantic activity with a quiet certainty.

There are no meaningful distinctions to be made between illusions; no matter what form they may take, the content is the same. Form is but the veil concealing content. You must learn to look past the veil and discern what lies behind it. The Holy Spirit will teach you to perceive truly, that confusion may leave your mind. He will guide your decisions and He always chooses what is good and true. As decision making becomes consistent with the help of the Guide God has given you, you will see the road rise up before you, stretching to the gates of Heaven.

Whenever a decision needs to be made, remember Whose function it is. This is particularly difficult for those who continue to assert their autonomy, the need to control life according to one's liking and preferences. What you like, what you prefer, is habit determined by past learning. Remember always that you were badly taught. You are unable to tell the difference between pain and pleasure though you think you can. You do not know what anything means, what it is for, yet are unaware of this fact. In your attempts to control life, you are always operating from the past with the ego as your guide. Allowing the one who knows nothing to guide your decisions is asking for disaster. It is extremely important to become aware of the ego's motives and its complete unsuitability to be your guide, and to face this fact honestly. Otherwise you will not relinquish your habitual dependency on the ego, leaving no room for the Guide given you by your Father to take its place.

Nowhere can you find happiness but within your mind. It cannot be found outside, for happiness is the true state of your mind and is independent of time or place. No special circumstances or conditions are necessary nor can real happiness be disturbed by events. To rediscover happiness while living in the world of separation, is not possible unless you are fulfilling your function here. Forgiveness is your function in a world where Love is denied, assigned you by God through the Holy Spirit, Whose function it is to teach you yours and help you fulfill it. Happiness is not possible without the commitment to Love; forgiveness is the demonstration and the expression of that commitment. In this world, all is Love or the call for Love. Your responsibility is to give Love always.

Teacher of God

Nowhere in the world is there reason to fear or to respond with anything less than Love. Your response is always based on what you think you are. This holds true for all times and all circumstances. If you think you are a body, housing a 'person' separate and different from everyone and everything, your responses to what arises in your life and mind will vary greatly. Variable response is the sign of an uncertain mind, unsure of itself and its course of action. The mind that sees itself under constant threat due to the apparent fragility of its self identity, cannot respond in a consistent manner. Consistency requires understanding and clarity, traits lacking in a mind riddled with fear. Those who identify with weakness will always suffer from the constant influence of fear, and their decision making will be distorted accordingly. What you think you are is the thought system that is the basis of your responses to yourself and the world around you. And you will project your beliefs onto the world you see which will then reflect them back, perception being always a reflection of what you want to be true.

Into this confused and uncertain situation come the Teachers of God to bring clarity and healing. Their task is to teach another way of thinking, living, and understanding. They do this in the simplest and most direct way possible through demonstration. By what they do and how they do it, what they say, how they treat all others with whom they come into contact, they demonstrate another way to live in all respects. Love, kindness, and non-judgment do they bring to all areas of life and everyone they meet. Unfailingly gentle, they show forth the strength that is gentleness and the patience that never fails.

The example set by the Teachers of God is not missed by those around them. Although they do not preach, their actions speak louder than words. A way of living is shown the children of separation, one that is the opposite of the worldly life in every respect. Their words are given to those who would hear them, their help and goodwill is given to all. The Teachers of God need not be concerned about what to say or what to do. Their mind is joined with the Teacher of Teachers; from Him, they receive their guidance in all things. The words they need are given them. What to do, the tasks of the day, are likewise given, and they receive all help they need to complete what is assigned to them. Nowhere is there any room for error unless they forget from Whom comes their strength and help. And then they remember again, and all errors are corrected and the consequences undone.

The Teachers of God rest content in the readiness to receive the gifts God has given them. Their trust allows the Holy Spirit to guide them in all they do and say. Their thoughts are given over to Love; what is not love is given over to correction. The Teachers of God know that everything that happens, whether within or without, is either Love or a call for Love. Their function is therefore very simple. They give Love to all and everyone and everything without exception. To what is Love they join, to the call for Love they respond with Love. Always do they answer the call for Love, and always do they let their answer be guided. A smile, a kind word, a helping hand, the form changes to fit the need but always is the content the same. A call for Love is recognized, and Love is given in the form most helpful.

No matter what happens, your responsibility is to respond with Love, forgiveness, and a willingness to help. There is no other way for a Teacher of God to live than in this manner. When once you accept that role, you accept responsibility for the world and everything in it. Your brothers need your help to recognize Truth and the way that leads to It. They call to you, asking you constantly to lead them out of hell, to help them see the cause of their suffering and the solution. You begin to help by seeing the one Light in your brother that also shines in you. Through your forgiveness of your brother and the world, you cease to lay upon them the burden of your guilt. By granting this freedom is it also given you. As your guilt is healed, so will all others appear guiltless in your eyes. Only the guilty condemn others for what they think they have done. The mind healed of guilt sees only the innocence of God's Son wherever it looks.

The task of the Teacher of God is to be helpful to all, giving help wherever it is needed. To this task we dedicate each day, resting in our willingness to learn the lessons the day brings. Through learning the day's lessons you are healed, and you are never healed alone. All the brothers with whom and through whom your healing takes place, are healed along with you. All you meet or see or chance upon over the course of the day will likewise benefit. No one is omitted, for healing is always given for all. Being aware of this fact, you rest in the certainty that whatever you do is done for the good of all, when you speak and act as you are guided.

Without the Teachers of God, there would be no salvation. They give form to the lessons the Holy Spirit teaches. For those as yet unable to turn to Him for help, they represent Him, offering His help in a form that can be recognized. There is nothing they cannot do; their trust and willingness given to the Holy Spirit makes all miracles possible. They offer miracles to all they look upon, one for every problem that appears. In their company, all tears are replaced with happy laughter, all sadness with gratitude and joy.

Miracles

Do not underestimate the extent to which miracles can change your life and set your feet on the path to God. Their purpose is to demonstrate to those lost in the darkness of the dream that there is a higher law, a law that supersedes the 'laws' of the dream. The miracle provides you with a means to correct all erroneous perception, and replace it with right understanding. As stated in *A Course in Miracles*, miracles wait in shining silence behind all problems you think you have. Let the miracle correct everything in your mind that stands between you and God. Its purpose is to bring you back to your Father through the demonstration you are under no laws but His. As an expression of Love, the miracle blesses giver and receiver. As corrector of perception, it demonstrates that nothing you perceive is what you think. Through its function of collapsing time, the miracle shows you that time is not real, that you are not a prisoner in a world of time.

Let miracles into your life through the acceptance of the One who brings them, the Holy Spirit. He will teach you all you need to know to allow miracles to transform life and perception. Miracle mindedness must be established in your mind to take the place of the fear that formerly ruled. When fear is replaced by miracles, Love will return to transform the mind. Do not keep It waiting; give your assent to the healing power of the miracle that Love may reclaim your life. Love, forgiveness, miracles, healing; these are but different names for the return of sanity and freedom.

Miracles are always available when your mind has been made ready to receive them. The Holy Spirit is the inspiration for miracles. He teaches you the conditions that must be met for miracles to be present in your life. Miracles are completely natural events. When they do not occur, something is wrong. In the human condition, miracles are not recognized or generally experienced, as the density of the mind of separation excludes the possibility of miracles. Miracles are expressions of Love; thus they bless the giver and receiver equally. If you would receive the power of miracles into your life, you must reach a state of miracle mindedness. This requires faith, faith in the unseen, faith in the Holy Spirit. He makes miracles available to you if you ask sincerely with an open mind and a pure heart. True forgiveness is itself a miracle that blesses giver and receiver.

Let all help be given you that you may be able to help those sent to you for healing. You are never healed alone; healing is for all and must be shared to be received. Do not refuse your brothers' pleas for help. They call to you to lead them out of darkness. Would you refuse to answer when you hold the key to deliverance in your hand? Alone, you are as helpless as they; joined with your brother, is all power given to you both. Joining in Love and shared purpose, together you walk the road back to God as the gates of Heaven open wide to receive you. No one enters Heaven except hand in hand with their brothers. Alone, the gate is barred by your own decision; the state of aloneness, separation from all others, is the denial of Heaven. In Heaven all souls are joined in a Oneness without beginning or end.

Love Always

Do not let the fear inherent in the state of separation, cast its dark shadow across the whole of your life. No part of human life is unaffected by the fear lying hidden in the mind. Thought, feeling, and perception; all are distorted and fragmented by unconscious fear. Human motivation is often driven by fear though it is usually not apparent. The different forms fear may take, the unawareness of its presence and influence, the dissociation from what you have suppressed, often hide from you the source of the motivation that drives your actions.

Love is a much better motivator than fear which replaced Love after the separation. Love's motivation brings us together for the good of all. Fear divides us, with each staking out his tiny kingdom and erecting thick walls for its defense. Love would break down all barriers that separate, and bring together its children into one big and happy family. Fear fragments the family of God, bringing chaos and conflict into all relations. Love only gives, and fear only takes away.

Always respond with Love no matter what occurs, and only good will come for all. To bring fear to any situation is to fragment and separate. Conflict then inevitably results. When Love is all you want to give, then Love is all you will receive. Never is there any need for anything short of Love, for Love is all there is. Everything that is not Love, is but part of a dream wherein you have lost yourself for a moment. Only Love exists; God is Love, and you are Love as you were created. Nothing God did not create exists at all. Fear, guilt, and the mad world that arose from them are imagination, shadows in the clouds that obscure your vision, nothing else. A nightmare still trapped in your memory and experienced as if here and now. It will not prevail against Love.

The End of the Dream

Now is the time to relinquish all nightmares, letting the Light shine through, dispelling the darkness. They no longer interest you; you have had enough suffering, enough pain and disappointment. Too much time has been wasted in idle pursuits that go nowhere and accomplish nothing. What is there to gain in a world where chaos rules and shadows play at being real? Abandon this madness before it drags you down once again to play the game of death, a game where only loss rises to meet you. The dream will end when you finally tire of it, not before. Learn to face its conditions honestly, let go of denial and dissociation. Remember the glorious Reality that waits for you beyond the dream. Remember your Father Who calls to you unceasingly. And remember the Holy Spirit, Whose care and concern for you are unceasing, Who guides you along the path He has chosen for you. The Holy Spirit will take you to the gates of Heaven. Give Him your complete trust, thereby do you learn to trust your Self.

In the discarding of all that is untrue, you will find the Truth. Your mind is filled with false ideas about yourself and the world. From this arises the partial perception and limited experiences of separation that characterize the sleeping mind. The Self has not left your mind; the Self is your mind, your real Mind. Only the configuration of your mind in a state of self invented illusion, based on attack and defense, conceals the Truth that still abides deep in your awareness. Hence you need not search for Truth outside your mind nor struggle to find It within.

What is needed is two-fold: become aware of illusion in all its forms and all its operations, and learn the difference between Truth and illusion thoroughly. The Holy Spirit guides this process, teaching you true perception and bringing you to genuine understanding. Without His help, you cannot break through the illusion you have constructed to limit your mind.

Withdraw your allegiance to the world you have made, to the illusion that characterizes your experience in every way. Without your active support, illusion will collapse, and that which it was made to conceal will shine forth.

Do not under any circumstances forget who you are and the help that is always available. The constant identification with the self you have made, and the operant belief that you are alone and must find your own understanding and solution to the problems you face, keep you frozen as the illusory self. Illusory beliefs must be raised to question and carefully examined. Willingness to let them go, to learn another way of being, of thinking and perceiving, must be cultivated and allowed to strengthen. All falsity must be honestly recognized and let go. This happens day by day, hour by hour, minute by minute, as you become frequently, even continually, aware of the content and activity of your mind. The process of letting go, of choosing again, is crucial. The false, the past, the illusion, must be chosen against in the present, in its activity and operation. Constant vigilance must be practiced for the mind is constantly active. The mind is continuing the past, the habitual, through its activity, or it is being corrected and directed towards freedom and Truth. There is nothing in between these two choices.

The Past

Do not allow the past in the form of habits and tendencies to continue its domination of your mind. You gain nothing by doing so. The same problems and misery will continue unabated until you learn to change your mind, to choose again over and over throughout the day, and set your life on a different course. The ego is firmly established in the past which is its home. The past is your home too until you recognize it for what it is and open your mind to the recognition of your true home. The ego's home is a prison with gaily colored walls and bars concealed behind the promises it holds out; a hollow shell that houses only death. Leave the dead and rejoin the living. You were never meant to inhabit the house of death.

You are life itself, eternal, joyous and free. You will return to your natural and authentic state. This has never been in doubt; God's Will assures your return. This can happen sooner or later according to your decision, for you alone determine the conditions of your life. They may appear to be due to outside forces, forces that lie beyond your control, but this is not true. You are the dreamer of the dream; you are responsible for what happens, you alone. You choose the feelings and thoughts you would express, and decide on the goal you would achieve. Do not waste time on goals that rise up before you like mirages, receding always just beyond reach. If you should attain such a goal, you find always you are holding nothingness; like sand it slips through your fingers. Choose the one goal that is possible to reach for it is always here and now. Salvation is yours any moment you truly want it. The Holy Instant is always available, waiting for you to let go the past and return to the present, to Love.

Whenever you let the past go completely, the present can be born anew, free of distortion and limitation. The ego represents the past; the ego is the past, the memory of all that has gone before. All the hurts, fears, slights, pleasures, and pains of a world born of separation from God, are carried by the ego and laid upon the present. You cannot truly experience now while carrying the burden of the past and perceiving through its distorted vision. Lay down all burdens, all memories of the past, and greet the present with empty hands, an open mind and a loving heart. Love is found only in the present for Love, like all Truth, is not of time.

The body's eyes see only the past, appearing as if it were happening now. A world imagined is what you look upon, a projection of your mind, a memory of what is over and gone. It lives on in your mind, out-pictured as if it were here still, that you may learn the lessons needed to take you to the end of learning where all memories end, leaving only Truth in their stead. Do not lose yourself in dreams by forgetting their purpose. Everything that happens in the world of separation has a higher purpose if you let it be revealed. The Holy Spirit uses all events, situations, relationships, and circumstances, to teach you what you are. There is nothing that occurs that He cannot use to guide you towards freedom and the end of suffering. Never is the form important in and of itself; it is the lesson it brings, the content, that you must learn to recognize.

Do let the Holy Spirit teach you the difference between Truth and illusion, Love and fear. You constantly mistake one for the other and have paid dearly for this error. You must learn to perceive with absolute clarity the Truth behind all illusion, all forms, and call It forth to witness. The bewildering variety of appearances and circumstances, the constantly changing parade of thoughts and images, the unpredictable moods and feelings that come and go; all the change going on within and without serve to confuse and absorb the mind, concealing the changeless Reality from your awareness.

You must learn to look past form and variation and find the changeless within the constantly changing. This cannot be done without the help of the Holy Spirit Who overlooks all illusion, seeing only the changeless. He will give you His vision when you are ready to join your mind with His. True vision will show you the Truth reflected everywhere in everything. Love, Light, and Unity, everywhere, embracing everything.

Forgiveness and Unity

Forgiveness will take you to the Unity that underlies the world of separation. The refusal to forgive, to love, maintains and reinforces separation, and keeps the belief in attack inviolate. What else but the release of what affirms separation and denies Unity could open the way for Its return? Into this open mind comes forgiveness, the affirmation of Truth. Forgiveness leads you to the recognition of your Oneness with the world and everything in it. The mind that forgives, that takes complete responsibility for all that happens without the need to project guilt and blame, has accepted all things as part of itself. In recognition and acceptance of the One Unity, you are set free to be your Self.

Without loving kindness, life becomes harsh and joyless. The unloving suffer from a sense of deep guilt that is projected onto their brothers, thus further strengthening the belief in guilt. To escape the belief of their unworthiness and the deep sense of guilt, they must engage in frantic activity, which keeps the mind diverted and strengthens the tendency to dissociate from the content of consciousness that arouses fear. As long as this is done however, that from which you dissociate remains in the mind, exerting its influence in many ways. All the content of consciousness, whether you are aware of it or not, affects the mind and the behavior that arises from it. Do not try to change behavior without changing the beliefs that elicit and shape it.

The Mind

All starts with the mind. Your awareness and its contents are your experience. Perception, emotion, feelings, thoughts, all take place in awareness, in consciousness. The world you see that appears as if outside of you, is like everything else in your mind. It has no reality apart from what you have given it. That this is not apparent is the result of a decision you have made to be separate from your Creator and your Self as He created It. There is no separation without form; thus a world was imagined, populated by many separate forms that move about, each with its own history and purpose.

You were created as Mind; even now Mind is what you are. All form is but image, projected and appearing as if outside of you. There is nothing outside of you. As you were created, you are whole, containing everything within you. Every mind contains all minds for all mind is One. Each contains and is the Whole.

Your mind is where a transformation must take place, nowhere else. There is nowhere else. In Truth, salvation, which is awakening, is not a change at all but a lifting, a clearing out of all that clouds your mind. Salvation is the return to awareness of what you are now and have always been. Driven from awareness by the wish to be as you are not, Truth merely waits until you are willing to welcome It again. Your experience of yourself and the world is transformed by awakening from your long sleep of forgetfulness. Until that blessed day, be vigilant for Truth and the Kingdom, remembering always your holy purpose.

What You Must Do

Do not look back and dwell on what you have done but look instead at what you must do. There is much to be learned, much to be undone, in order for freedom to be restored. Each day, and each experience of each day, is an opportunity to learn the lessons the Holy Spirit teaches and unlearn what is taught by the ego. Patiently, step by step, you retrace the steps you took in the descent into separation, undoing each in turn. When all are undone, your Father will take the last step, and you will return to the Kingdom forever.

There are many journeys you may take in the dream of separation, all leading nowhere but for one: the journey back to God. In truth, it is not a journey at all for you have never left God's Mind, yet in this world does it seem to be a journey whose destination waits in some far off future time. And journey you must as all are destined to return; of that there is no doubt. Only in time does the outcome seem uncertain and time itself is an illusion. Do not rest content with some future idea of salvation. Salvation is always now and now only. Neither in the future nor in the past will you find Truth; Truth is not remembered or imagined but is directly experienced as what you are now. How and when you attain It is but part of the dream. You have always been the Christ, the Holy Creation of God, and forever so will you remain.

To refuse to do what is asked of you by the Holy Spirit, is to refuse to act in your own best interest. The mind asleep does not know what is in its highest interest. You do not recognize what will bring you pain, for you cannot distinguish between pain and pleasure, often confusing one for the other. The search for security, which dominates human life in the world of dreams, is a futile attempt to deny the insecurity inherent in life as a bodily identity. Living as a fragile body in a world of constant change, of rapidly shifting circumstances and conditions, constantly arouses a sense of threat, of danger. The search for security, the erection of defenses, the attempt to control the present and maintain stability into an unknown future; all these are the response of the ego to what it perceives but does not understand. If you continue to see the world through the ego's eyes, you will remain a prisoner to its misperceptions and wrong understanding. Your security cannot be found where there is none, or in a state of identifying with what you are not. All that you will find in an illusory world is the continuation of fear, pain, conflict, suffering and death.

Do not let the mistaken beliefs of the past continue to dominate and shape your life. Turn to the One Who shows you the way to Truth and freedom. With your consent, He will take you there. The only thing you need remember is that you know nothing. This thought, kept clearly in mind, will serve as a reminder to let go all old ideas and beliefs, and open your mind to learn what the Holy Spirit teaches. The mind must be emptied of the old, of the past, to be ready to welcome the new. The Holy Spirit teaches you to recognize all that you have learned is meaningless. With that realization firmly established, and your mind empty and open to receive the new, learning will inevitably follow.

Learning and Experience

Learning that is not of this world is something entirely new. It is not just a replacing of the old beliefs you have carried so long with new ideas. New ideas must point to, must represent, experience that is not of this world. This experience is what the learning of the Holy Spirit's thought system will lead you to; experience that takes place in the world of separation, but Whose Source is beyond. What is beyond will remain beyond; It is reflected here for those willing to perceive It. Through the wholeness of perception, and a consistent and uncompromising commitment to forgive, the Love, Light, and Unity of Heaven are reflected in the dream. The real world is the new home of those whose feet still walk the earth, but whose minds have reached the gates of Heaven.

To do what must be done may seem difficult at first due to the egoic resistance. You have been long accustomed to devoting your time and energy to remaining asleep. You have worked very hard to make the meaningless meaningful, to find value in what is valueless, and to avoid the Truth that lies as if buried deep within you. All of your life has been a movement away from the Self. Now you must turn around and begin the journey that leads in another direction. You must move towards Truth and not away from It. This requires a training of the mind, the mind that is fundamentally undisciplined, at the mercy of its unconscious fears and desires. Confusion, unclarity, and conflict, are the hallmarks of an untrained mind. To undo, to correct the false and meaningless thought system of separation, everything you have believed and the mental habits and tendencies that are part of it, is indeed a daunting task. Remember Who goes with you every step of the way.

Just when you need help, it is given, not before. All things are done when and as needed. Let all things be given, let all be revealed. There is One Who knows all, Who guides you always. Accept the plans He gives you in place of your own; His will work, yours will not. There is no reason to doubt His knowledge and beneficence. He will never desert you or you Him. You may delay and resist, postpone the final reckoning; you cannot stop it or avoid it forever. Your Father wills that you return to Him; what He wills is already true. You but wait for the recognition of that fact to reach your mind. God does not wait on time. In truth, neither do you.

Do you know the way you must follow? Are you aware of what needs be done, and how? To admit you do not know opens the mind to receive the necessary guidance. To recognize your ignorance is the prerequisite for knowledge to return. Learn to remember always, at all times and in all situations, that you are not alone. Do not try to understand anything in isolation, by yourself. Nothing is understood alone; always your understanding is shaped by the thought system to which you adhere and the guide you thus choose. Learn to remember to ask always, at all times, the Guide your Father has given you to help you understand. Let Him guide your thoughts, words, and actions, that you may become a Light unto your brothers, a lamp to shine the Light on the way they too must follow. You listen to the Holy Spirit not for yourself alone; all that you are given is to be shared with your brothers.

A New Life

To teach you how to recognize what is necessary and what is not, what is helpful to the accomplishment of your single purpose and what hinders and obstructs it, is the purpose of this teaching. To that end, you are being guided by both the words before you and the intent from which they arise. Words do not only carry meaning, they give form to intent. I am asking you to join with me and all your brothers who have accepted our part in God's Great Plan of Atonement. We need your help. Each and every one of you has an important part to play. The Great Plan is not complete until everyone has accepted their part and completed it.

You can delay as long as you want, wander down a thousand dark alleys that go nowhere, keep yourself endlessly busy doing nothing. Sooner or later you will have had enough of suffering; your pain threshold will be reached. Not until then will many of you be willing to look for another way to live, a real solution to conflict, pain, and suffering. A solution that carries you beyond their reach forever. And some will recognize the Light that calls to them and respond, recognizing that conflict and suffering are unnecessary, thus shortening their journey immeasurably. Do not wait my brothers, do not delay. All delay is a needless prolonging of fear and misery. Do not resist the inevitable return of freedom and Love. Do not cling to fear and suffering as the basis of your life. You never wanted this; you have been dreaming a dream of forgetfulness. Surrounded by dream figures, you have forgotten who you are for a moment. Now is the time to let the memory of what you are return to your awareness, transforming your life and returning you to the Kingdom. Now, only now.

Begin a new life this very day, a life dedicated to Love and Truth. Leave fear and conflict behind. They will wither away as you withdraw your interest and belief that you gained something thereby. Life itself awaits you. What you have been experiencing as life is a pale shadow, a sickly distortion of what you are meant to be. Fear not you will be asked to give up what is near and dear to you. What you value so highly has come at the expense of everything that has real value, and has never brought you anything but loss and sorrow. No real sacrifice is asked of you. Can it be a sacrifice to give up what is meaningless and valueless? You are merely asked to lay aside the cause of pain and suffering, and accept peace, freedom, and Love in its place. Can that be a difficult choice to make? Any difficulty around this choice is but the resistance to see what you have valued so long for what it really is.

Do not wait any longer in the vain hope you will find fulfillment and peace of mind in a world that lacks both. There is too much to be done to waste time in vain imaginings. Take up the thread of spiritual life, turn over decision making to the One Whose function it is, and learn of Him what must be done. Let go the empty conceit that you know anything of value. Let your mind be emptied of all that came before, of all that is past. Learn to greet each present moment, each new day, with a happy mind and an open heart. Be ready to listen and willing to learn always. And above all, let peace and forgiveness be your gift to everyone you meet.

Do Not Be Concerned

What is the next step to take after your mind has been reoriented and turned towards Truth? You must begin to understand what is required of you, what is needed for salvation. Certain changes must take place in your mind. This purification cannot be avoided. Purification may be described as the emptying out of your mind and heart of all that is false; the beliefs, ideas, and the habits of thought, feeling, and action that characterize the mind self-identified as an ego occupying a body. This process is direct and constant, requiring a total commitment on your part to be completed. Love and forgiveness must replace fear and guilt, and all need to attack and defend must be relinquished. Only then can you discover where your real safety lies. Only then do you become capable of welcoming Truth as it is.

Do not be concerned if at times you seem to falter, if your dedication wavers. This is a natural part of the process, for you are learning to accept and trust a new Teacher while still operating from the lessons you learned in the past. This back and forth, this movement in fits and starts, will usually characterize your journey until you began to see unequivocally the real value of what is true, and the actual suffering that results from every choice for illusion. You have not been completely aware of the consequences of all thinking, feeling, and action that arises from fear, from egoic motivation. In fact, you have not been aware of how deeply fear pervades your mind and influences your life. The mind in separation must dissociate from the fear and guilt at its core in order to function at all. Yet it will not allow them to be healed, for they are the basis of separation and the world you see.

It is essential that you become completely aware of the condition you are in, of how you would feel if your true state were not disguised by dissociation and denial. The habitual and unconscious actions of your mind keep the ego's control in place.

In fact, they are part of the ego's solution to separation, a solution that is no solution at all, but rather a temporary escape that lessens anxiety just enough to keep you going as its host. Fear must be avoided and controlled, but never completely released, or you would not need the ego as your guide and teacher. Without fear and guilt, Love would arise to your awareness, and the memory of God would not be far behind.

Do not give up hope ever. Do not be discouraged. The way may seem long and hard, the road stretching out before you to the far horizon, but you are not alone. Your Guide and Teacher goes with you, angels are your constant companions. The holy instant is available at every moment to lift you out of this world, giving you a taste of Heaven. Patience, infinite patience, is needed as long as you still journey through time. Yet time is illusion; Truth is never absent. Do not forget what awaits when you reach the gates of Heaven: a glorious homecoming, a celebration of the return of Light and Love and freedom. Nothing you have experienced in this world can even faintly compare with that bright moment.

CHAPTER NINE

Time and Purpose

Now is the moment when Truth returns. Now is when real learning takes place. Healing and release are always now. Forgiveness happens now, though it heals the past and releases the future. The eternal now, where time meets eternity, is the only moment of time that is real. Hence it is the only time that Truth can penetrate and reach your mind. The ego would have you live in the past, overlooking the present and chasing the future. In the present the ego does not exist; it must avoid the present at all costs. The Holy Spirit brings your mind back to the present, that you may hear Him and began to experience life in a new way. You must return to the present, that the burden of the past be lifted from your mind and the future set free to continue the present. What is new and alive must be allowed to flower and grow in your mind, replacing what is over and dead.

Give time the Holy Spirit's purpose. He knows how to use it to free you from the past you made to limit your mind and obscure the Truth. The ego uses time to perpetuate illusion, to maintain the bondage to fear and suffering. It would have the future be the continuation of a past that was over long ago.

Trudging slowly along a road that goes nowhere, each day a stale repetition of the one gone before, until you are too weary to go on, with only the strength left to sink into oblivion and death; this is the ego's goal for all who depend on it for direction and meaning.

Do not follow the guidance of one that knows nothing and leads you nowhere. Turn away from death and welcome life again. Your Father has given you a Teacher and Guide Who will lead you gently back to the promised land. To follow Him is to follow the Will given you by God in your creation. You have no other will. Yet it seems as if another will, apart from God's Will, has taken Its place. As long as you believe your will is separate from God's Will, you will resist doing what is necessary for salvation. You will think the Holy Spirit demands sacrifice of you, and your progress will be slow.

Is it a sacrifice to give up pain and suffering? Is it sacrifice to let go of what is valueless? Does it make sense to base your life on what is valueless, meaningless, incapable of bringing lasting satisfaction and fulfillment? Surely it is not sacrifice to give up the things of this world, illusory images without substance. The Holy Spirit will take nothing from you. He will wait until you recognize what is worthless and unnecessary, and withdraw your investment in illusion. Then He will teach you what is real and of immeasurable value to take its place.

Willingness to Learn

To do what must be done is the simplest thing in the world, yet for the mind of separation, it is the most difficult. The projections of your mind, both the imagery you see before you and your interpretations, complicate your mind to the point where real understanding and clarity are not possible. Projections of right and wrong, like all judgments, distort the mind and introduce varying and constantly changing criteria by which to understand the events and situations of life. Honest consistency becomes impossible; that is why no one can be consistently fair in their interpretations of the behavior of their brothers. Shifting and inconsistent thinking, evaluations that vary greatly from one situation to another; this is the state of your mind and your responses to the many events that occur in your life. And to this we may add the conscious and unconscious moods, feelings, and egoic defense mechanisms that are always in operation.

In such a state, even the recognition of what needs be done to free the mind of the self induced madness in which it is seemingly caught, is impossible without help from beyond the circle of insanity. How that help is given depends on your willingness to learn from the Holy Spirit, and the willingness to surrender your life, to turn it over. He is always available to you if you make yourself available to Him. An open, receptive mind, making decisions with His help, ever ready to be guided, always listening; such a mind easily receives the Holy Spirit's direction and acts as guided. This releases the power of Spirit into your life, and the transformation of your mind is the inevitable result.

Willingness to recognize and accept that you know nothing is essential. The belief not only that you know, but that it is even possible to understand Truth from the standpoint of separation, is a great obstacle. Reliance on yourself alone, on the image you have made to take the place of what God created as your Self, is what has deprived you of the awareness of Reality. In order to return to that awareness, what is responsible for its loss must be relinquished. You must recognize the falsity of the whole thought system of which the self is an expression. As these beliefs are relinquished, investment is withdrawn from the self-identity. Eventually, after a period of disorientation, the self becomes empty and transparent, and the Reality of what you are begins to shine into your mind. Do not allow the sense of disorientation to frighten you. It will pass, as will all states and conditions of this world. Fear is never justified in any form, being the sign you have identified yourself with the state of separation. As such, it is simply an error, a forgetting of who you are, a remembering of the past as if it were still here now. The past cannot affect you unless you hold it in memory and give it the power of your belief.

Do not let the habits of a life time continue to hold you prisoner. Freedom awaits your choice. Once that decision is truly made, and with the Holy Spirit's help, nothing can stop you from attaining freedom. The choice for freedom is the choice for the Self, as the Self is forever free and beyond limits of any kind. The Self is Love, and Love cannot be bound; there is nothing that can hold It or obstruct It in any way.

What price freedom? How can that which is your birthright require payment of any kind? To recover, to return again to what has always been yours, is the result of your decision to let go of what has temporarily taken its place. Nothing given you by your Father has been lost. What you have been given by God you will always have, for what you have is what you are; you cannot lose or be apart from what you are except in dreams, and dreams will not last. The journey back to the realization of Truth but seems to be a journey. The distance you traverse from where you find yourself now to where you have always been, takes place in time as if eternity were not here now. You are standing at the end of time, imagining a journey that is not yet over, awaiting only your decision to let go all illusion and be again what you have always been. All teaching and learning, everything the Holy Spirit gives you, the slow development of willingness, the correction of your mind and perception; all this has a single purpose: to bring you to the point where this decision is remembered.

Cause and Effect

There is much to do but there is not much time to do it. Within you is the key to your dilemma of separation. Within your mind is where separation occurred and where it is still being maintained. The 'external world', being the effect of your thinking mind, reflects separation back to you. The world outpictures what you want to be true, and provides the 'proof' that you are separate from your Creator and your Self. The world provides you with a means to hide from God, while you continue to usurp His Function and fear His retribution. Both your thinking and its effects, the world you see, will change as you allow your mind and perception to be corrected. Your experience of yourself and the world will be transformed, for experience is the result of what you want to be true.

When you allow the Holy Spirit to teach you what you want to learn, you will begin to see yourself and the world in a new way. You will see the real condition you are in right now without fantasy or denial, and you will accept your responsibility for it. Without accepting responsibility for what you see and experience, you cannot be free of its effects. The refusal to recognize that you are not the helpless and innocent victim of the world that appears around you, keeps you an apparent prisoner, subject to the many events and conditions that occur.

The ego's response to the world it sees is to perceive threat everywhere, and counter it through a continuing strategy of attack, defense, and projection. Its strategy cannot bring you peace, safety, or fulfillment, though you believe it can for that is all you know. The Holy Spirit's function is to help you see all beliefs and strategies arising from the ego as meaningless, ineffective, and ultimately self destructive. Your safety does not depend on outward conditions or circumstances. No security can be found in a world of constant change and chaos. Within you, waiting to be allowed back into awareness, is everything you need or will ever need.

All your apparent problems, internal or external, begin with the one original error you have made. All other errors stem from this one. In the separation from God were the myriad problems, difficulties, and every kind of pain and suffering born. In the attempt to grapple with what are simply the consequences of your original error, the cause of all problems is veiled and hidden by continuing denial. You will never solve all the problems which appear in your life by responding on the level of form. Form is effect while mind is cause. Problems must be solved by removing their cause, not by responding to effect which will simply reappear in another form if the cause remains.

The Holy Spirit teaches you to overlook all effects that appear as problems by remembering where the problem, the one problem you have no matter the form, truly lies: separation from God. And there is one answer to them all given you by God: the Holy Spirit. He will provide the specific answer to all appearances if you ask. In a world of differences, of specifics, your one problem appears in many different forms; the one solution must then likewise be given in the form most appropriate.

Thought and Awareness

Do not allow unbelief or doubt to limit your mind. Mind itself responds to your decisions. Your intent directs it where you want it to go. Choose against doubt by recognizing its source. The ego doubts, delays, and resists all real change. You must learn to be aware of the origin of all thought that enters your mind. Thoughts given by the Holy Spirit will express peace, kindness, and Love. They will direct you towards Truth and away from fear. You are strengthened always by listening to the Holy Spirit and following His guidance.

Egoic thought covers a wide range of topics, of feelings and emotions. The ego consistently focuses on the past or imagines a future. Judgment and condemnation are ever present. Always egoic thought is based on separation, on the position of a separate being, and the importance of your needs, your desires, your likes and dislikes, your comfort and security. Always the ego fluctuates between fear and desire, attack and defense. The whole movement of egoic thought is self-obsessed, chaotic, and at times contradictory. Frenzied thoughts come and go in rapid succession, tripping over one another. There is no peace to be found while you identify with the constant parade of madness in your mind.

Truth comes to a quiet mind, a mind made ready for Its coming. The constant inner noise and activity of the egoic thought process drowns out the still, small voice of Spirit that would call you home. You cannot listen to two voices just as you cannot serve two masters. The choice is yours as always. Listen honestly to the thoughts that cross your mind unceasingly. Become aware of what they represent. Ask yourself is this what I truly want as my guide to action and understanding? Do I want chaos, confusion, and contradiction, to dominate my thinking and deciding?

There is another way along which the Holy Spirit will lead you. Truth, peace, and Love will accompany you, and true reason will be your guiding light. You must develop the practice of being constantly aware of the thoughts, impulses, feelings, and images that crowd your mind, the constant activity and momentum of the past. You have been carried along by this process for so long that you identify with it, believing yourself to be the source, the thinker of these thoughts. There is no thinker. There is only the memory of the past, playing out constantly in your mind as if the past were happening now. The ego is the source of the inner process of thought that dominates your awareness. It will never speak truthfully to you, being itself an illusion. Yet its constant activity convinces you that it is you. Thus has the belief arisen that egoic thoughts are your thoughts, that you are thinking them.

Let the Holy Spirit help you be continuously aware of the activity of your mind. Let Him teach you the difference between His communications which are true and helpful and lead you in the direction of Truth, and the ego's communications which are false and lead you away from It. You will learn over time that you no longer want to be a body, an ego identity whose chaotic and frantic thought process does not give you a moment's peace. As this understanding becomes established, it will lead to a progressively increasing rejection of the entire thought system of separation and its expression as the egoic thought stream that flows constantly through your mind.

Constant vigilance is needed to undo the habitual identification with the egoic stream of thought, and free your mind from its domination. You must be aware of what passes through your mind, and maintain a sense of being beyond the thoughts, if you would be able to choose the thoughts you want to think. To be aware, as thoughts pass through your mind, from the vantage point of an alert, quiet awareness is essential. You will find as you progress with this 'mind watching', that it will become increasing clear to you these thoughts of which you are becoming aware, are not your thoughts despite their obvious familiarity. You will also begin to notice their repetitive nature; the same thoughts and feelings repeat themselves over and over again. And it is not unusual for thoughts to conflict with and contradict each other.

The more consistently aware you become of the continuous stream of thoughts, feelings, and images, the more clearly you will see the chaotic and insane nature of the whole process. It is a process whose purpose is to occupy your mind, dominate your attention, and keep you self identified as a mind in separation with its own private thoughts. None of the thoughts of which you are aware, are real thoughts; they are not from God. Nothing that is 'private', belonging to you alone and incapable of being shared, is real.

Your real thoughts are only those you think with God; they cannot be described for they are not conceptual. The thoughts you think you are thinking are taking the place of your real thoughts, thus obstructing your awareness of them. While the egoic thought process is absorbing your attention, your mind is effectively blank; the Light cannot shine in and through the mind while it is occupied by illusion. What can end the domination of illusion is the consistent vigilance against it.

Being aware of the constant activity of your mind will free you of it. You are free to choose your thoughts only when you are aware of them as they arise. By learning what is Truth and what is illusion, and the difference between them, you have a sound basis from which to choose. Vigilance, being aware moment to moment of the minds activity, enables you to choose the thoughts you want to keep. Being able to choose what you want to think on the basis of what is true, will eventually free your mind of the ego's chaotic, meaningless, and self destructive thought process. This is not an easy task but it is a necessary one.

Choice and Habit

Due to the lingering effects of all choices made without the help of the Holy Spirit, the momentum of illusion will continue even after you have turned resolutely in the direction of Truth. Nowhere is this more apparent than in the habitual nature of your responses to the changing events of everyday life. To respond effectively is to respond from a position of moment to moment awareness of the mind's content; yet this readiness does not stop the flow of thoughts from the past and their influence on your mind. All that is false and all its effects must be skillfully undone by the Holy Spirit with your cooperation. This undoing must go on throughout each day, day in and day out, until the mind becomes quiet, empty, and free. Nothing must remain to sully the purity of your holy mind.

Only the resolute and consistent response of Truth to falsity will free your mind from the effects of illusion. Illusion has surrounded and ruled your mind for so long you know nothing else. It is as if a spell has been cast over you like a kind of hypnotism . You see what the hypnotist tells you to see, and all else you overlook and ignore. While you prefer fantasies to Reality, sleeping to awakening, you will continue to sleep walk through life, imagining yourself to be something you are not, reacting to the shadows you think surround you. They are not there. Be willing to have this shown to you, and you will walk out of the world of shadows into the bright sunlight.

Let the Holy Spirit take you by the hand and show you the dark shadows that seem to threaten you are your imagination, not to be feared but forgiven. Let Him show you the bright and shining Truth that waits behind every fearful dream you have ever had. You have hypnotized yourself into seeing what is not there, and not seeing what waits to set you free. As the self-hypnotism is lifted, the world before you will appear very different. Its natural brightness will become evident, and in time real vision will develop, revealing the Light that is in everything.

Whatever you do, do with Love. This will bring power and meaning to all your doing. A state of mind in which you remember to regard all things with Love, appreciation, and gratitude, will do much to set you free. By remembering to offer Love only, you will learn that you are Love. When Love is all you want, then

Love will be all you see. Those who give only Love are truly blessed, for they are giving only what blesses to their brothers.

To bring all that you are back into your life will reveal your aliveness in all its fullness. Without awareness of all that you are, you are living partially, your life is incomplete. No matter how you try to find meaning in a state of incompleteness, you will not succeed. Your wholeness, your completeness, is your meaning. Meaning need not be sought somewhere outside of you. Like all that is real, meaning is within you, part of your very Being. The search for meaning is the great, yet unconscious motivation that drives human seeking. All such seeking will end in failure, for humans do not know what they seek. To search for you know not what, will lead to nothing but frustration and disappointment.

Do not let the force of habit rule your mind and limit your perception. Habit dulls the vision, casting a grey veil across everything you see. It robs life of its freshness and immediacy, reducing experience to dull routine. The mind of the self functions in habits, as habit. If by habit we mean a pattern of thought or behavior that repeats itself regularly and more or less automatically, then we could describe the entire ego mind as a configuration of habits. To function automatically, habitually, in repeating patterns, is to be acting from the past, as the past. The present is covered over, and all it has to offer goes unnoticed.

The Power of Willingness

Do you want to awaken to the Truth of what you are? That is the question you must answer. The answer you give determines the course of your life in general as well as its many details. To answer that question affirmatively will lead you to everything that is real and lasting. To answer in the negative, whether consciously or unconsciously, will lead you on a journey to nowhere. Salvation is the only goal worthy of attainment. Every other purpose is nothingness disguised to appear as if it were something. Would you go nowhere or would you make the only journey possible of completion? And if the answer is yes, all of Heaven will rejoice with you.

To all of your efforts on behalf of Truth are added the mighty strength of the Holy Spirit. He responds to the slightest inclination, the smallest effort, with all the power of Heaven. No desire for Truth, no opening in your mind, goes unnoticed or unsupported. He waits with infinite patience for your willingness to take even the smallest step in the direction of Truth. All He needs is your little willingness; to that He adds His own, making it a mighty force for Truth. Without your willingness, the Holy Spirit can do nothing, for only willingness can open your mind to receive the help it needs. Nothing can enter a closed mind; Truth can come only where It is invited.

Do not underestimate the power of willingness to accomplish miracles. Everything starts there. Willingness is the positive response of the one freedom left to you in the state of separation: the power to choose. Willingness or unwillingness informs every choice you make. Do not allow weakness or apathy to paralyze your willingness to choose the miracle. The miracle would deliver you from all weakness, all falsity. Do not let what the miracle would save you from, prevent you from accepting the help it brings.

Fear and Illusion

There is nothing to fear in the world of illusion. Threat, like all illusion, is non-existent. What is non-existent can have no effects. In thought, you can choose to believe the effects of illusion, and this will make them real for you. The apparent effects you experience are not real effects; they are as illusory as their source. The birthplace of all illusions is the mind that cherishes them as an escape from Reality Itself. Without the support of your mind, illusions would disappear and their effects with them.

Is this what you want; to be free of all illusion in every way for always? There is no freedom but the freedom of true existence. As the Self, as Spirit, you have always been and always will be free; nothing can limit you in any way. This was God's gift to you in your creation. His gifts can never be lost; they are what you are. Being Itself cannot be lost or changed in any way. Do not despair if freedom seems lost to you. It is but a seeming loss, a temporary state of confusion in your mind about who you are. Like all of illusion, it will be corrected, leaving only Truth to be Itself.

The undoing of illusion, the correction of the falsity in your mind, is the only thing you need be concerned with. All else will take care of itself when your commitment is given wholly to the realization of Truth. Accept the Atonement for yourself without reservation, and everything needed will be provided; nothing will be lacking. Your Father knows what you need, and the Holy Spirit translates His gifts into the forms you recognize.

You live in a world of form and difference; thus your needs appear to take many forms. God's One Answer appears as if in different forms to address the needs you believe you have. Yet is His Answer still One. Love will provide and keep you safe through the changing circumstances and conditions of life. Never will you be left comfortless or lacking. If this appears to be the case, be sure you have cut yourself off from the possibility of receiving the help you need. Now you must examine your mind and become aware of your motives. Somewhere in your mind, you are refusing the help that is available, and choosing misery and isolation in its place. Help cannot be received without willingness and clarity. The willingness to do your part is always necessary.

Give and Forgive

Do not refuse to do what the Holy Spirit asks of you. To refuse to give will block your receiving. Give all you have and then give more, and your cup will always be running over. Those who are blessed with the gifts of God will give all that they have received. By giving away what you have been given, it becomes yours to keep. Your store will be continually increasing; the more you give, the more you will have. You have an inexhaustible supply of gifts to give, your storehouse is always full.

Those who have accepted their part in God's Great Plan recognize the importance of giving to all. Your Father only gives. "Be you perfect even as your Father in Heaven is perfect." Give all to all, and forgive the world and everyone and everything in it. Give and forgive; let this be the rule that guides your life. Thus will you be doing God's Will, and bringing Heaven's blessing to a tired and suffering world.

Let all those who come to you be comforted. You are meant to be a help to all, bringing God's blessings to a world that has lost all hope. A Teacher of God is a Light shining in the darkness, illuminating the way for others to follow. You must accept the responsibilities you are given; that is how you fulfill your part in the Great Plan. In completing your part, you are released from all illusions and returned to your eternal condition of peace and freedom. Only you can complete the part assigned to you, and only thus are you made whole and complete again. Doing God's work is not a burden; it is joy itself. You will never be happy unless you are fulfilling the function given you by God. To do what God wills is to follow your true will, for your will <u>is</u> God's Will.

A Teacher of God has a single purpose, and it is to this he devotes his life each day. All the day's activities are seen in the light of this single purpose. No difficulty arises, whether within or without, that is not easily resolved through the power of love expressed as the willingness to love, to forgive, and to heal. Miracles are the Teacher of God's constant companions for he has welcomed them into his life. What you have welcomed with an open mind and heart, you will be given, and what is given you can be given to all.

Your Father's Will

Let the indivisible Unity of which you are a part be the guiding influence in your life. Life lived as the Whole rather than as a separate part, is perfectly fulfilling. You are the Whole; you contain and are contained by everything. There is nothing that is not your Mind.

Apparently separate existence is but a dream you are dreaming. While you continue to sleep, the dream seems real, much as your nightly dreams seem real until you awake. Then you see clearly that you were dreaming and you do not mistake those dreams for reality. When you awake from the sleep of ignorance, you will know that the world you see and everything in it was nothing more than a passing dream that is now over. The spiritual sun is rising, and its Light shines away the darkness of the long night's sleep. Step forward into the Light and take your rightful place as the Christ, God's holy Creation. Even now you are the Christ as you have always been. The dream cannot affect your Reality, only your awareness of It.

To do your Father's Will is to do your will. You will never be happy by following an alien will that leads you only to death. Do not mistake the familiarity born of long association for Truth. You have lived in an unnatural way for so long, it seems natural to you. Eyes long accustomed to darkness do not remember the Light. What is gone even from memory is not missed. However, a world bereft of the Light and Love of God's Presence is not your home.

Your Father calls to you unceasingly but you do not hear Him. Your ears are closed to the song of Heaven for you prefer the din of earthly life. The constant noise of the ego drowns out the cries of suffering that surround you. You do not hear the pleas for help from your brothers lost in the darkness. They call to you to save them. You are their savior as they are savior to you. Do not leave their call unanswered; to respond to their call is to hear your own. You cannot hear your Father calling unless you recognize your brother as yourself. Heaven's call goes out to God's One Son; it is answered by the many fragments who are still One though they have forgotten. Each one who answers, answers for all. You cannot respond to Truth from separation. One Son of God is awakening though It may appear as the many.

Grace and Willingness

When the time comes to let it all go, will you be ready? To let go is to relinquish all attachment, all need to hold on to something. The end of suffering is the release of all that causes it. What are the causes? False beliefs about yourself and the world. What else could bring about a state of suffering in the mind created perfect by God? Suffering is illusion; the mind that thinks suffering real, has forgotten what it is and imagines itself to be something else entirely. That something else is a body, housing a mind with which it is identical. Could such an identity shift truly occur? Only in dreams where you seem to be as you are not. All authentic spiritual thought systems attempt to teach that you are not a body, separate from everything you see and your creative Source. You are Mind and Reality Itself. Only your ignorance of your eternal Reality, a kind of amnesia that is actively maintained, keeps the true experience of your Self from your awareness.

Do not let this ignorance, this forgetfulness, continue; it is a willful ignorance. If you have made a choice to forget, to banish from your mind, you can choose again to let what was denied return. The purpose of this teaching is to help you make this choice. You need help to recover what you have apparently lost, for your mind is limited and distorted by false beliefs. This has led to a state of mind and experience that is self convincing and self justifying, and you cannot see beyond it. Only the One Who is outside of the narrow little circle of illusion and rooted in Truth, can help you to free yourself from the effects of ignorance.

All that must be done, is done through grace. Without the grace of God, you would be lost forever in the dream you have made. You must be willing, however, to accept His grace, to welcome it into your life and allow it to work. Willingness is indispensible; without it nothing can be done.

One of the goals of this teaching is the redirecting of your willingness from illusion to Truth. For a long, long time, you have been willing to live in a state of separation from your Creator and your Self. You have chosen to be apart from your brothers and all that surrounds you. You have sought safety in various defenses, physical and mental. Fulfillment has been sought through the attainment of personal goals and accomplishments; pleasure and stimulation of many kinds have been fervently pursued. And you have tried to find Love in special relationships which exclude all others. Guilt, fear, and sorrow have been your constant companions. At the end of this senseless series of journeys, death waits to finally release you from what you have made. Or so you think.

CHAPTER TEN

You Are Not Alone

Do not be afraid of what you have made; it is not real. Its hold over you is but part of the dream. You have given it the power it seems to have, and you can withdraw it at any time. Nothing need trouble you; despite appearances, you are not in danger and cannot suffer loss or be deprived in any way. All such experiences are the result of wrong understanding. You do not see the help that is always with you; you do not hear the Holy Spirit Who is always guiding you. Behind every problem, every experience of fear, pain, or suffering, stands a miracle waiting for your acceptance that it may enter your life and set your mind free.

All of life stands ready to join with you in singing hymns of praise and gratitude to your Creator. Everything is communicating its Self to you, but you must be willing to enter this communion. There is no separation here. Even while dreaming the mind is One. Everything you see is a part of you; all bodies, all forms, are but images that appear in your mind. Nothing is separate. Open your mind to receive the communication that fills the universe. Open your heart to Love that you may join with your brothers and offer salvation to a tired world that longs for the Light. Remember who you are and who your brother is. Separated from each other, you are afraid and powerless; together, you will leave this world and walk hand in hand through the gates of Heaven.

Whatever you do, remember this: you are not alone nor do your actions affect you only. All are affected by what you think and do. There are no private thoughts or actions in isolation; you are always thinking and acting for the Whole. You are responsible for the whole world, not just for yourself alone. To fulfill this responsibility rightly, you must recognize the importance of everything you do and think. You cannot be careless or casual in anything. Your life is your gift to all your brothers as their lives are to you. The only gift worthy of being given to any Son of God is Love.

Love and Fear

Your true desire is to be helpful to all, and this is accomplished through Love. No other motivation is truly worthy of you. Your brother is yourself, and you love him as you love yourself, or you would, if you but let yourself love. Fear of your brother keeps your mind and heart closed to him, and obscures the Love you really feel. All your actions and perceptions have the aim of maintaining separation and the belief your safety lies apart from your brother. Guilt must be maintained to uphold the specialness you feel and justify your failure to love.

The failure to love is not just a problem in itself; it also contributes to the maintenance and continuance of the allegiance to guilt, which preserves judgment and the belief in attack and defense that follow. When Love is absent, all manner of errors rush in to take Its place. Yet are all errors but forms of fear no matter their appearance. In this world, fear has taken Love's place, even masquerading as Love at times. Fear is not Love whatever the disguise it may be wearing. Only those who have forgotten the meaning of Love could possibly make that error.

Clearing your mind of the basic confusion and misunderstanding around Love and fear is essential. Little progress can be made while you continue to love fear and fear Love. This confusion has made peace impossible and conflict inevitable. You live in a state of constant conflict, within and without, that has left you feeling vulnerable and in a state of constant anxiety. Under these conditions, believing yourself open to attack from all around you, you have adopted a posture of attack and defense that greatly distorts communication. Your relationships are never free from the need to limit and control communication. This control makes real openness impossible; without real openness, Love will elude you.

Nothing can be done without real surrender. To surrender to the Higher Power, to trust, and to turn over decision making to the Holy Spirit, is essential if you are to free your mind and return to Truth. The idea of giving up control of your life arouses great fear in the separated ones. The control you attempt to exercise over your life and mind arose as a response to the terror of the original separation, and you have tried to maintain control ever since. Yet is this control just another part of the illusion. The belief in control helps maintain the illusion, but does not keep you safe, which is its intended purpose.

The fear you would keep hidden and protect yourself from, lives on in your mind and exerts a constant influence on your life. You can, temporarily at least, keep naked fear from awareness and seem to be comfortable and secure. This state or condition cannot last. The instability of ego mind and the many external conditions beyond your control, make the whole idea of controlling life just another ego fantasy, impossible of accomplishment.

Your safety lies not in the futile attempt to control but in the relinquishment of control. Surrender to that which alone deserves your allegiance, will bring you the security you try vainly to achieve on your own. The attempt to control life according to your liking, is the attempt to establish as real the identity you have made. Here is the real failure of all egoically motivated activity. What is illusion through and through can never be made real, no matter how much energy and effort is expended for that purpose.

One of your greatest fears is that you have no real existence. Some have seen this clearly, but were unprepared, and descended into madness. Yet at this time is your greatest opportunity to break through the barrier of fear and reach the Love that waits just beyond. Help is needed to make this transition; it will be given if you are willing to ask for help and accept what is given.

Surrender to the Love that is what you are and fear will disappear. The Light of Love shines away all darkness. With fear gone, you will realize that you are safe and always have been. Your Father holds you safe and secure within Himself, where you abide eternally.

The Light of Truth

Do not let the stories you tell yourself interfere with what you truly want and need. All stories are meaningless, meant to keep your mind too busy to notice the state you are in. Do not believe the tales the ego has invented to keep your allegiance and cloud your mind. Everything the ego has told you is not true. Your belief in what is not true has robbed you of your sanity, your freedom, and your Self. Do not continue this pointless charade. Nothing can take the place of Truth in your mind. To lose awareness of Truth is a loss too enormous to comprehend.

If all you know is of existence on a very small island surrounded by fog, the vastness of the ocean around you cannot be comprehended. If someone were to tell you there is a great ocean surrounding us, you would not believe as you are unable to understand what is so far beyond your experience. The mind asleep is like that, unable to recognize anything beyond its dream world. Yet there comes a time for every mind when the desire for Truth, so long repressed, begins to rise to awareness. This desire must be nurtured that it may strengthen and develop into real commitment. To let the longing for Truth be lost among the many conflicting voices of the ego, is a great tragedy. Do not let the Light of Truth go out or wither away when once It begins to shine.

The Light has always been a part of you, the natural radiance of Christ Mind. The Light is not visible or accessible, however, while you are asleep and dreaming, for you have chosen darkness to take its place. Like all of Truth, the Light cannot go where It is not welcome; Truth enters not into conflict with illusion. When you have cleared your mind, making a clean and empty place for the return of Truth, It will be there. Your mind is Its rightful home despite your willful ignorance.

There is no need to search or struggle to find Truth for it has not been lost, it has been forgotten. All true spiritual practice is the seeking out of all obstructions to Truth in your mind, and the healing of them. To heal is to release, to renounce and let go of what denies Truth and actively prevents Its return to awareness. This is the purpose of the Atonement. The Holy Spirit, the Mind of the Atonement, is the means by which this is done with your help, dedication, and cooperation. Illusion cannot withstand your commitment to let it go. Only through your support and continuing defense of illusion, does it maintain its apparent hold on your mind.

The Solution

What is the solution to the apparently false condition in which you find yourself as a human being? It begins with the willingness to recognize and accept that what I experience is not the Truth, is not real. The identity I have given myself, a self in separation, is not what I am. You must be willing to accept at least the possibility that all you thought you knew is not true. You know nothing. This willingness is essential, that you may begin to make room for what the Holy Spirit will teach you. He cannot teach a mind that is full of its own ideas and beliefs and unwilling to let them go.

Purification is the letting go of all that is false, of all that denies, obstructs, and attacks the Truth. To let go is to renounce, to withdraw your investment and expel from your mind. The cessation of the false identification of yourself as a body, must be accomplished before your true identity can be revealed. You do not have two selves, one real and one unreal. There is only one Self, the Self of All. The self you have made is a dream, nothing more, despite its apparent existence.

Whatever the distance you are asked to go, do it. The Holy Spirit does not ask of you lightly; all He asks is for your own benefit. Do not refuse Him the cooperation He needs to lead you to freedom. He alone knows what is needed at all times and in every situation. If you would learn to trust and to cooperate in every way, He will show you again and again that your trust is completely justified. Do not give in to doubt. Doubt is of the ego; it will come and go. Remember its source and let it go, for doubt will simply delay the restoration of freedom. It has no other purpose.

Do your best to become aware of the various delaying tactics of the ego. Try not to let the resistance in your mind get in the way of what must be done. Too often do you choose against your own best interest. Resistance always arises from fear and the belief in sacrifice. To give up what you never wanted, what has brought only suffering and limitation, is no sacrifice. You are never asked to give up what is truly valuable and necessary. So long accustomed to value what is valueless and deny what is of immeasurable worth, you do not recognize the difference between them. Thus do you have no real basis from which to make the only choice that can be made.

The power of choice must be used wisely. Used wrongly, in the service of the ego, choice maintains illusion and perpetuates separation. The ego would have you choose where choice is not possible; to choose nothingness is but the illusion of choosing. Used rightly, guided by the Holy Spirit, choice is used to set you free. You must learn to choose against what brings pain and sorrow, and choose instead what will bring freedom and happiness.

The Present

Today is the only day there is just as now is the only time. To recognize this is very important. The future is like a carrot the ego holds out before you to hypnotize and divert your attention from the present. By operating from the past, from accumulated memory, and keeping your eye on the future, attention is focused on what is already over or what does not yet exist. The present is effectively bypassed, leaving you always somewhere in limbo. Thus you are always in actuality nowhere. In this state of confusion, your life is limited by the past and lost in the future. Is it then any wonder that you become exhausted by the ego's constant demands? Never are you focused and resting in the present wherein are your strength and Being. To have no access to the Source of life while being constantly busy but never present is exhausting. To keep you busy and distracted chasing shadows, is the ego's strategy that assures its continued existence.

If you were present, really present in full awareness, you would discover the ego does not exist. The source of the continuing experience of separation would be seen for what it is. That this is not your experience is obvious. Yet this is a choice you are making, a choice to identify with the past and project a future that is the continuation of the past. Thus is learning in the present limited by what was found acceptable in the past.

Real learning takes place in the present independent of the past, and with no already established reference to the future. Real learning is not determined by past likes and dislikes, but is rather an open-ended process of receiving in the now. The mind must be open, free of clinging to the past, and receptive without preconditions. Real learning takes place in a mind that recognizes it does not know, that opens itself to the unknown. Only then can that which comes from beyond the mind be received without fear.

To learn what the Holy Spirit would teach, requires just this openness, receptivity, and presence of mind. You do not understand what you need or even why. He will lead you to where you want to go, to where you need to go. You must give Him your willingness to learn and your trust. He will provide the rest.

Freedom is always freedom from the past. It is the memory of the past that imprisons you now. The past and its history of separation lies across your mind like a heavy weight. Like a dark and cloudy lens, it obscures and colors all you see and experience. The core of this lens, this distortion, is the self, the identity you have given yourself to replace what God created as you. The self, the ego's expression in experience, cannot be anything other than a distortion of your mind in every way, and a severe limit on your experience. In addition to its constant busyness which distracts your attention from the now, the only moment in which you can truly and directly experience, the self is in itself a contraction of fear that prevents true openness.

An Open Mind

Real openness is necessary for authentic learning to occur. An open mind is receptive, free of pre-established limits on what it would receive. This allows its horizons to be expanded, knowledge far beyond its previous limits of experience to be given. All true learning aims at taking the mind back to its true nature as the Self. This is the only learning that is truly helpful. All other learning is based on and maintains separation though it may be helpful in day to day life. Let yourself be given what you need, and learn to let go of what you do not need. Only what is truly helpful in the light of your highest purpose, is of any use to you at all. You will be shown the difference between what is helpful and what is not. As you learn to recognize this consistently, you will have a real basis from which to evaluate every choice, every decision that seemingly needs to be made. Until you have established in your mind a stable understanding of what benefits you and what hurts you, you will be unable to consistently choose rightly. From right understanding, you are able to look past the bewildering variety of forms and circumstances that confront you and perceive the content of every choice. Until this consistency of perception stabilizes, your choosing will likewise be erratic and inconsistent.

Do not underestimate the importance of accurate perception for your life's purpose. So long as perception proceeds from past associations, from memory and habit, so long will real understanding be absent from your life. Without authentic understanding, your mind will simply fluctuate within the narrow limits established by the ego and accepted by you long ago. Perception must be purified, must be corrected, to free your mind from its narrow range of experience. This tiny space in which your life seems to take place, is nothing but a dream of separation and limitation. To be separate from everything you see is to live in fear. To live in fear is to suffer. Is this what you want? You have lived in a state of fear and suffering long enough. Too long has Love and the healing It brings been absent from your life. This need not be. This need not be.

If you were to seriously consider whether you are happy living the way you have always lived, what would be your conclusion? Happy or unhappy? Do you think happiness and fulfillment can be found by continuing down the same dusty road? Have you ever found a peace, a sense of contentment that was lasting, no matter the changing events and circumstances of life? Perhaps it is time to consider the possibility of traveling a different road, of marching to the beat of a different drum. Your life is the result of the choices you have made, and these choices are determined by your beliefs, by your thought system. Your mind determines the conditions of your life, nothing else. If you are not happy with what you are getting, then it's time to change your mind. Your life will change accordingly.

Now is the time to begin again, to find another way. There is a way to find the real meaning of life, and to live in accordance with it. Do you know where that way lies? Within you is the way home and the destination. Nowhere else can it be found; do not look outside yourself. Nothing is outside yourself, everything is in your mind.

What is the next step to take after the recognition that change is needed? Just listen. Just listen. Openness is essential. Openness will take you far. The human condition is the opposite of openness. The mind is closed, imprisoned by its false beliefs. The heart is closed, limited by the fear of Love. Feeling is contracted, limited by the senses and the misuse of the body. All in all, the human being is in a state of contraction, configured in a dynamic of attack and defense. This is true on all levels of experience, both obvious and subtle. The thought system of separation is a kind of prison you have built around your mind to keep out Reality, to keep God away. And it has succeeded, but at what cost? It has cost you happiness, peace, and freedom. Your relationship with your Creating Source has been lost. Your true strength lies in God. To lose the awareness of your Father's Presence within you is to live in a weakened condition. Thus is fear inevitable.

Fear has taken the place of Love in the mind of separation. It cannot be otherwise. To exclude God from your awareness is to exclude Love. Where Love is absent, fear rushes in to take Its place. Life in a world of separation can be characterized most simply as a condition in which Love has been replaced by fear. In the Great Reversal, Love returns to banish fear, Truth returns to banish ignorance, Light returns to shine away the darkness. The spiritual journey leads to the undoing of all that is false, the reversal of all the thinking of the world, and the return of Truth to the mind that forgot It for a little while.

Openness and the willingness to listen will take you far. As the mind opens more and more to the Truth it needs to learn and directly experience, the false beliefs that have crippled it begin to fall away. The limitations on experience that arise from the false belief system began to dissolve. A momentum develops that begins to feed on itself. Openness lets more experience in, and greater experience leads to more openness. Crucial to this whole process is the willingness to listen. Help must be given and received. The Truth lies forgotten deep in your mind. Help is not needed to be what you are for that was established by God. However, help is needed to reach the Truth, for you have driven It from your awareness and have erected many defenses against It.

Use Time Well

The Holy Spirit is ever ready to help. Without the help He brings, you would be lost indeed. He will direct you in every way, informing you always of what you need to know in any given situation, at any given time. He will guide your thoughts, words, and actions. To stay in communication with Him is essential as you go about your day, for He gently and surely guides you along the journey homeward until the goal is reached, the journey over, and His help needed no more. Until that day, remember the help that is available and continue to invite it into your life.

The now is crucial in the understanding of time's purpose. Time must be used, and used well, if you are to free yourself from the limitations it imposes. Whatever you do in this world is subject to time and the changes is brings. The task is this: you must discover and open to the timeless while living under the laws of time. The changeless must be realized in the midst of the constantly changing. The eternal is always with you in the present, but is not noticed. The mind is very busy, so preoccupied with the past and the future that the present is overlooked and passed by. So long as you identify with the ego, with the constant activity of the mind, with its unceasing stream of thoughts, feelings, images, impulses, and desires, so long will you bypass the present. Your life takes place now, not in the past or future. If you would reclaim your life as it really is from the illusion you thought it was, you must return your attention to the present. Nowhere else does real learning take place; nowhere else can your mind be healed.

Self Imposed Limitation

All the limitations self imposed on the mind will be lifted when you no longer want them. To identify with and cherish the body is to cherish limitation. To identify with the sense of separate self which is the ego, is to cherish limitation. To act out the constant attack and defense scenario of the ego, is to cherish limitation. To hold to the belief in sin and guilt and the projections it fosters, is to cherish limitation. There are many different ways by which you cherish and maintain limitation. All attachment to being a separate identity, a body, is a vote for limitation. To accept is to perpetuate for there is no desire to change. The changing of your mind, freeing it from what has held it prisoner for so long, requires real determination, real understanding, and real intent. Without the intent to free yourself and persistent effort, no real change is possible.

To uncover all the hidden motivations and attachments that help maintain the sense of separate identity, you must apply yourself to the task. For too long has your mind been ruled by habitual patterns of thought and feeling. Yet you remain unaware of them in any deep or true sense; this unawareness keeps you a prisoner to the past. What you are unaware of can and does hurt you. What drives your behavior and shapes your mind can hardly be considered harmless. Yet that is what you unconsciously believe when you let the ego's agenda control your life and determine your future. There is no road to real freedom that does not lead you into greater awareness of your own mind and all that is hidden there.

True Purpose

What you need to learn, you will learn if that is your intent. Whatever you learn to value, will become part of your life because you want it to be. Greater awareness and the freedom it brings must be valued or you will not make the necessary effort. All your life has been spent using great effort to maintain the position of mind, the state of mind, that you have always known. Tremendous energy has been expended to continue the past and avoid what waits for you in the present. You can just as well use that energy in service to a true purpose.

However, you must first accept the idea that a true purpose for life is a possibility, and that it is valuable, infinitely valuable, or you will not be willing to take the necessary steps and welcome the necessary changes. As always, willingness is an indispensible part of the journey; without it, nothing can be done. The Holy Spirit's task is to help arouse in you the willingness needed, and He adds His willingness to yours, thus making it a mighty force for change.

The first step in the journey back is the recognition of both the necessity and the great value of living in the light of life's true purpose. The only purpose of life in this world is to awaken to Truth, to recover the memory of who you are and your real relationship with your brothers and your Creator. No other purpose is worthy of you, for you were not created to crawl across the surface of the earth for a little while, lost in the darkness of sin and guilt, till your little life ends with your return to the dust from which you came. This is not the Truth of God's Holy Son, but a dream arising from the fear and madness of separation.

When recognition of life's purpose has led to willingness and determination, the journey back begins in earnest. Now the Holy Spirit can take you by the hand and show you the way and its requirements. The way the journey unfolds is highly individualized, yet the same requirements must be met by all, and the mind purified of everything that obstructs the Truth. The undoing of the mind is a process that takes time; its purpose is the ending of time. When the mind is clear and empty, open and receptive, Truth will return and eternity will bring time to a close.

Today is the only day there is. To remember this is to use the time each day gives you well. Every day provides you with the opportunities to remember Truth by practicing forgiveness and seeing the Light in your brother. If you rise each morning with a prayer of gratitude on your lips, you will be ready for whatever the day brings. Throughout the day, remain in contact with the Holy Spirit, always remembering your single purpose. In the evening, before sleeping, give thanks to our Father and the Holy Spirit after reviewing the events of the day to clear any unforgiveness that may remain. A day so spent is a day well utilized to further your life's purpose. Do not waste a day or even an hour by forgetting who you are and why you are here.

To do what must be done requires that you know what must be done. As you know nothing, you must learn what is required of you from the One Who knows. The Holy Spirit is the Source of all guidance and help. If you are willing, He will teach you everything you need to know.

Freedom and the Present

The question you should ask yourself is this: Do you want to be free? Do you know what freedom is? Obviously, in order to attain something, you must have an idea of what it is, that you may move in its general direction. No one in the state of separation has a real answer to this question. So long accustomed to living under the constraints of time and space and the limitations of a bodily identity, freedom, if thought about at all, is considered a result of physical conditions that are favorable or as a state of acting out your desires as you wish. Acting out your desires and impulses, however that may look, is not freedom but slavery. Your desires and impulses arise from the ego, and have as their purpose to keep you in a state of bondage to illusion. Bondage is the state in which there is no freedom, only the perpetuation of the past. To live in the past, which is the condition of ego based bodily identification, is not freedom. Only in the present can freedom be found, for it is a part of what you are in Truth; and Truth is always and only in the present where time and eternity intersect. Thus is freedom not limited by the bonds of time or the conditions of illusion.

Always and only in the present will you find the freedom that is your birthright. Freedom has nothing to do with the body; in fact, freedom is the recognition that you are not a body. Freedom is of the mind and is entirely independent of physical conditions of any kind. Thus is freedom unlimited and not subject to the restrictions of this world. As Reality Itself, you are free and have always been. Even now you are free, though it is hidden from your awareness by the false identification with what is in bondage.

Do the bonds of time and the limitations of space have any real effect? Only in your mind are the restrictions of any kind experienced as real. This is due solely to the power of belief through which you give illusions reality. You cannot make illusions real but you can make them seem real in your experience, and give them effects that are as strong as Truth. The mind believes in what it makes; through this belief, what has been made is experienced as real and seems to have real effects. Withdraw your belief in and your investment in illusions, and they will disappear and their effects along with them.

The Real Question

When is the time to give up what was never real and has brought you nothing disguised as something, pain disguised as pleasure, and loss presented as gain? How about right now? There is not only no time like the present, there is no time but the present. The past is over and the future is imagination. To refuse to begin right here and right now is to postpone the only thing worth doing. To postpone is to lose time and happiness. Nothing is gained by waiting. Because you do not see rightly, you think you can take your time. You do not realize the condition you are in, and what you lose by refusing to act now. In the condition of separation with its uncertainties and constant changes, you do not have the luxury of wasting time. The belief that you do is part of the illusion and keeps you bound to it. Whatever else you do, do not postpone the only thing here worth doing. To delay is to lose ground, for you are either moving in the direction of Truth or you are moving away from It. There are no neutral thoughts or actions. Everything you do, say, or think, supports Truth or multiplies illusion. There is no neutral ground.

Do you believe that Truth, freedom, and peace are worth having? This is the real question. No one will seek or expend effort for anything unless it is seen as valuable. If you recognize that it brings you something you want, you will desire it and try to obtain it. Do you want freedom, peace, and the end of suffering? Do you truly want to be happy? Every human being desires happiness; this is intrinsic to the mind. The question then becomes where do you think happiness can be found? This is the point where the search can and does flounder. The mind wedded to illusion and unwilling to look elsewhere, will seek happiness where it cannot be found. It will seek and seek, and seek again, but never will it find.

Happiness cannot be found outside yourself for it is not there. Happiness is a state of mind, a part of your real Mind. Happiness waits for you within; it waits for you to reestablish the conditions under which it can return to awareness. You have thrown happiness away by choosing separation. Yet it has not left your mind, for the Holy Spirit holds it for you and gladly returns it when you are ready. If happiness be your true desire, and you are willing to begin letting go what has taken its place, it will return to your awareness.

CHAPTER ELEVEN

God and You

Whatever you do makes you happy or unhappy, fulfilled or unfulfilled. To operate from Love will always leave you happy. To act unlovingly will always make you feel guilty. You may not be aware of the guilt, but the feeling you will have will be some form of fear. Fear is pain, and pain never stops as long as you are fearful. You are long accustomed to fear; your mind has dulled itself in an attempt to lessen the effects of fear. You have given its different forms many names in order to disguise it and dissociate from it. Fear cannot be escaped; it forms the very core of the identity you have given yourself. To heal and release all fear brings the self to an end. Where there is no self, Love will rush in to take its place.

Whatever you do takes you closer to God or away from Him. God and illusion never meet, yet you who are surrounded by the illusory creations of your mind, can yet find God if that is your true desire. God is not far from you; you are far from Him, not in fact, but in your experience which is as illusory as you are. You rest in God, move in God, and have your Being in God. Your Mind is part of His, and your life also. The Light that shines so brightly within you is God's Light, and the Love you feel and express is His Love.

God has never forgotten you but you have forgotten Him. It is a deliberate forgetting and must be just as deliberately undone. This undoing does not happen all at once, for the fear of God which lies deep within your mind, can seldom be directly uncovered without preparation and purification. All the fear that lives in your mind has taken the place of Love; it must be healed though the practice of forgiveness and non-judgment before you are ready to face the deepest fear of all. When you are ready, with the Holy Spirit's help, you will stand before the final veil between you and your Father; it will be penetrated by your willing awareness and you will be free.

In no other way can you return to the freedom you once knew than to become aware of the self created bonds that deny your freedom, and let them go. No other has taken your freedom from you; it was given up under the impact of the belief in separation and the fear it engendered. Only your fear has robbed you of freedom and peace, for fear took Love's place in your mind. There is no freedom without Love; Love is unconstrained by anything of this world. It knows no boundaries or limitations of any kind.

Nothing you see in the world of form and separation means anything in and of itself. The things you see are like the experiences you have; they are not bad or good, they are meaningless. Nothing in this world calls for judgment of any kind. Through the act of judgment and discrimination, you make the world around you real, and give it seeming solidity. Let all judgment go and the world you judge will disappear. Forgiveness does not judge. To forgive is to recognize no judgment is necessary or possible; in that recognition, you are freed of all need to judge. When you lay down all judgment, never to pick it up again, you will find a happiness you have never known.

Happiness is impossible while you judge your brothers, for judgment is condemnation and condemnation is attack. To attack your brother is to attack yourself; to attack yourself is to be fearful, not happy. While you expect attack and justify your need to attack in defense, fear will never be absent from your mind. The purpose of judgment is to keep fear alive in your mind, that you may not see your brother as he is, and thus not know the truth about yourself.

Fear has usurped the place of Love and kindness in your mind; it has taken on the role of motivator in your life though you are not aware of this fact. Fear is the hidden motivator in much of human life. It does not matter whether you are aware of it or not, if fear drives your motivation as is so often the case, suffering and limitation will be the result. And you will wonder why happiness eludes you no matter how much you try to establish the conditions under which you think it will be found. Fear and happiness are mutually incompatible, as is fear and Love. Love brings happiness as surely as fear begets sorrow.

Now is the time to remember your Father for His call goes out unceasingly. All the activities you use to avoid hearing the call, are meaningless and as nothing compared to God's Love. If you truly felt His Love, even for a moment, you would drop everything you are doing, let go of all that you value, and turn towards God with all your heart and mind. Nothing else in this world is even remotely valuable in comparison to your Father's Love. Through His Love were you created, and through His Love you will return to Him. There is no other place to go for God is your Being and your very life. The search outside yourself for satisfaction and fulfillment is the search for something to take the place of your relationship with God. There is no substitute for God. When that becomes your realization, you will avoid Him no more.

Self Destruction

Whenever you feel the need to do something you should not, something you know is harmful to yourself, stop and ask yourself this question. Do I really want to attack myself and thereby cause pain and suffering? Is this an intelligent and rational thing to do? You must learn to look honestly and with open eyes at all your actions. The self destructiveness, the self hatred, that lies hidden deep in your mind, must be uncovered and brought to the Light. The purpose of the Atonement is to correct your mind. All the levels of your mind that have been given over to illusion must be brought to awareness and healed. Everything in your mind, whether conscious or unconscious, is the result of a decision you once made. All decisions of the mind remain in effect until they are changed; they cannot be changed unless you become aware of them.

Only by becoming completely aware of your thoughts, feelings, and actions, will your mind be revealed to you as it is. Through the willingness to know your mind as it is, not as you wish it to be, the deeper levels of mind below the threshold of consciousness will be uncovered. As you become aware of them, you will be able, with the help of the Holy Spirit, to choose again. All that is false, all fear, hatred, and guilt, must be undone and released. All illusion must be healed that your mind be made clean and empty, a fitting vessel to which Truth can return. Your holiness must be restored to your awareness, that the memory of God may return and set you free.

The desire to hurt and destroy yourself is not natural. This is a part of the madness that came over you in the separation from Reality. The belief in the reality of separation produced the ego, which became both your 'new identity' and the solution to the terror and guilt of separation from God. You have experienced yourself as an ego, a separate identity complete in itself with its own will, ever since.

The ego is not you. It was invited into your mind and given your allegiance at the time of separation; it appears to be who you are because you have forgotten, and think you are something else instead. The ego is the part of your mind that believes in separation, and has chosen the body as its home. The core of the ego is fear, its foundation stone is guilt, and its purpose is to maintain separation from God and your Self at all costs. The ego bases its argument for the reality of separation and your identity as a body on the reality of death. In fact, the ego believes you merit nothing but death, and leads you steadily and inexorably to your destruction.

Even now in the condition of insanity that prevails in your mind, you need not cooperate with the ego in your own destruction and death. The ego is but a part of your mind, and has existence only because of what you give it. Withdraw your allegiance and protection and it will disappear, leaving your mind whole and undivided once again. The Holy Spirit will guide you in this process of freeing and healing your mind; you must learn to trust Him and give Him your full willingness and cooperation if you are to return to Truth. Let Him do His part, and be sure that you do yours.

The Uncreative Use of Mind

Now is the only time there is, do not waste it. Your mind is constantly wandering in the past or imagining a future that is a continuation of the past. All such thinking is meaningless and without substance. Seldom are you present and fully aware in the present. The energy of your mind is used to go nowhere and do nothing. The most powerful and creative force in the universe, is used in an uncreative and wasteful manner. The good you could do and would do, is not done. That which you should not do, which brings you nothing, is given all your time and energy, and therein you accomplish nothing.

You who share the creative power of life with God Himself, are not using it. Your mind is used uncreatively to maintain the illusion of a futile existence that does nothing but perpetuate itself in an endless circle of repetition. Is this what you truly want? Would you continue if you were able to stand clear of insanity, even for a moment, and really see what you <u>are</u> doing? Caught in an endless cycle of life and death for so long, you do not remember the Truth that was yours nor the life that is eternal. The deep peace and joy that is yours is long forgotten, beyond hope of recall.

The Mind of the Atonement

You cannot reach the memory of Truth that lies buried deep in your mind without help. Help must come from beyond the dream of separation. Help is given from the realm of knowledge, not perception, though the One Who aids you must be aware of both. The Holy Spirit was created by God in answer to the loss of communication with a part of Creation. He is in God's Mind, the realm of knowledge, and He is in your Christ Mind, the part of you that is real. He is aware of the realm of perception, the dream world in which you seemingly find yourself. He holds for you the memory of your Father and your Self, while also being aware of the illusions that characterize your present experience. Thus is He the perfect and complete Answer to all the problems you think you have, including the one problem of which all others are just variations meant to disguise their content. Separation from

God is the only problem you have, and to this the Holy Spirit has the only answer.

The Holy Spirit is the Mind of the Atonement; He will guide you unerringly through the undoing and correction of your mind until it has been freed of all illusion. He is unfailingly right because He is part of Truth and has all knowledge. The Holy Spirit is unfailingly patient and gentle, for He knows the illusions under which you suffer, and the fear, confusion, and ignorance that make real learning so difficult for you. Do not be afraid to turn over decisions to Him. His function is to guide your decisions, as yours is to turn them over to Him.

Become Deeply Aware

The present is the only time when you can get to know yourself. You cannot understand yourself in the past or in the future for neither exists. Something can be learned by evaluating past behavior, but such learning is only superficial. To become deeply aware of your own mind, its constant activity, its compulsions, desires, and motivations, you must be aware of it in action, as it functions in the present. This requires an alertness you do not possess unless you commit to the process of self awareness, and train your mind to be aware of itself. In and of itself, this is not a difficult process, but the mind as you have made it is very undisciplined and constantly wandering.

When you begin this discipline of watching your mind, you will quickly notice two things. The mind is always busy, amazingly busy, like a dog chasing its own tail. And, if you really pay attention, you will notice the repetitive and unnecessary nature of much of your thinking. Over time, it will become clear to you if you are honest, that much of the thought process that dominates your mind seems to have its own agenda, an agenda that is not necessarily the same as yours.

Your basic and continuous thought process is, in fact, an expression of the ego's agenda. Although you identify with the ego and its chosen home, the body, you are not the ego. You have given it your mind and your allegiance; consequently it seems to be you. Yet is the ego not you but a part of your mind, a part of your belief about yourself. The ego seems to be all of your mind, yet it is only a part. If you would be free of the fear and uncertainty that plague human life, you must take back your mind from this stranger who claims to be you. Until then, you are caught in a repeating pattern of action and reaction determined by the past, for the ego is of the past and devotes itself to maintaining the past at all costs.

Nothing to Fear

You must learn to see your mind as it is, with complete honesty. Only then is it possible to free yourself from the habitual and constant restraints it imposes on you; restraints on your freedom, happiness, perception, understanding, and behavior. So much of your life is simply a repetition of the ego's agenda. Over and over, in many seemingly different forms, you act out the maintenance of separation, attack and defense in many different ways, pursuit of pleasure, and the avoidance of fear. Never do you look seriously within and question why you do what you do except in the most superficial way. Though your thoughts, feelings, actions, and responses seem to change constantly, the content remains the same: avoidance of the deep fear and emptiness within. Thus the fear which darkens your days and literally poisons your mind, is never recognized for what it is and what it does. In this condition, a true and lasting happiness is impossible though you seek it unceasingly.

My brother, there is nothing to fear in this world. Your belief that there is, keeps fear alive and unhealed. There is nothing you fear more than the actual experience of fear. Fear in all its forms is experienced as unpleasant, uncomfortable, even intolerable. The direct experience of fear is universally avoided. Whatever you need to do to keep fear from your awareness, you will do.

Your life is built around the need for security, for protection from the uncertainties and instability of life as you have known it. Although you think you are thereby avoiding the circumstances you fear, and to a certain extent this is true, what you are really doing is protecting yourself from the fear within. Virtually all human activity, all motivation, carries within it the stain of fear. Life in the condition of separation is inherently fearful. Without the original response of fear to fear, separation could not have occurred. Separation is based on fear, and all life in separation carries its mark. Existence as a separate and fragile bodily identity in a world seemingly filled with possible danger and indifferent to your welfare, induces an unconscious sense of threat that reinforces the fear within.

Fear is thus multilayered and all pervasive in human life, and in the human mind. You can deny it, dissociate, suppress, and avoid it, but you cannot escape it. It is impossible to escape from anything that is in your mind. Fear can be healed and released, it can be transformed, but it cannot be escaped through denial. Fear is a part of your mind for it makes up the core of the ego, your chosen identity.

To renounce the ego is to renounce fear. The process of ego renunciation, of undoing the entire egoic belief system and its thought process, is the undoing of fear and guilt in all forms and all expressions. To do so is required, for there is no other way to recover your true identity. The self you have made, the ego, is both a substitute for the Self and the defense against It. The ego is the denial of Truth in every way; that is its purpose, function, and expression. Constantly it is busy maintaining its position as your identity, and defending its interests which are not yours. Because you do not realize this, you act out the ego's agenda faithfully. Your actions and understanding stem from the egoic thought system of separation, for you have accepted its belief that attack is salvation, and is necessary to protect yourself from the attacks of others. There are no others! Certain it is that in the dream, separate figures seem to go about pursuing different interests, and taking turns attacking each other. They are simply doing what you have assigned them to do.

The world of separation is made real through the projection of guilt and the apparent necessity to attack and defend. This purpose was given it when it was made and projected from your mind. Perception goes out to seek what it would find, to seek what was put there for it to find. Nothing could be further from the Truth than to believe the world is 'out there', independent of your mind, with its own objective existence. The world does not exist outside of your mind; you are responsible for it in every way. To really accept this fact absolves the world of all guilt and blame, and places responsibility for all that happens to you squarely on your shoulders. In this lies the escape from all fear and guilt, for who could be afraid of what he had made and endowed with the attributes of reality? Nothing can attack you unless that is your request. You have forgotten that you are dreaming, and so have given the dream figures a terrible autonomy that seems to threaten you. It is not so my brother, it is not so. Do not fear the imagery of your own mind; it is only your own thoughts that seem to attack and injure and kill.

Vision and Forgiveness

The Holy Spirit is the guide to salvation. This is His function given Him by God. He fulfills His function perfectly, and never ceases to offer the help needed in each and every situation. He knows your strengths and weaknesses, and how to work with both. To fulfill your function perfectly, you must turn over decision making to Him consistently and in all ways. Do not hold back some areas of your life that you would still control. The 'you' that would maintain control is the egoic identity. The ego opposes the Holy Spirit and salvation in every way. Do not place your trust where it is not warranted. The ego is not your friend.

You do not know the way back to your Father and your Self. You have wandered alone and friendless through an alien land, seeking what you cannot find. It is not here. Yet there is a Friend Who walks with you and will never leave you comfortless. Take His hand and let Him lead you down the way of peace, which leads back to where you are at Home. Heaven is a state of Unity, of Oneness with God and all He has created. So far beyond the world of separation even the imagination cannot conceive of it, Heaven is always close at hand. Not within the dream, yet is It reflected here if you would have it so. The Holy Spirit will show you the real world, the forgiven world, wherein the Light of Heaven is reflected, if you will accept His vision in place of your own.

Your vision is not vision, it is image making. You see what you want to see, what you put out there to see. What is but projection and imagination driven by desire, can hardly be called vision. The Holy Spirit will give you real vision, a unified vision that sees truly. You must be willing to share His vision and release your own if you would see the Truth that is reflected everywhere.

Through a unified, purified vision, you will set yourself and your brothers free.

The consistent practice of forgiveness will lead to the Vision of Christ. To see truly, you must be willing to see the Truth, the Light in your brothers. You must be willing to see them as they truly are, in the shining Light of their innocence. They are not bodies nor are they guilty. Your eyes were made to see bodies; your mind judges them and finds them guilty. So long as you are willing to see your brother guilty, reduced to a bodily appearance, so long will real vision be impossible for you. Your brother is as guiltless as you are. He is not a body as you are not a body. To see him as what he is not, is a denial of what he is. You will not see the Christ in your brother while you prefer to see him as something else.

Do not underestimate the gifts forgiveness provides. The world does not understand true forgiveness nor is it aware of its many gifts. Forgiveness will transform your mind and set you free. The power of Love Itself flows through forgiveness, transforming both giver and receiver. To forgive without conditions is to love unconditionally. Love will bring you back to your Father and your Self; nothing else will accomplish this. Do not make the mistake of overlooking what will restore the memory of God to your awareness. God is Love as are you. Only through the acceptance of yourself as you are, will the Self be able to reclaim your mind.

True vision will be given when you want it above all else. The body's eyes cannot see truly, for they were made to perceive illusion and establish it as real. Do not rely on the body's senses. The ability to see comes from God, and is a part of your mind that is beyond the ego's reach. Real vision occurs through the mind, not the senses. Through the Mind of the Holy Spirit does vision reach to you, allowing you to see the Light that is reflected everywhere. When once you begin to see the Light in your brother, you will not close your mind to vision ever again. The loveliness that is your brother will replace the mask the body's eyes see; you will find the same Light in yourself, and It will lead you Home.

Surrender

There is no need for help to be the Truth, the One Self, the Christ, for you have always been that and always will be. You cannot help being what you are. However, you have lost awareness of what you are and invented a substitute in its place. Through the identification with the false self you have made, you have surrounded and filled your mind with false beliefs about yourself. These beliefs are like a wall that encircles your mind, keeping it a prisoner to illusion. You cannot find your way through this wall without help, for it is experienced as part of your reality and is beyond question.

Help is offered you from beyond the heavy veil of illusion that obscures your mind. You must accept it if you are to leave your prison behind and reclaim the freedom you replaced with a dream of death. There is no single more important understanding to reach than this: I need help for I know nothing. All I have taught myself is false. This realization, when truly accepted, will bring you to surrender to a Higher Power. No matter the spiritual path you walk, surrender is fundamental, the basis for real awakening. Without surrender, you are relying on yourself and what you learned in the past. In other words, you are following the ego as your guide.

The ego will not take you beyond the prison walls; the ego is the prison walls. Would you ask your jailor to show you the way to freedom? The ego knows only the way to nowhere and there it gladly takes you, keeping you busy along the way so you will not notice what waits for you at the end. Death waits at the end of all roads you walk with the ego as your guide.

Surrender is the key to spiritual consciousness. Without surrender to a true teaching, one of the forms of the universal curriculum, you will continue to wander in ignorance, acting out the past over and over. This cannot be over emphasized: unaided, you cannot find your way out of the self created prison that holds your mind. To try to do it yourself is to continue employing the ego as your guide. This will continue and perpetuate the condition in which you find yourself. Help comes from a level of Mind that is beyond your reach. Whether from the Teacher of teachers, the Holy Spirit, or a teacher in human form who represents the Holy Spirit, help will come. Do not waste any more time following the voice of ignorance, the ego. Realize and accept your own ignorance and make the only choice that can be made. The world is weary, weighed down by suffering and sorrow. Your brothers need your help. Do not abandon them but remember they go with you on your journey. You do this not for yourself alone. Your awakening benefits all; your Love goes out to all. When you are healed of your separation from God, you are not healed alone.

Only the Truth

Do not let the cares of the world weigh you down. It was made to be a place of sorrow and woe, where fear and death rule supreme. The belief in fear and suffering makes the world real in your mind and chains you to it. To see pain as real hurts your brother also for minds are joined, and in their mutual recognition of illusion, they confirm the reality of suffering to each other. Refuse to see all illusion as real; do not reinforce your brother's belief that binds him to sorrow. Set him free by offering him the Truth, by seeing the Light in your brother that proclaims his innocence. His Light will join with the Light in you and set you both free.

Only the Truth has the power to return you to the state of freedom you once knew. Illusion has made the chains that seem to bind you. In the healing of all illusion that limits your mind, does the Self become your identity again. The Self is forever free, unbound by illusion, joyous and at peace. Only as the Self will you be free. The quest for freedom is not a quest within the boundaries of the past, the known. It does not take place within the constraints represented by the ego. The movement towards freedom is a movement beyond the ego, beyond the identity you have known, into Spirit Itself. To awaken in Spirit is to find the Source and the home of freedom. Nowhere else can it be found; not within the experiences of this world or the physical conditions of life in separation. Money will not buy anything that is truly precious including freedom. The body will never be free, as it was made to take away your freedom and replace it with nothingness. Let the Holy Spirit show you where freedom awaits, and take you there.

Nowhere in the world of separation will you find a home. All the homes you have labored so hard to construct are but temporary shelters, easily washed away by rushing waters or blown down by the next mighty storm. They will not withstand the winds of time, nor will they protect you from the vicissitudes of life. To build a home as a refuge from chaos and constant change, is to labor in vain. You cannot find what does not exist but in dreams. Give up the meaningless search for what cannot be found.

Your home is in God. This is a fact not to be disputed or argued against, but to be accepted. Allow the Holy Spirit to gently guide you through the chaotic maze of your own mind, past the resistance of many lifetimes, beyond the fear that veils the Truth, to the memory of your Father that He may take the last step that returns you to your true Home forever. God has always been your Home; you rest in Him in deepest peace, undisturbed by idle dreams and passing fantasies. The constant noise of this world, the cries of pain that arise from the suffering ones, the clash of arms and the constant conflict; all this cannot reach you or diminish the peace and security you experience when you rest in God. Nothing can reach you there but what belongs to you in Truth, what is part of you forever. My brothers, you are not forsaken; you have not been left comfortless. Even in a world of dreams, you carry your Home with you always. Within you It waits for your recognition, that It may shelter you from the battle that rages without. Please accept It now, turn within and find peace.

CHAPTER TWELVE

Two Answers

Do not make the mistake of not taking your life seriously. Life is not given you to spend in idle pursuits, chasing after pleasure and fame. The most you can accomplish in such a life is to keep fear away from conscious awareness, and the idea of death suppressed. Stimulation of all kinds, goals to be achieved, and the collecting of possessions and accomplishments, do nothing but fill your time and provide the illusion of meaning. The meaning of life does not lie within the limitations of bodily existence. Within that narrow context of living and experiencing, all activity has but one purpose: to keep God away. It need not be so. All the activities of your life, mundane or otherwise, can take place within a frame of reference that is meaningful, and will bring real happiness. For that, a change of mind is necessary; a change of focus, perception, and understanding.

Everything takes place in mind, in awareness. All of your life is a play of consciousness. The essential point is this: where do you direct your awareness? How do you conceive of yourself in relation to life, the world, and 'others'? What do you value above all else? All of these questions are really the same for they all arise from the original and most basic question: What am I, and what is the purpose of my life? Your answer to that is your life, and all of its conditions and circumstances are determined by the answer you have chosen.

There are only two answers to this fundamental and all important question. One answer is true and one is false. Sure it is there appears to be many, even an almost unlimited set of possible answers, yet that is just the confusion engendered by the many apparent forms that experience takes. Do not let the multiplicity of forms confuse and cloud your mind. That is their purpose, yet can you look beyond form and see the content the form conceals but represents. The content of all form, all activity, all experience, all thought, feeling and perception, is always and only one of two possibilities: Truth or illusion. Thus the answer to your question is always a choice for Truth, for your real identity and a life of true meaning, or it is a choice for illusion, the illusory self identity you have invented, and a life based on what has no meaning.

Which answer do you prefer? Life, and all its conditions, are always the result of choices you are making, though in both general and specific ways, that is not apparent to you. You think you have simply found yourself in a world not of your own making, into which you were born without any consent on your part. This forgetfulness and lack of recognition of total responsibility for your life in all its details, is a part of the dream. Ignorance allows the dream to continue unquestioned, with you playing the role of helpless pawn at the mercy of forces beyond your control. As long as you prefer the role of 'victim', however you may choose to glorify or grapple with it, you will be choosing illusion and meaninglessness.

Let's make a clear, simple, and unmistakably accurate declaration: you are always doing exactly what you want to do. Always it is your choice that determines thinking, feeling, action and reaction. Though you may seem to be acting under duress, or forced to act against your will, you are nevertheless responsible for the conditions that seem to be forcing your choice. Hence you are still responsible for your decision. You would not react at all to the events of your life if you remembered you were dreaming. Your responsibility is total. In that lies your salvation.

Will you choose salvation by accepting Atonement for yourself, or will you choose to wander off awhile down the paths that lead nowhere? Even then you will be brought back eventually to the only choice that can be made. Why waste time? Choose now or choose later; one choice arising again and again, appearing as many due to the illusion of time, yet always one, always the one and only choice that can be made. The content of all you do, think, or experience, is either Truth or illusion. This is inescapable. In that is our salvation, for what could be simpler than to choose always, no matter the appearance, between two alternatives? And of these two but one is real. Please remember this, remember this always.

Only that which is real has any lasting significance for your life. All else, no matter how valued and esteemed at the time, will pass away and be no more. This includes your body which is not your home, but is rather a temporary learning aid, a means to learn and teach the Truth. Real communication is the body's only function as the Holy Spirit sees it; therefore it is the body's only function in truth. Use the body as He would have you use it, and its health is assured. If you do not misuse the body by assigning it roles it cannot fulfill, it will serve you faithfully as long as you have need of it.

Do you know the purpose of your life? The purpose of life, which is its meaning also, should be the foundation from which you live. Without a foundation, a real purpose, life becomes empty and meaningless. There are not many different purposes as the ego would have you believe. Chasing after various purposes, trying to find the one that is 'right' for you, is the way to avoid facing life's only real purpose. The ego encourages you to do this, assuring you that purpose is yours to decide. Do not believe this. It is no more your role to assign life a purpose than it was your role to create yourself. The One Who created you and all life, has given that life its purpose.

Your role is to learn this purpose from the Voice for God, accept it fully, and build your life on that sure foundation. The purpose of life in this world is to return to God. The act of separating from Him, followed by a conscious decision to forget, resulted in your present condition of separation from all that is real. Separate from God, you have no real purpose though you have invented many. All are meaningless. You must return to Truth in which all meaning is found. The only purpose to be found in a world of separation is the escape from illusion and the return to what is real.

As has been so often stated in *A Course in Miracles* and this teaching, you cannot do this alone. God has given you the Answer to the dilemma you are in, and you must accept It if you are serious about restoring your life to what is meaningful. Let His Answer guide you in the ways of Truth. You do not know Truth from illusion; this you must learn and learn well. The sure understanding and recognition of the difference between them is absolutely essential. You will not learn this all at once; it takes time, perseverance, and consistent effort. If you truly want to learn, and apply yourself to the process, refusing to give up no matter what happens, you will learn what is needed and it will set you free.

Now is the time to devote yourself to doing what must be done. There are certain requirements that must be met in the journey back to God. They cannot be bypassed or ignored for the mind of separation, the self you have made, must be undone and all that is false corrected. Though the way the journey unfolds is highly individualized, the same corrections must be made and all the conditions of Truth must be met by all who would awaken. You cannot bargain with God nor evade His laws, and you cannot bargain with the ego in any of its forms. The ego must be renounced, its thought system undone, and all traces of its hold on your mind must be healed and released.

Do not try to make decisions on your own but let yourself be guided in all things by the One Who knows the way. He will lead you surely through every pitfall, past all resistance that arises in your mind, and give you the solution to all problems you may encounter. There is nothing you cannot do with His help. You cannot fail if you deeply and truly, with all your heart and mind, want only to be the Self created by God once again. If your purpose be strong, dedication unwavering, and your willingness reinforced and augmented by the Holy Spirit, you will gain the Kingdom.

The only thing you need do on your own, and even here you have help, is to turn over decision making to the Holy Spirit. This decision is only yours to make, and it must be repeated many, many times, for it is a process of surrender that proceeds gradually over time. Decide that you will not decide for yourself, but ask for His guidance in all things. The more consistent you are with this, the more quickly will you reach the goal. Nothing is more important than to consistently do, in all areas of your life, what you are guided to do. You may be asked to do something you do not understand. Do it anyway. You may be asked to do something you do not want to do. Do it anyway. You do not perceive your own best interest, but there is One Who does. He will guide you unerringly through all the dangers and obstacles that seem to block your path. He has the answer to all difficulties, the solution to all problems.

If you are to realize your true Self condition in this life, you must desire this above all things. Anything you would accomplish takes much time, effort, and right application of your mind in the learning process. Unless you strongly desire to achieve a result, you will not be willing to devote the necessary time and energy. To realize the Self is the only goal worth devoting your life to. Unlike all other goals, it must become the central focus of your life, and all other aspects of life must be arranged in right relationship to this goal. In other words, the other aspects of life must not hinder or obstruct, but rather support the accomplishing of spiritual awakening.

In truth, most of the factors of worldly life as is commonly lived, have as their purpose to conceal or deny spiritual reality by maintaining and reinforcing the experience of separation. This need not be. Much of what you have invented to take the place of Reality can be reinterpreted by the Holy Spirit and used instead to help bring about the ending of separation. You must, however, be willing to accept His interpretation, and learn how to use the factors of your life in a new way. To give something a new function which includes a different purpose, requires that it be used differently. This means learning.

Life in the world of separation demands constant learning due to its constant changes and often bewildering complexity. You have taught yourself to live as something you are not in a self invented context called the world, and in a condition that is the opposite of Truth in every way. This is a gigantic learning feat that establishes your remarkable ability to learn when you are motivated. You have learned your way into the condition you are in, so you will have to learn your way out.

This process requires you to 'unlearn', to let be undone all you learned before, that you may then learn what is true. The Atonement is an undoing, a correction of false thinking and perception that Truth may take its place, leading to a transformation of mind. Learning was invented to take the place of knowledge. Learning is variable and what you learn constantly changes. Knowledge is invariable and changeless. Learning is uncertain, knowledge is always certain. When you learned to be something you are not, knowledge was banished from your awareness.

The purpose of learning is to bring you to the end of learning that knowledge may return. When learning has accomplished its purpose, it is needed no more. Until then, you must learn, and learn well, all the lessons the Holy Spirit teaches. He will present you with true ideas, concepts that are expressed in words, yet are pointing to that which lies beyond the reach of concepts. Truth must be directly experienced; the purpose of conceptualizing about Truth is only to send you in Its direction. Your direct experience of what is real will bring conviction; and the Truth, when fully experienced, will free you from the bonds of earthly life.

To do what is necessary, you must first know what it is. You do not understand the way that leads out of illusion or what is required. A blind man cannot find his way out of a maze. He needs someone who stands above the maze, who sees the whole picture, to guide him to the exit. I am not exaggerating when I liken your position to that of a blind man. The mind of illusion is like a maze in which you are trapped. The maze is guarded by the ego whom you have chosen as your guide. The ego directs you so as to go round and round in circles, that you may not escape the maze, for its existence depends on it.

The first step out of the maze is to let go of the guide who helped you build it for the purpose of keeping you trapped forever. This is the obvious thing to do, yet is the obvious often the most difficult, due to the complexity and ignorance of the mind of illusion. So long identified with the ego mind, thinking of yourself as the body that houses the mind, you do not realize the absolute shift in identification that is required, nor do you have any idea of how to go about it. This is why the Atonement is an undoing, not a doing. As the ego, you are always involved with doing, hence the necessity of shifting to undoing.

The ego's thought system must be undone thought by thought and its dark cornerstone, the belief in sin and guilt, must be healed. The fear which underlies and pervades its entire thought system, must be uncovered and recognized in all its forms. This requires time and consistent help from the Holy Spirit. The process of undoing can be painful at times, even disorienting, but you must go through it until you come out the other side. To stay where you are is also painful, though pain is often masked as pleasure. The pain of spiritual awakening, though intensely experienced at times, will come to an end and suffering will be no more. The pain of continuing bondage is unending.

To attain salvation, what is false must be given up entirely. All false beliefs, all values rooted in nothingness, all commitment to illusion in any form, must be renounced that Truth may take up its rightful place in your mind once again. Do not think you can keep the illusions you like and have Truth as well. To hold on to any illusion is to keep all of it. Illusion opposes Truth in every way. This will never change for illusions were made to take the place of Truth. One or the other, but not both, will rule your mind.

Hold no exceptions to Truth as valuable, for Truth is one seamless Whole. Its nature is to be all inclusive, without exceptions. Truth is all encompassing; what is not part of Truth is illusion. Anything that seems to stand outside of Truth is but projected illusion no matter how convincing the appearance or experience. The Truth as God created It, is all that is real; nothing unreal has been created by God, all that is unreal is not Truth and does not exist.

Your desire for illusion in place of Truth results in appearances that are real to you because you made them. Do not believe what your senses tell you; they were made to show you what is not there. Nothing your eyes see is real despite its appearance. A partial and fragmented perception will never allow you to see what is really there. You can learn to see Truth reflected in the world of illusion, if you are willing to let the unified vision of the Holy Spirit replace the way you see now.

All vision shows you the outpicturing of your state of mind. Through the body's eyes you see the projection of the illusion of separation and its consequences. This picture of a 'world' is what you have chosen as your reality for so long. Never has it given you safety or Love. Never has it given you peace of mind and it never will. The world of separation represents the insanity that has gripped your mind since that moment of terror so long ago. The world cannot but outpicture the chaos, fear, and uncertainty, that characterize the mind that has rejected its Creator. To reject God is to reject Love, leaving only fear to take its place. Never have you seen the Truth reflected in this place of desolation, and you never will through the eyes that were made to look on fear only.

Real Vision, the Vision of Christ, is the Holy Spirit's gift to those who want Truth, not illusion, and are willing to do what is necessary. Like all perception, even the unified Vision of Christ is illusion, meant to last only while it is necessary to fulfill a mighty purpose. There is one important difference however, between real vision and all other perception. Through the unified vision of the Holy Spirit, you see the Truth reflected in the world of illusion. His vision shows you the Light that is in your brother and all things. Unified vision is not knowledge, but it does not oppose knowledge in any way, and like knowledge, it is whole. Thus it is close enough to knowledge that it leads to knowledge and the end of perception.

To see the Light in your brother is to see him truly. In that shining Light, his innocence is reflected for you to see beyond the shadow of a doubt. The one Light and the innocence of the Christ shining there are also in you; through the willingness to see your brother as he truly is, you are able to see the Truth in yourself. This the gift every brother holds out to you. Accept it gratefully that you may be joined together as One, and together you will leave the world of fear and separation.

The present is the only part of time in which you actually live. This is self evidently true as you clearly do not live in past time nor are you living in future time. The present is the only moment in which you are actually here. Yet, strangely enough, the present is the part of time that is least experienced. If you were to watch your mind carefully, it would become very evident that you are seldom fully present. Your thoughts fluctuate wildly and unceasingly, absorbing your attention and diverting it from the present moment, from here and now. There is no way to be fully present to any great degree while you tolerate your wandering mind and let it dominate your awareness. To be present is to be aware, not lost in thought.

The constant activity of the thought process has the purpose of preventing you from being aware in the here and now. The untrained mind, stuck in a habitual pattern of remembering the past and imagining a future, can live an entire lifetime and never experience being fully present. Why is this so?

The mind of separation is a restless, chaotic process of constant thought, feeling, and impulse. Driven by unconscious fear and the need to get, to acquire, it is always in motion, never at rest. With little or no understanding of even its basic motivation, the mind is at the mercy of the past which drives it, and the conditions that surround it. Its responses are determined by past learning and associations that have become habitual tendencies through which it expresses and reacts. There is little room for spontaneity or real learning, both of which can happen only in the present. Such a mind is as good as dead as it lives out the past and plans for the future; never is it fully alive in the present, the only place it can be. To be alive is to live in present time, leaving the past behind and the future open.

What if there were no such thing as time, as past, present, and future? What if time were not sequential unless you imposed that order upon it? What if all time were over and gone, and you were just living out a memory of events long since vanished? This is actually what you are doing. Holding a memory in your mind of a moment of time in which everything that could happen to you in separation did happen, you are standing at the end of time, reviewing the journey in your mind, imagining that you are making it again, and breaking up time into past, present, and future. What happened simultaneously in that one moment of time is now broken up into discreet events that you review one by one, producing the illusion of a life lived in sequence from past to present to future.

You are thus retracing your steps in a journey that was over and gone long ago. Even what seems to you to have not happened yet, is past. If you have not yet reached that point in your memory, your review, there appears to be a part of time you call the future. Time is but illusion, a trick you play upon yourself. In your hands, time is a way to prolong a journey that never happened, so that life in separation can seem to continue into a far off, indefinite future.

The Holy Spirit has a better use for time. He can collapse time for you, and bring the end to your imaginary journey much more quickly if you will cooperate with Him. If you learn the lessons He gives you, and allow the correction of your mind, time becomes less and less necessary, for its only purpose is to aid your true learning. Eventually you will reach the end of learning; at that point, time is needed no more and it will come to an end. All of life in separation is the repetition of a journey that was never necessary. Due to your belief, however, the journey must be made until you want and need it no more. The sooner you realize its futility and become willing to let it go, the sooner it will end in the return to Truth.

Eternity intersects time in the present. The only moment of time that is real is where your life takes place, even in the dream. To let your mind wander, and keep your attention in the past or the imaginary future, is to avoid your own life. Living through a screen of chaotic mental activity, threading your way through the mass of egoic projections, is to spend life in a haze of distractions. You cannot afford to let the tendency of mind to overlook the present dominate your life; in so doing, you are assured of the continuation of the fear and confusion that make happiness impossible and suffering inevitable.

Through the return to the present, you are brought face to face with your own mind. Here is where it operates, now is when you can become aware of your mind in action. To see it as it is, in its continuous activity, is necessary if you wish to free yourself of its tyranny. Your awareness and attention are dominated by the ceaseless stream of thought, feeling, image, and impulse. While this is so, you are not free to experience your mind as it is, to understand yourself to any great degree, or to change the way you think and live. You are bound to an automatic and repetitive set of feelings and responses determined by your individual past and the general egoic mechanisms.

To return attention to the actual present and rest in awareness itself, is essential. Be vigilant in your mind for God and against the ego. You have been vigilant for the ego and against God. You must reverse this orientation, and begin to choose Truth over illusion, God over the ego. The ego is the source of the constant thought activity that so absorbs your energy and attention. You must make the decision to take them back; only thus can you return to freedom. There is no need to sleep walk through life, absorbed and controlled by what appears on the screen of inner awareness. Take back your mind, take back your attention. You will be amazed at what there is to discover.

To know your mind as it is, in its constant and unceasing activity, is your responsibility. You think that to have a mind is enough to understand it. You do not understand your mind; if you did, you would be free of the fear, conflict, and confusion that dominate it and keep you prisoner to what you do not understand. Your mind operates in a kind of automatic fashion, sweeping you along day after day. Living within the rigid and repetitive patterns that dominate your mind, deprives you of real understanding and true freedom. The mind of separation is a creation of fear whose purpose is to exclude Love.

Love is not mechanical like the mind of separation. A mind operating as Love's expression is free, spontaneous, and very alive. Always and only giving, the mind of Love is not concerned with getting. Love is fullness itself; giving to get as the ego does, is foreign to It. When your mind is filled with Love, overflowing with compassion and goodwill towards all, you will realize that you have everything. The motive to get, to take, to bargain, will disappear. You will live in the quiet certainty that you have all you need. Why would you want more than this? Contentment and gratitude for what you have, will fill your mind with joy and peace. What need have you for more than this?

"To those who have, much will be given." What does this mean? Those who have the peace of God, who live in a state of Love, have become like an open door through which the gifts of God may be given to the world. Those who truly have, understand that the gifts they are given are not for them alone. God's gifts are for all, and must be freely shared if you are to have them for yourself. God only gives, and what He gives is unlimited and all encompassing. That is the nature of His gifts. To give away what you have been given, is the recognition and acceptance of the gifts of God for what they are. Nothing can be accepted except as it truly is.

The ego cannot accept anything for what it is. Always it must control and adjust, modifying everything to fit its perceived needs. In all your relationships is this evident. You do not accept your brother as he is; you reduce him to an image that pictures what you want him to be to you. To this image, made up of what you want him to be, you relate. The image you make of your brother always represents what you would have him be. It also represents what you think yourself to be.

The body is the basic image through which you think you live. From this image you relate to all the other images that seem to surround you. You have forgotten that you put them there for you to see. And so they seem real and independent of you, able to affect you against your will. They must then be controlled, not allowed to penetrate the defenses you have erected around your mind.

My brother, nothing can threaten or harm you ever under any circumstance. You are not the image you have made. There is only Love surrounding you on all sides. Your foolish defenses against what cannot attack, only strengthen the fear in your mind they were made to protect you from. The one thing they do, and do well, is keep Love away. That is their real purpose, to keep fear alive yet seemingly under control. As long as fear rules your mind and drives your behavior, Love will not be welcome.

You do not realize that Love is total, without exceptions of any kind. You think you can continue your allegiance to fear as motivator, and still have Love. This is impossible. While it is true that Love penetrates even the dream and makes its presence known, it is but a glimmer of what Love truly is. To know Love as It is, as Itself, you must refuse to countenance fear in all its forms, and choose Love as your only motivation. To choose Love only will lead you inexorably to the practice of forgiveness.

Forgiveness, not as the world understands it, but as it is in truth, is the highest form of Love attainable on earth. Forgiveness is given to all regardless of appearances; like Love, of which it is a part, its meaning lies in its all inclusiveness. Do not question the value of forgiveness; it will lead you back to God and perfect freedom. Without forgiveness, you are like a blind man trying to judge what he cannot see or understand, groping his way along through the darkness in which he lives. Forgiveness illuminates the darkness of human life, shining it away while restoring your mind to Love.

What in this world could offer you anything remotely as valuable as forgiveness? It will undo the hell which you have made; a place of fear and hatred, marked by conflict and sorrow, ending in death. Forgiveness will heal your mind of the deep sense of guilt you have carried so long. It will relieve you of self hate and the sense of unworthiness that drives you to project guilt and the need for punishment onto your brothers. Forgiveness ends the dream of conflict and pain, of lovelessness and isolation. It will bring you back to where you belong, where you become a shining beacon, lighting the way for your brothers to follow.

CHAPTER THIRTEEN

The Way to Heaven

Here is the way to Heaven, the state of Unity you once knew and will know again: surrender, patience, unwavering trust, perseverance, and constant willingness. These qualities, these capacities, must be developed to transform the way you live now. They must be applied to the process of returning to Truth, and withdrawn from their dedication to upholding illusion. Until now, your faith in the ego has been unwavering and consistent. Likewise your perseverance in following the ego's goals and accepting its interpretation of the world you see. This has only hurt you, and has given you a few paltry rewards that are fleeting and meaningless.

Surrender is essential in spiritual life. The ego bound personality is accustomed to living the way it chooses and making its own decisions, or so it thinks. In actuality, no decisions are made on your own. Every decision is made in concert with the guide you have chosen. There are only two, and of these two, only one guides your decisions so as to strengthen you and lead you away from pain. The decisions you think are made on your own, are always determined by the understanding and value system of the ego. Their purpose is to maintain separation and fear, and keep egoic defenses intact.

There is no more effective way to begin to free yourself from the egoic misidentification and its consequences than to turn over decision making to the Holy Spirit. This is what is meant by surrender. You have relied on the ego as your guide and identity for too long, and it has cost you dearly. The most effective way to withdraw your allegiance is to turn your life over to the Guide God has given you. He will not fail to lead you out of the trap you have made and back to freedom in God.

Can you surrender to the Higher Power is the important question? You do not realize you have already surrendered your life to an alien will not your own. You seem to be an independent entity, capable of making your own decisions based on the exercise of 'good' judgment. Your cherished right to decide for yourself is jealously guarded and protected from the infringement of other egos. Yet all along, while you are making decisions supposedly in your own self interest, you are actually supporting the ego's interests rather than your own. Due to the fundamental confusion of identity, you do not realize they are not the same.

You are not the ego though it lives in your mind as a part of your mind. You invited it in as a solution to the overwhelming fear arising from the first experience of separation. The ego is the belief in separation; inviting it into your mind to become part of you made separation 'real', and led to the further development of separation until the world you see arose. Your true identity was lost to you though it never left your mind. Yet is it buried so deep in your mind, you cannot remember or reach it without help.

The Holy Spirit has the function of restoring the awareness of your true identity, the Self, the Christ. This is not difficult to do if He has your full cooperation. However, full cooperation takes time to develop in most cases; this delays the successful completion of the learning process. Once the decision is made for God, for Truth, and the recognition of its inestimable value dawns on your awareness, the end is certain. Do not delay my brother. Do not hesitate to make the only decision that can be made.

Salvation, or spiritual awakening, is the only purpose you can pursue that will lead to a truly beneficial outcome for you and all your brothers. Everything that supports this purpose will only help, and all that does not will only delay. The means given you through this teaching is the practice of forgiveness, and a conscious relationship with the Holy Spirit. The Holy Spirit is a part of every mind, but how many are aware of this? And of those, how many actively pursue the establishment of clear and consistent communication with Him? He is always with you, waiting for your willingness to accept His help. Whether to make use of it or not is your decision. Always is He willing and able. Are you?

Please do not turn your back on salvation when once you become aware of it and what it brings you. You will not find happiness here, you will not. You may continue to seek it where it is not, but you will find only frustration and disappointment. All things of this world will pass away, all accomplishments and honors will become as ashes, leaving only their bitter taste in the end.

You have heard it said, "Patience is a virtue." Patience is more than a virtue; it is a necessity for patience is a part of surrender. To be patient is to forgo demands on the present, on anyone or anything. Patience does not try to control what happens or force possible outcomes to be achieved into a timetable of its choosing. The ego mind is always trying to reach its goals according to its idea of time. Time is used to get as much as possible as quickly as possible. The ego tries to use time in its own way regardless of the wishes of others. It sees time much as it sees everything else, as a limited quantity that it must control in order to meet its perceived needs. Under the ego's influence, you are always rushing through time, never present here and now.

To be aware in the present requires the exercise of patience. The mind must be checked in its headlong flight through time, not by opposition but by relaxing in the present, by slowing down its race to the future. Release of the inner tension must be achieved, that the mind may become capable of being quiet and present. You must give up the need to force outcomes or set timetables for results; in other words, you must develop patience. As is stated in *A Course in Miracles*, "Infinite patience brings immediate results." The patient mind has surrendered the egoic preoccupation with the future that prevents it from experiencing itself as it is now.

A quiet mind, resting in the present, is ready and open to receive Truth. Truth cannot enter a mind that is busy, driven to distraction, filled with its own ideas and goals. In such a mind, there is no room for Truth nor would It be welcome, for the restless, constantly active mind is interested only in itself, its needs and wants. Virtually all spiritual practices aim to achieve just this quietness of mind that is the condition in which Truth can be experienced. Patience is a part of preparation, a quality of mind that must be developed, that awareness be able to rest quietly in the present. Patience rests on surrender and deepens it until they become one.

There is no place in the ego mind where the din of constant activity is not heard. Do not allow this clamor to drown out the voice of reason. The still, small voice of Truth cannot be heard through the continuous noise that fills your mind. To hear this voice again, the desire for constant escape from the present must be recognized and given up. Then and then only, when all activity has ceased and the mind relaxed and quiet, will the Voice for God be heard. The Holy Spirit has spoken to you since time began, and He will continue to speak until time is over. Do not fail to listen; His is the voice that will lead you to freedom. Leave the shrill voice of the ego, the guide to fear, and follow the Teacher God has given you to bring you home.

Now is the time to begin the journey that will lead you out of the world you have made, beyond all pain, suffering, and sorrow, to the very gates of Heaven. You have a Guide Who will not fail you; the only question is one of time. You will leave time and all it entails and return to God. When that moment comes is your decision and yours only. The Holy Spirit will take you there, but He cannot decide for you. Just as you decided for separation long ago, you must decide for Unity now; nothing that happens to God's Son comes but by His decision. This world was born of judgment; lay judgment down and you are free. Separation was the result of a choice for fear and the denial of Love. Renounce fear in all its forms big or small, and Love will return to heal your mind of all the consequences of what never was. Take off the mask you have worn since time began to hide the face of Christ. Release the self you have made back into the nothingness from which it came, and step into the Light so bright It illuminates the universe. Now is the time, only now. Do not delay.

All goals deemed attainable are reached through means in which you place your trust. Even the belief that a goal is attainable is a statement of trust. You will not set a course towards anything you desire unless trust is invested in the means and the attainability of your purpose. If you are investing worldly means and goals with trust, if you are trusting the guide you have made, the ego, a guide who knows nothing and leads you nowhere, how much more does the Guide given you by God deserve your trust and faithfulness?

Let us consider what God has given us. He has given us a Guide Who cannot fail, the Plan of Atonement which will bring separation to an end, and the means by which the plan of Atonement is completed: forgiveness. All that is needed to free ourselves from the prison of separation that we have made, has been provided. We need only avail ourselves of the help we are given, and add to that our own little willingness, and salvation is assured. Yet how many are actually using what has been given them to leave suffering and separation behind? Why the reluctance to let go of pain and fear, and turn towards joy and Love? Surely even a child would see the desirability of such a decision.

"Except you become as little children, you cannot enter the kingdom of Heaven," as stated in the Bible, is an admonition to become simple in your thinking, and learn to trust as children do. The ego mind is heavily over conceptualized. Its thinking is not only complicated, convoluted, and often conflicted, but it covers over experience with a haze of concepts that further deadens and complicates. The Truth is simple, straightforward, and easy to understand for those who seek true understanding. Before understanding can be attained however, the mind must be corrected and purified. Until then, the heavy clouds of guilt, complexity, and confusion, that characterize the human mind will make real understanding impossible.

Understanding in the spiritual sense is not a matter of conceptualizing, of clever argument, or reasoning based on the past. True understanding cannot be reached by a mind that is not present or self aware. Learning as a process relating to spiritual understanding, is an entirely different undertaking than all learning that takes place in the worldly context. The faith required is a part of this process, as is the surrender that follows faith. Ultimately, no real and authentic spiritual understanding can be reached without direct experience of what is being taught. Direct experience is not mental; it has nothing to do with concepts, it is not mere thinking. Spiritual experience takes place directly in consciousness without the mediation of symbols. Spiritual experience is an entirely new kind of experience that falls entirely outside of the ego's sphere. You will become established in the awareness it brings over time if you persist. This new awareness will become the freedom of your mind; it will expand and grow until the Self reveals Itself as you.

The trust of a child is strong, innocent, and unwavering. A child does not question its parent's ability to take care of it and protect it. This frees the child from unnecessary anxiety, and leaves it free to learn what must be learned. Your relationship with God should be like this. Know that you are safe and taken care of always, and your mind will be free of the fear that clouds it and makes real learning so difficult. Know that your Father, through the Holy Spirit, knows what you need and will always provide. For every problem you perceive, the help you need and the solution are given. If you but knew the constant concern the Holy Spirit has for you, and His infinite Love, you would leave all doubt and fear behind. Your trust is well placed if given to Him, and misplaced if given to the ego.

Trust has never been lacking in your life. You trust implicitly in the identity you have given yourself. Your faith in sin and guilt has never been questioned, and your trust in the defenses you have made is likewise very consistent. Yet to trust, to have faith in what is constantly changing, is surely not reasonable. The self you have made has a thousand different moods that can shift instantly from one to another. The perception on which the self rests, is marked by constant variability, a variability that can change from day to day, even minute to minute. The same object of perception can be seen differently, according to your mood or state of mind. Judgment, on which perception rests, has no consistent standard other than what you consider valuable, and this too shifts with every goal. Nothing is more unreliable and less trustworthy than what you commonly place your trust in.

Contrast this with the Holy Spirit, in whom your trust is well placed. He does not depend on the erratic and uncertain process of partial perception; His perception arises from knowledge which is wholly consistent and unchanging. He always sees truly, perceiving only the reflection of Truth in the dream world. And His judgment is wholly true and never varies: you are the holy Creation of God, created in Love, as Love, forever innocent and shining in the One Light. The Holy Spirit perceives the difference between Truth and illusion, and never does He confuse the two. No matter the form, illusion is illusion; he overlooks all illusion and sees the Truth that shines just beyond it, the One Light. He understands everything that seems to happen in the world of separation is either the expression of Love or a call for Love. Never does He perceive anything other than these two possibilities. His response to both is always the same; He gives Love to all always.

There is nothing in the world to which you should give your trust. Only the Holy Spirit, Who stands beyond the world, is worthy of your complete trust. With His help, you too will go beyond the world of separation, back to the Truth you left only in dreams. He will bring you to the end of dreaming if that be your true desire. If not, He will help you, wherever you are, to turn in the direction of Truth. No positive and helpful thought, no hint of Love that appears in your mind ever so briefly, will go unnoticed by the Holy Spirit. He will always respond, reinforcing every little step you are willing to take, augmenting your little willingness with His. He cannot give you what you are unwilling to accept. Always are your learning limits respected, though He yearns to give you every gift of God He has been keeping for you since time began.

The Holy Spirit is the Teacher of teachers; all teachers of God simply represent Him in outward form. You can have a personal relationship with the Holy Spirit if you make the commitment, and follow it up with honest effort and heartfelt cooperation. The cooperation that is needed is simple and straightforward. Recognize and accept that you know not the way back to God; you know not what is required. Remember always that you know nothing, but that you have a Teacher Who knows everything. He knows your strengths and weaknesses, knows how to strengthen you in every way, and bring you beyond all weakness to the strength of Christ within you. He will shorten your journey, and go before you to clear the way. God has given you the Answer to separation and all the problems you seem to have, the solution to all pain and suffering. Why would you look for another when this One Answer contains all answers? Turn within and decide for peace. Begin the process of making all decisions with the help of the Holy Spirit. Learn to listen to the Voice for God in your own mind, and follow the direction you receive.

The only way to reach God is to surrender. The egoic identity is not in a condition of surrender to anything except its inclination to seek pleasure and avoid pain, and its habit of projecting guilt onto others. Your belief in guilt is not what you should base your life upon, for it brings you only pain, conflict, and discord. Life, to be meaningful, must be based on that which is true and good, that which helps you rise above fear and limitation.

There is something within you that is true, soaring high above the pain and strife of this world. The purpose of life is to find this within yourself, and live in the Light of That. Do not seek It outside yourself, It is not there. The Truth lives deep within you, far beyond the mind of separation, far beyond the reach of the ego. It has vanished from your awareness long ago. Yet It has never left the mind where it was placed by God. To reach this long buried Truth, you need the help that comes from beyond the little circle of illusions you have erected around your mind.

God has given you the Answer, the One Who will lead you back to the Truth you have always been. The most difficult thing for you to do, and indeed the only thing you must do, is to learn to surrender. From true surrender, comes all the qualities, the capacities needed to awaken from the dream. Your mind must be purified, freed from all the falsity that characterizes and dominates it. The Great Plan of Atonement is an undoing, an unraveling and emptying of the delusory mind of separation. Your mind must become clear, quiet, and empty, freed from its dependence on the past that Truth may find welcome. Only if welcomed without resistance or reservation will It return to your awareness. You need not seek for It; you need only become aware of everything in your mind that denies and opposes Truth, and give it over to be undone.

Do not delay or resist what is inevitable. Everyone without exception will return to God. God's Will, which is also your true will, will be done. The longer you live in the condition of separation from God and the Self, the more suffering you will have to endure. There is no substitute for Truth. Always you have tried to find what can take Its place, and always you have failed. Why go on trying to find what does not exist? Illusion will not satisfy you no matter how attractive the form or temporarily gratifying the experience. All form, all experience, passes away in the end, leaving nothing behind but fading memories and shattered hopes. And death waits for all who come here for that is why they came: to prove death victor over life and the ego victor over God. This is madness plain and simple, and never will it bring you anything but pain and suffering.

You do not need to continue as you have always done since time began. You can change your mind about who you are and the purpose of your life. All the help you need will be provided if you decide for Truth. God's grace is always available, but you must be willing to receive. Effort is needed on the road to Truth. You have exerted yourself with all your might to maintain and defend separation. Now you must engage in the effort to bring about its end. You are not alone in this task; mighty companions will be given you, the Holy Spirit will help and guide you in all things, the Truth within will draw you into Itself. Success is assured if you are willing to surrender, trust, persevere, and cooperate with the help that is given, the guidance that is received.

Whatever the cost of freedom, are you willing to pay it? The price that must be paid is nothing less than all you hold dear, for what you cling to so tenaciously has enslaved your mind. The state of separation is a self imposed state of limitation and bondage. Bondage to what is not true, what has only hurt you. What you value, what establishes the basis of your life, has robbed you of your freedom. Yet are you a willing victim, for you choose what you value and decide upon the means of attaining or keeping it. No one outside of your mind has deprived you of anything. You have voluntarily chosen illusion in place of Truth, fear in place of Love, and limitation in place of freedom. You can just as well choose again, and you must if you would be free.

The belief in sin and guilt is the foundation of the ego's entire thought system. From this arises projection, judgment, the need to defend and attack, and the misuse of all relationships. To the ego, all relationships have the purpose of keeping guilt alive and separation unquestioned. All relationships must be limited, tightly controlled, and based on what you can get from them. The giving they require is always a kind of exchange, a bargaining in which you decide how much you will give for what you get. Love, if It enters at all, is present in an incomplete and distorted form, and is used as one of the bargaining chips by which each of you decides the value of what you exchange.

A holy relationship is the opposite of the ego's relationships in every way. Its purpose, given it by the Holy Spirit, is to bring an end to guilt and replace it with Love. It does this by joining rather than maintaining separation, by learning to see the other as innocent, which is to see your brother as he truly is. A holy relationship has the goal of bringing Truth into both your minds that Heaven be restored to you. It has no other goal than this, for there is no other goal worthy of you. In the holy relationship, you learn to give without concern for what you get. The emphasis on exchange, so characteristic of the ego, is absent. Love only gives, It does not exchange for It already <u>has</u> everything. The inclusion of Love and the purpose of Truth will establish holiness rather than guilt as the foundation of your relationship. The holiness which you look for and see in your brother, will restore you to the Kingdom and bring Heaven to earth. The ego will not prevail against the will to unite in Love.

Nowhere in this world will you see the results of your actions as clearly as in a holy relationship. Its transformative power is literally limitless in its capability to restore Truth to your awareness. Recognizing that your brothers interest and yours are one and the same, releases the healing power of the miracle into both your lives. The holiness of your relationship will spread until it covers your whole life, bringing all of your relationships to Love. When Love is the purpose and foundation of all you do, life will become an expression of holiness in action, and you will offer only God's Blessings to all.

In all you do that you value, in learning what you want to learn, you demonstrate perseverance. Very little can be accomplished unless you persevere. To learn what you must learn to replace illusion with Truth, requires great perseverance exercised over a long period of time. The undoing of your mind, the false mind of separation, requires constant dedication to a single purpose. This purpose must become the guiding Light that illumines your entire life, clarifying all the factors of existence, putting everything in proper perspective. There is not your spiritual purpose and your other purposes to which you also give time and attention; there is only your one true purpose and the relationship of all parts of your life with that purpose. Eventually, everything you think, do, or say, must be evaluated in relation to Truth. Does it support your journey back to God, or does it hinder you?

Ultimately, you cannot avoid the necessity to make an uncompromising decision for Truth if you would awaken from the dream of suffering and death. No compromise is possible between Truth and illusion, between God and the ego. You are always choosing one or the other with every thought, word, and action. The uncompromising commitment to awakening must be an active one, for you are called upon to choose the Self or the ego a thousand times a day. The perseverance required is way beyond what is needed to accomplish worldly goals. The goal itself, to realize the Self that is your true nature, is of immeasurably greater value than any worldly accomplishment. Whatever you accomplish in the worldly sense, no matter how seemingly glorious or worthwhile at the time, will pass away. Illusions do not last no matter how stable they may appear for a little while. All things in the world of separation are temporary, ephemeral, and destined to return to dust.

Even the body, your most prized possession, is temporary and subject to decay, disease, and death. No goal whose purpose centers on the body, is anything but a fleeting memory in time. Your life does not depend on the body, nor does it begin or end there. Life is One, and all who live share that One Life with God. He is the Creator of all that is real; what He created not does not exist. The body is your invention, made to be the symbol of separation, the 'proof' that you are not what you were created to be. The body is a thing of madness, meant to surround the mind with a wall of flesh, and separate it from other minds.

Mind is continuous; it cannot be separated into little disconnected pieces unless you want that to be true. Your body appears to separate you from your brother whose body likewise separates him from you. That is but a choice you make, not a fact. Your minds are still joined as One. To know this, you must be willing to accept the fact that you are not a body, you are Mind. The entire experience and context of separation rests on the belief that what you are can change and become something unlike itself. You believe that Mind, formless and unlimited, can take on and become form which is limited. This is the basis for the "I am a body" idea.

Despite the persistence of this belief, you are not a body and never have been. Yes, it is true the body is a part of your experience, and used rightly according to the Holy Spirit's purpose, it will not hinder but will support your awakening. In your awakening, you discover that you are not a body. In fact, you are not even in a body; the body, like the world you see, is in your mind. The body is but a projected image, used to apparently surround your mind and wall it off from other minds, thus keeping you safe from Love. The body is the home the ego has chosen; as long as you continue to identify with the ego, with separation, you will think you are a body.

The body need not limit you nor separate you from your brothers. In itself, the body is a neutral thing, incapable of feeling or purpose. It does what you assign it to do, nothing more and nothing less. If you would use it to separate, it becomes your prison, reducing your mind to a tiny location in space. From this tiny place of nothingness, you look out at all the other tiny fragments of mind likewise confined, for as you see yourself you will see your brothers. This need not be.

If you so choose, the body can be a learning aid, used to help you learn the lessons that end separation. It can be used as a teaching aid, to communicate the Truth to your brothers who still think they are bodies. The body will fulfill the purpose you give it. Why not accept the Holy Spirit's purpose and use it to help set you free?

Mind is continuous, extending everywhere without hindrance or limit. In the world of separation, mind appears to be broken up into separate discontinuous fragments whose communication with each other apparently takes place through bodily forms. The continuous communication that joins all minds appears to be interrupted, occurring sporadically, chaotically. The illusion of separation thus appears to rule the mind as well as the body. In this condition, each separate fragment seems to be isolated, complete in itself, with its own private thoughts unshared with any others. This will indeed be your experience if this is your choice: to live in a world of sleepwalkers, each lost in his own dream, pursuing his own goals at the expense of all others. Is this what you want?

In truth, all minds are joined in a state of continuous communication with each other and their Creator. Nothing can interrupt this communication but the wish to be separate and alone. Even then is the experience of non-communication nothing but illusion, yet illusion is what you experience as real. Only the wish to be as you are not maintains the illusory experience of non-communication with all that is. You can choose again, and you must if you would have Reality restored to your awareness. To do what must be done to bring you back into full communication, is the task of the Holy Spirit. He knows all minds are joined forever, and He recognizes that you have lost awareness of this fact.

Through true vision, you are shown the Truth in your brother, the One Light that shines in everything that God created. As you see this Light through the Light in you, the Light in your brother will extend and join with you. Thus is communication restored and the illusion of separation and discontinuity proven false. The Light, like Mind, like Love, is One and nothing can interrupt or fragment what God created One. Nothing in Heaven or earth is separate from God or its true nature as the One Self.

CHAPTER FOURTEEN

Light and Creation

Whatever stands in the way of your freedom needs to be thoroughly examined. What you are unaware of nonetheless exerts an influence on your mind. The many obstructions to the return of Truth, collectively make salvation impossible. Essential to your awakening is the uncovering of all that denies it. All the dark places where unforgiveness hides in your mind must be exposed, that the Light of Love may shine on what they conceal, and forgiveness replace all grievances. The many fears that lurk beneath the threshold of conscious awareness must be brought to the light of day, that you may see the insanity of your mind, and let all fear be healed. All the mental tendencies and habits of a lifetime must be clearly examined, and evaluated by the standards of Truth. Those found wanting must be given over to correction, to be replaced by what is helpful.

You are the One Self whether you are aware of It or not. Your mind functions by means of a Light that comes from beyond it. The Light of the Self pervades the mind of separation; without this Light, there would be no mind. You cannot use this Light of Mind creatively however, for the mind reduces this creative power of the universe to partial perception, conceptualization which it regards as thinking, and habit patterns of thought and feeling. It is as if you took the power produced by a huge dynamo and used it to run a toy train. Very little of the power potentially available to you is actually used in your life. Even that is misused to make sure this greatly reduced mode of functioning is maintained.

The Light within you is brighter than a thousand suns, brighter by far. Yet you do not access It, nor is It available to the mind devoted to separation. When Truth was driven from your mind, the Light of your mind also became unavailable, for Truth is One. Truth is Spirit, Mind, Light, Love, and peace. All of Truth vanished from your awareness when you chose illusion. Nor can It return; no aspect of Truth can return to your awareness until you choose all of It. However, a little point of Light remains, waiting for the day when It can blaze forth and illuminate the darkness in a world of pain and limitation. On that day you will rejoice, and your brothers also, for the Light is given you that you may illuminate the path that all must walk.

Real creation is unlike what is considered creation in this world. To create as God does, and only this is real, you must extend your whole Being, the Light and Love that you are. In that way is Reality extended and thereby increases. Only the increase of Truth is true creation. The purpose of the Light is to create by extending Itself forever.

In this world, as you open to the Light in you, It is used to communicate Truth by joining with the Light in your brothers, and used to make a unified vision possible that perception be corrected and brought close to knowledge. God is the Light in which you see. Without the Light of God within you, you would not see. Your present way of seeing is through the body's eyes. Seeing through the eyes of an image you have made to take the place of the Self God created, is not seeing, it is but imagination. You are literally seeing what is not really there. There is no difference between hallucinations and the way you see now. The seeming stability and continuance of the world you see prevents you from seeing it as the projected illusion it is.

Perception is always the result of a decision you have made about what you want to be true. This fact you keep hidden from yourself that your world appear as 'reality', something that is really existent, separate from your wishes. The means by which perception appears to take place, the body, is also an invention of the mind. Thus the means and what it perceives arise together. They are co-dependent; without one, the other would not appear to exist. Such a closed circle is indeed convincing, for you cannot see beyond it. The means to see, and the world that is perceived, seem to reinforce each other's reality, leaving you convinced of the reality of both. Nowhere can you find your way out of this closed circle.

To see beyond the illusions of perception in which you are trapped, help is needed from beyond the illusion. The Holy Spirit sees truly. He is not fooled by appearances, by form, for He sees beyond the form to content. He responds only to content, not form, for He recognizes form as illusion and always will. He looks past what is meaningless in itself, and the vision He gives you allows you to look past the form and see what it conceals.

The Light of Heaven is reflected here in everything you see. The form matters not; it cannot conceal the One Light unless you wish it so. Like partial vision, spiritual vision is also the result of what you want to see. However, it differs from how you see now because it is a decision to see truly, to see the Truth reflected here rather than to see what has replaced Truth in your mind. The Light in what you see will join with the Light in your mind for the Light is One, and this Light will brighten the world of darkness and show you the way home. Darkness will disappear in the presence of Light; you will cease to give it your belief, and it will hamper you no more.

The Creations of Light make up the real universe. The One Creative Light that fills the universe is what you are. You, who carry the Light within you, have the power to shine away the darkness in the world of illusion. In the dream, the only truly creative action of mind is to awaken to its reality as Mind, and extend the Light and the Love that It is to the world of separation. This is done by extending Light and Love to your brothers through the vision of Christ. By giving Truth away, It is strengthened in your mind and in the mind of your brother simultaneously. To see the Light in your brother, and to join with that Light, is the greatest gift you can both give and receive.

What would you do if you suddenly realized you were living in a dream, that none of this is real? This is the realization everyone will come to in time. The total meaninglessness of all you are doing cannot fail to break through the egoic defenses and dawn on your awareness sooner or later. You cannot avoid this. However, the sooner you stop your active avoidance of the real state of your existence, the better it will be for you. No matter how you try, how successful you are at the ego's game of defense and attack, you will not escape the penalty of pain, suffering, and death. You will not.

There are those who realized all at once the extreme futility and meaninglessness of their life, and, overcome by despair, descended into madness or attempts at self destruction. To see the state you are in is not enough, for the response, whatever it may be, will be a continuation of the same error, the belief in separation. What is needed at this time is a solution to the hopeless situation in which you are seemingly trapped.

The Truth will set you free, but first you must become aware of Its at least theoretical existence. Generally, for most minds, the movement towards freedom is a gradual one that may unfold over a period of many years. It will take just as long as you want it to, no less time than this. The strength of your desire for Truth is the determiner of the duration and the conditions of the journey. You may have other desires that compete with Truth for your allegiance. These may contradict or even oppose the attraction to Truth, resulting in slow and uneven progress. Salvation is not just another goal, one among many that may attract your efforts; it is the only goal worth aiming for as it is the only one worthy of you, and the only one whose attainment is wholly positive and lasting. And it is the only goal in the world of illusion that restores Reality to your experience, ending fear, pain, and suffering forever.

If you could make a choice right here and now that would end pain and sorrow forever, would you? The sane answer to this question would be yes, yet the ego bound mind can seldom respond in a straightforward and uncomplicated manner. The ego, always suspicious of what is offered, insists on controlling every decision, and censoring always what would enter the mind. Do not listen to the ego. You have chosen it as your guide by the act of identifying with a body. Through your obvious experience of separation, you have come to identify with the belief in separation that holds the center of your mind and the whole thought system that arises from it. The ego, the personification of this thought system, is suspicious of everyone and everything, for it believes danger surrounds it and attack will come at any moment from any direction. There is nothing that can be done to change this attitude, this position; the ego is itself a personification of fear and the hatred that always accompanies it.

The only thing that can be done with the ego and the thought system of separation, is to let it be undone with the help of the Holy Spirit, that Reality may be revealed to you. You need not oppose the ego or struggle against it. The ego is a part of your mind that has an illusory existence that you believe real. Illusion need not be opposed; opposition merely strengthens it. By your opposition you make it real, and this is a continuation of the problem not a solution. The belief that illusions are real is what gives them their seeming power over you.

Let the Holy Spirit teach you the unreality of illusions, and do not resist His teaching. You have believed in illusion since time began; your mind is very attached to what it has made. Illusions will not disappear in a day. With patience, and the willingness to learn what is true and what is illusion and the difference between them, all illusion will be steadily undone through the consistent choice of Truth with the help of the Holy Spirit. Nothing more is needed but also nothing less. Your true desire is to return to the Truth hidden deep in your mind. Nothing can prevent this if you apply your willingness to this goal consistently and persistently.

Pain and sorrow are constants in human life; they are never far away. Pain takes many forms, constantly exerting its dark influence on your life. Much human behavior and energy is devoted to avoiding pain, controlling pain, or suppressing it. Yet it cannot be escaped while living in the state of separation. Separation is itself a state of fear and pain, but much of it is suppressed and kept from awareness by egoic mechanisms such as dissociation. The loss of your relationship with your Father, Who is the Source of your very existence, is a wound so deep and lasting that you cannot face it; sorrow would overwhelm your defenses and flood your mind. You fear the deep emptiness within, the result of the loss of God, and much of your activity has the purpose of covering it up so that you do not have to face it.

Yet there is something that you fear more than the emptiness, more than the sorrow. Under this, and beyond the fear of God deep in your mind, is the Love you feel and have always felt for your Creator. This Love for your Father is so deep, so powerful, that were you to feel it again, you would rush back to Him, forgetting the world of separation and all you thought you held dear. Everything you have valued, everything you have learned through the ego, would vanish instantly in that moment when Love returns to Love.

This return to Love, the ego fears more than anything, though it does not understand what it fears. Yet it does recognize threat, and it is to threat of any kind that the ego devotes most of its attention. The return of the Love that you are to your awareness, would be the end of the ego's domination of your mind, and thus the end of its existence. The day will come when you will choose Love over fear unequivocally, and on that day you will be free.

The Self is what you are and have always been. The Christ in you has never been absent, even in the dream, for the mind with which you think you think, functions by virtue of the Light arising from the Self. It is as if you have closed off what you are, and allowed only a tiny little part of it to be experienced as you; even this tiny fragment of mind is not allowed to be itself, but is distorted by form and the action of perception which has replaced knowledge in your experience. Nothing of this tiny sliver of mind that has been sliced off from the Whole, is allowed to even reflect the Truth, and it has been further divided into many levels of awareness that are cut off from each other.

The surface level of awareness we call the conscious mind; beneath it are levels of subconscious mind from which the impulses and thoughts arise that drive the actions of conscious mind. Yet even here, in this dreary arrangement of littleness and divisiveness, there is hope, for the Holy Spirit abides in a deep level of the subconscious mind beyond the levels inhabited by the ego, and He is also able to communicate with the conscious mind when it permits Him to do so.

There is an additional reason for hope, which, along with the help of the Holy Spirit, is the way out of the labyrinth of illusion. Awareness is in itself of the essence of Mind. In the state of separation, it becomes the basis of mind, being used for perception and delusory thinking. Constantly distracted and filled with the activity of perception, thought, and feeling, awareness becomes absorbed in and identified with the content that appears in it. Thus is its fundamental nature lost to experience. As mind in separation, you seldom if ever experience the basis of your mind which is awareness; even then, it is only a fleeting, momentary experience quickly swallowed up by the maelstrom of thought activity.

Awareness in its fundamental nature as itself, is quiet, open, and empty. It need not be constantly filled by frantic activity nor need it be identified with such. How often is it said in *A Course in Miracles* that Truth comes to a quiet mind. This quiet mind is nothing more than the quality of awareness freed from its false identification and absorption in delusory thought, resting quietly in itself in a condition of openness and receptivity. In such a mind, Truth is easily reflected, like an image appearing in a mirror.

How is one to attain the quiet mind? Mind is ceaselessly active, filled with a constant parade of thoughts. This activity goes on automatically. You have no real control over your thoughts or their source, the ego, because you are so constantly identified with both. The nature of ego mind is to be busy, filling awareness with a stream of thoughts, feelings, and impulses that go on without interruption during the so called waking hours. If this frantic mind is what you are, and that is what you believe while you identify with it, then the state of a quiet mind is impossible to reach. You will be what you think you are, and you will act it out.

Fortunately for you, you are not the frantic and fearful ego mind nor the sense of self that arises from the false identification. There is no self. There is only awareness that mistakenly identifies with the content that ceaselessly demands its attention. The unconscious identification with what you are not, gives rise to the sense of personhood, a thinker, a bodily identity. This identity is a fiction, an imaginary entity. As long as you think it real and continue to believe in it, you <u>will</u> seem to be the thinker of thoughts and a bodily identity. The power of belief will make it real in your experience.

The solution to this dilemma is, as always, to step outside the circle of illusion that seems to hold you fast. With the Holy Spirit's help, the false mind can be undone. Through the practice of constant vigilance, your attention will move from absorption in the thought stream to resting in awareness itself which is its source. Generally speaking, the mind that would be free must go through a process of relinquishing all that has been learned before and all that has been valued. You have been badly taught by one who knows nothing, the ego. How could you learn anything but what is meaningless from the guide who does not know what is meaningful? As you give up all false beliefs, they will be replaced by true ideas, thoughts that support and point to Truth.

An important part of this process is getting to know your mind as it is, in action. Here is where vigilance is applied in the form of becoming constantly aware of your thoughts, feelings, and reactions. By becoming aware of this movement as you go through your day, you will see the constant choices you are making that are shaping your life and determining its experiences. You will also see how fear in all its forms, the activity of attack and defense, and the projection of guilt and judgment, are distorting and agitating your mind, making peace impossible.

What is the cost of sin? What does the belief in sin and guilt demand of you? The loss of happiness and peace of mind, is the cost of believing what is not true, of replacing Truth with illusion. Nothing you can do is as important as giving up the belief in guilt and sin. Their complete renunciation is perfect forgiveness. Through forgiveness, you will heal all sense of guilt and sin in your mind by offering this healing to your brothers. If you believe you are guilty, that is how you will see your brother, for what is seen and believed within will be projected without.

There is a kind of reciprocity at work in all partial perception. How you see your brother is how you see yourself. You will believe you are what he is, and he is what you are.

No more perfect example of this exists than the beliefs around the body. If you believe you are a body, it is impossible not to see your brother as a body also. As long as you see him limited to a body, so long will you be so limited. You cannot see the Sonship except as One, though you are no longer aware of this fact. How you see and think of your brother will always be how you see and think of yourself. Your brother is likewise bound by this principle. All projection is always a projection of yourself onto yourself. You are always and only seeing as real what is in your mind.

The perception of sin and guilt in the world, in the figures that come and go in your dream, is always a projection of the guilt that lives in your mind. It cannot be otherwise. That is why you must forgive the world and everyone and everything in it, for only thus do you forgive yourself. Only by healing all guilt and sin wherever you perceive it, is the sense of sinfulness and guilt in your mind healed. This naturally follows from what was stated earlier. The Sonship is One, you are a whole part of that Oneness; therefore, to heal and free your mind, you must offer healing to the Whole as It appears in little bits and pieces in the condition of separation. All these apparently separate bits and pieces are actually part of you, and you will be healed in your entirety or you will not be healed at all.

Do not let guilt cloud your mind any longer. It brings you nothing but suffering and death. Guilt drives Love from your awareness and leaves you alone and friendless in an alien land. The belief in guilt has robbed you of all that is good and valuable, yet you remain a willing victim to this loss as long as you cling to guilt. It exerts a strong attraction on you; through the projection of guilt, you maintain your identity in separation and justify your attacks on your brothers. Because you are consciously unaware that you are always the first victim of your attacks, you continue to judge and condemn your brothers, thinking that attack on another brings you something of value. Attack brings you nothing! This cannot be overemphasized. If you were aware of the total loss you suffer with every attack on your brother, attack would lose its attraction for you.

The attraction to attack is the choice of fear over Love, of conflict over peace. My brother, now is the time to stop this insane war on yourself, and lay down your arms. You never wanted to attack yourself or your brother. It was simply an error, a mistake in identification, easily corrected if that is your will. To give up insanity is impossible until you honestly recognize that you are insane, that you are acting insanely. Ignorance of the mental condition of insanity protects and perpetuates it. You cannot say that you are still unaware of your mental state or the mad behavior that results. There is nothing to do now but turn your back on the madness of the past and choose Truth. Reason tells you that to stop attacking yourself will bring an end to the pain and suffering that seemed to come from outside, yet was always self inflicted.

Forgiveness is the solution to all pain, all fear and conflict. Forgiveness ends the dream of death, for it leads to the perception of a forgiven world where all are loved and blessed by its kindly Light. There is a world beyond the world of darkness and strife, seen only by those who have laid down their weapons, renounced all attack and judgment, and chosen Love instead. You can live in the kindly Light of the real world if you would exchange it for the one you inhabit now.

The real world appears to those who see not only with the body's eyes. It must be seen through the eyes of Love, through spiritual vision shared with them by the Holy Spirit. He has been holding this vision for you since time began. The readiness to see truly arises only in the mind that chooses forgiveness for all, leaving all judgment to the Holy Spirit Whose function it is. He, and only He, always judges truly, for He sees only the holiness in all of God's children. Everything else is simply an error; He helps you correct all errors in your mind until only Truth remains.

The real world appears to those who have let their perception be corrected. Through the body's eyes, the world appears to be a place of attack and conflict, ruled by fear and driven by the need for vengeance. Threat lurks everywhere, and nowhere can safety be found, for vengeance may strike at any time. In such a world Love is absent; It is not welcomed by those who prefer attack and judgment. Yet those who see with the Holy Spirit, look upon quite a different world. Everywhere they look, the holy Light of God stands revealed; It shines from within everything they see, and lights the world with its kindly glow. There is no threat anywhere; only Love and mercy await them everywhere they go.

The real world is a forgiven world, where judgment is forgotten, replaced with the vision of Christ that sees only the reflection of Truth everywhere. The Oneness of all things is apparent, and Love is offered to all without exception or exclusion of any kind. The real world, like the world seen by the body's eyes, is also a projection of the mind that sees it, but there is one important difference: The Love of God is not excluded, so it contains the reflection of Truth. There is no doubt or uncertainty where Truth prevails. The real world extends to the gates of Heaven. Freed of sin and guilt, doubt and uncertainty, illuminated by the Love of God, you may rest there a little while until you are ready for God to take the final step.

Those with spiritual vision do not trust the body's eyes to show them the reality of what they see. The body's eyes see only the external, the form, never the content of what appears before them. Forms differ and change over time; they may come and go, but never does the content change. Content is always and only one of two possibilities; Truth or illusion. The body's eyes cannot make the distinction between the two, but the mind that has chosen Love and forgiveness has let itself be corrected. Its vision is whole, not partial, and it sees directly without the mediation of the eyes that see only form. The lovely Light that is Truth's reflection, is easily seen by those who are willing. To see this Light is to join with It; in this union are all blessed as One.

To see the Light in your brother is to know It in yourself. To forgive your brother is to forgive yourself. Only through the relinquishment of judgment and the offering of forgiveness to all, will you be set free from the limitations of your self-made identity. There is nothing you can do in this sad world of pain and suffering that is as meaningful as forgiving your brothers. Only action that arises from Love has any lasting effect on you and the world. Either you will act from Love or you will act out fear. One will lead you in the direction of Truth, the other away from it. One will set you free and bring suffering to an end, the other will strengthen the bonds that bind you to suffering, and deny your freedom.

Forgiveness is your function as long as you are in the world of appearances and separation. This world is the projection of your thoughts, reflecting back to you what you want to be true. As long as you maintain the wish to be separate from your Self and your Creator, you will be at the mercy of your unconscious guilt and self hatred. To be guilty is to hate yourself for what you believe you have done, for your unworthiness. Guilt demands punishment; the guilty will project both their guilt and the demand for punishment onto their brothers in a vain attempt to relieve their burden. Your brother is yourself. To see him as guilty will reinforce your belief in your own guilt, and never will it be gone from your mind.

The mind must be freed of guilt if you would return to Love and freedom. Your function of forgiveness is the way out for you from the prison you have made. Forgiveness will set you free and your brother along with you. To fulfill your function, to reclaim your freedom and return to Love, you must deny guilt in all its forms. No matter where it seems to appear, guilt is still always and only in your mind. To forgive your brother is to forgive yourself; to forgive the world is to forgive yourself. To forgive yourself is to forgive yourself, the world, and your brother as One. The mind that has let its guilt be healed, will see no guilt anywhere. In your healing is everyone healed.

The time for forgiveness is now. As you go through your day, if you are paying attention to the movements of your mind, you will see little irritations and judgments come up again and again. It matters not the apparent cause or the circumstances; if there is an upset of any kind, there is unforgiveness, there is a grievance. Perhaps you think that mild irritation or a sense of dislike is harmless, especially in regard to certain situations. Not so. All grievances, no matter how mild they may seem, are a refusal to love. They represent the belief in and projection of guilt regardless of the details.

All grievances are affirmations of the desire to remain separate, providing the justification for attack and condemnation. All attack, no matter the mask it wears, is the intent to injure and kill. And always it is yourself who suffers the effects of your intent. There is no such thing as a mild attack; all attack carries the same intent and will have the same results. All irritation, no matter how mild it seems, but masks the rage underneath that would attack and kill. As you learn to become aware of your mind and its unconscious movements and motivation, you will see clearly what you now deny.

Forgiveness offers you a choice as to how you feel about yourself and your brother. The choice of guilt has left you in a state of mind where you hate rather than love yourself. To hate yourself is to hate your brother, for those who hate are unable to love, and must project how they feel about themselves onto their brothers. Forgiveness is a choice of Love over hate, and a rejection of all attack in any form.

The belief in attack has made the attainment of peace impossible. Forgiveness makes possible the return to a state of peaceful mind. A mind at peace within itself, having forgiven itself and everyone and everything it sees, can offer only Love to a world made dark by hate. Through your forgiveness, the world is blessed. A blessed world offers you only sanctuary and mercy; the help you need at any time and in any way will always be given. Those whose minds are ruled by forgiveness, whose hearts are filled with Love for all, see a world ruled by kindness. Everywhere they look they see the reflection of Heaven; Heaven's gates stand wide open to receive them. They know the way is short, and time is almost over; they will remember their Father, and leave the world forever behind them.

What could offer you more than forgiveness? There is nothing the world can give that is worth even a tiny fraction of what forgiveness makes possible. All worldly gifts and accomplishments are temporary, fading from your sight almost as quickly as they appear. Everything you think you now possess will be left behind, forgotten, even the temporary learning aid that is the body. The Love you give through the miracle of forgiveness, will return to you multiplied manyfold. It will remain to bless you through all eternity, for Love has always been a part of you. Through forgiveness your mind is healed, and you return to the awareness of what you have always been. Forgiveness simply brings you back to what you are and where you are always. That is enough.

Remember always the gifts held out to you by the practice of forgiveness. Never forget that forgiveness is the answer to all fear and suffering of any kind. To forgive is to be free; free to Love, free to bless. Through forgiveness, you become One with the world and everything in it. In its gentle sight, your brother will appear as he is in Truth. His innocence is revealed, and the One Light that shines in him will become visible. As the Light in you extends to the Light in your brother, you will feel a touch of Heaven.

There is a very practical question that arises in relation to forgiveness. How are you to actually forgive when your mind tells you forgiveness is not warranted? You have been attacked, seemingly injured in some way. You have suffered loss at the hands of another due to his unfair and unprovoked action. In truth, you cannot forgive what has really happened; the ego will not allow it. The human mind by itself will never be able to forgive its brother. Forget maybe, even overlook occasionally, but forgive? Never! What you believe has really happened to you is unforgiveable by all worldly thinking. The thinking of the world is based on the belief in guilt and the necessity of judgment. The continuing 'reality' of what you see depends on it. If attack were real and loss possible, if you could be unfairly deprived of anything, if injury could be inflicted upon you, forgiveness would have no meaning and no basis. However, you are not a body, and the 'reality' in which you seem to live and move, is but a dream. You cannot attack or be attacked, and everything that seems to happen to you is imagination. Forgiveness as taught by *A Course in Miracles* and within these pages, is based on Truth, not dreams. Reality is not the result of idle dreams of separation and death. The domain of Spirit is the basis and Source of what is real, not the wishful projections of a mind lost in the nightmare of its own fearful imagery.

Forgiveness is rooted in and arises from the understanding of Truth. As such, it reflects the Truth in the world of dreams. Forgiveness takes the place of all illusions that cloud the mind of God's holy Son, folding them all into itself until only Love remains. Forgiveness is the operation of Love in a world that was made to keep Love out. The return of Love in the form of forgiveness, brings an end to evil dreams of hate and malice that have kept you a prisoner of fear and suffering.

Whatever you believe will be true for you. Believe in illusions, and they will be your reality. Withdraw your belief and faith in them, and they will collapse into nothingness. The Truth need not be believed to be real. It is real in and of Itself. Yet It must be believed and accepted in order to enter the realm of your experience. The refusal to accept Truth is the choice for illusion, and what you choose you will experience, even if only in dreams. Dreams are real to the dreamer and Truth is lost to him, replaced by a distorted wish to be separate from his Source and his Self. Neither the Creator, nor anything in Creation, will go against your wish to be what you are not. Truth does not oppose. It does not attack or do battle. Truth merely overlooks what has never occurred, and lets it go down to nothingness. You can believe in dreams or in the Truth, and whichever one you choose will be your experience. That is the law of Mind. Never will you make illusions true, never will you make them into Reality. The power of your belief will make them seem real, and the experiences they bring will be 'proof' of their reality, but this is only seeming. The stuff of dreams will convince the dreamer as long as that is what he wants. Change your mind, and the whole flimsy edifice of your 'reality' will come crashing down. Without your support, it cannot exist in your experience.

The Light is what you are in Truth, being the natural brightness, the radiance of your Whole Mind. The extension of Light is the creative action of Mind. Light naturally extends Itself, and thereby creates like Itself in the true condition of creating with God. For this you were created. The awareness of yourself as Light was lost in the separation. Mind became split, reduced and distorted, cut off from its wholeness. Its natural radiance was lost, and it became dim, dull, and lifeless. Yet the Light remains, reduced to a tiny point, lost to awareness and imperceptible to the mind that thinks itself separate.

The natural radiance of Mind that is Light, is your truly creative energy. When this is lost to you, you are left with the uncreative use of mind. Mind is then used to perceive and to think thoughts it does not share with God. What is considered creative in the world of perception is, at best, but a pale shadow of the true creativity given you by God. That glory can perhaps be mirrored in a small way, as have some of what are considered great masterpieces of art. You cannot however, create in the manner given you in your creation until you return to the awareness of the Light that is you. The radiance of this Light outshines everything in the world of perception. It lights up the universe with a glory that cannot be imagined by anyone who lives in the dimness of perceptual mind. When you are ready, you will recover the awareness of the beautiful Light that shines in you and all things. Pray that day be soon.

Love, like Light, is part of what you are in Truth. It has also been lost to your awareness except in distorted form with few exceptions. Yet is Love always present, for you are surrounded and sustained by the Love of God. You become aware of God's Love, Which is everywhere and in everything, through the practice of forgiveness. Forgiveness mirrors Love as It truly is, for it is given to all without conditions or exclusion. True forgiveness sees no one and no event, circumstance, or happening, as evidence of guilt or sin; it sees only the perfection of everything reflected in the dream. Love, as it exists in Heaven, is reflected here in every act, every thought of forgiveness. The practice of forgiveness will return Love to your awareness, and where Love is, the memory of God cannot be far behind.

True forgiveness is the most powerful force for healing your mind and setting you free. As the highest expression of Love on earth, it heals your mind of all that is not Love, and paves the way for Love's return. Extended to all your brothers, it restores the Oneness in which all are joined. Due to its all encompassing and uncompromising nature, it undoes the ego's hold on your identity, for it gives the ego no place to turn and undoes guilt, the cornerstone of the ego's thought system. Forgiveness removes the basis for attack and defense, and gives judgment back to the Holy Spirit where it belongs. It removes all fear from your mind, for it is the choice of Love and the renunciation of fear.

Work, effort, and struggle: these are the basic conditions under which human life takes place. Everything must be sought, accomplished, and then maintained, that its usefulness continue. All things in the world of separation are in a state of constant change. Nothing is as it was even a little while ago; all is changing whether you are aware of it or not. Only that which is valued, and in which you invest belief and effort, appears to offer satisfaction and a sense of security.

Your mind, constantly active and changing, shifting its focus here and there, subject to various moods that follow each other like the clouds drifting across the sky, offers no security and peace in itself. You respond by seeking them in external circumstances and conditions, in goals, attainments, and experiences. All of these have no meaning in and of themselves. Your mind gives them all the meaning they have for you. The same mind that is constantly changing, at times contradicting itself, and does not understand its own workings and motivation. This mind is what gives all things in your life whatever meaning and purpose they may appear to have. Is there any basis for life, for security and satisfaction, more unstable and erratic than this?

Despite the investment and effort you expend in controlling and responding to the external, that which appears outside of you, you have set yourself an impossible task. You are looking in the wrong place for what you need. Life begins and ends in the mind. Everything you do and experience is experienced through awareness. You determine the value of all things to you in your mind. The mind determines what is valued, what will provide satisfaction and security. The external circumstances of your life are a result of how you use your mind, what you choose, and what you choose against. Your mind determines the goal, how to attain it, and directs your efforts. It decides when a goal is attained, and how satisfying that should be. If you really look at the whole process and dynamic of your life, and the role played by the mind, it would be obvious to you that what happens in your mind is the key to everything.

Yet you are, for the most part, oblivious to this fact. You do not know or understand that which is most central to your life and experience. Perhaps you think using your mind to make decisions and judgments constantly, is enough to understand it. No so. If you would look honestly at your life, the decisions made, the conflicts and so called failures and successes, you would see the erratic patterns of thought and response by which you live. Much of human life is determined or shaped by various unconscious habit patterns of which you are at best dimly aware. The awareness that is the fundamental characteristic of mind, is absorbed in and dominated by the continuous stream of thought, feeling, and impulse, that fills it. Never is there a moments respite from this constant activity. The source of this activity is the levels of mind that lay beneath the threshold of conscious awareness. In other words, you are dominated by the unconscious content of your mind.

The more superficial levels of the unconscious mind are the domain of the ego. The ego is not you although you think it is. The ego is a part of your mind, whose core is fear and whose thought system is the crystallization and development of the belief in separation. The ego is only a part of your mind, and yet has seemingly taken over all of your mind because of your identification with the sense of separateness, and its chosen home, the body. The ego has its own agenda of which you are not aware; it acts always to pursue its own interests which are not yours. Due to the lack of comprehension of what the ego is and its goals, you accept its goals as yours, thinking it is in your interest to pursue them. Hidden from your awareness is the ego's beliefs about you. It believes you are guilty, unworthy, and deserve punishment and eventual death for your sins.

The ego's goal is to take the place of God, of Truth, and make sure that your mind and life are dedicated to maintaining this illusion. This means that as long as you identify with the ego and its chosen home, the body, you will be denying and excluding the truth of what you are from your life and experience. The ego does not know Love; it regards Love as an enemy, a threat to its existence. It does not know peace or happiness or kindness. To the exact degree to which you give your life and mind to the ego and its goals, you will not know Love or peace, and happiness will elude you.

Surely it is insane to cast your lot with the one who plots your death, rather than the One Who gives you life? Yet this is exactly what you do when you defend and maintain the separation between yourself, your brothers, and your Creator. It does seem as if you are self-evidently separate from all others because you experience yourself as a body. However, the body separates you from your brothers only if that is your choice. The body is a neutral thing; it does not separate or join. It responds to the purpose given it by the mind; it is the mind that separates or joins according to its purpose. If the purpose chosen is to maintain separation, guilt, sin and attack, that will be your self-validating experience.

The mind cannot be cut off from all that surrounds it; the wall of flesh that seems to limit it is but illusion. Unless you want the illusion of a body to imprison your mind, it cannot. Even asleep, the mind is still One, and continuous without interruption.

Bodies appear in the mind, mere images without substance. Mind is not contained by appearances, by form. It cannot be separated into fragments, kept apart from each other by the projected images of bodily form. Withdraw your dedication to illusion, cease your fascination with the hallucinations that seem to people your world. There is nothing out there separate from you. Everything is in you and you are in everything you see. There is no objective world separate from the mind that perceives it.

When you are willing to see your brother as he is, the Light in him will join with the Light in you. In that moment, the whole world is blessed, for the Oneness of God's holy Son has been affirmed. Let go the illusion of separation and all the misery it entails. You never wanted to suffer, alone in an alien world, separate from your Father and your Self. It was simply a mistake, easily rectified if that is your will. In any moment, it is possible to leave this world if only for an instant, and be once again the pure Light of Heaven.

What you think and do today will affect you in every way; its effect will continue until you change your mind. This is true of every day, every hour, even every minute and each moment. All you think and do echoes through time, accompanying you until time comes to an end or you choose again. Ideas leave not their source and continue to influence the mind in which they live. Everything you do is the result of an idea in your mind, and reinforces or cancels that idea accordingly. Every act, every thought, affects the whole world for mind is One.

There are no neutral thoughts, words, or deeds. Each one either multiplies and reinforces illusion, or supports the Truth. There is no in between nor any other effect. Each moment you are choosing Truth or illusion, Love or fear, freedom or imprisonment, and you will always experience the consequences of your choosing. Thus is it imperative that you be aware of your choices moment to moment, if you would choose wisely and well. The decisions made by the sleeping mind are responsible for all that seems to happen in your life. To be aware of and accept that fact is very important; otherwise you will continue to be at the mercy of your unconsciousness. The sleeping mind is the slave of time and human destiny.

If you would free yourself from the parade of events and situations that drive your responses, you must become aware of the activity of your mind. The mind is always active; always choosing the thoughts it would follow, the feelings it would animate, the actions it would carry out. Much if not most of this activity of choosing, goes on below the threshold of conscious awareness and is determined by past habit. You are thus unconsciously acting out the past in the present, which assures a future that is a continuation of the past. As long as this continues, you will be stuck in the past, destined to repeat it over and over, and never will you know the freedom that is your birthright.

Do you want freedom or don't you? Do you want to become aware of your own mind or continue to activate the past habit patterns that control your responses? These are really the same question. Freedom and unconsciousness are incompatible; where one is, the other isn't. Freedom is restored to those who earn it by their efforts. It comes to those who truly want it. Like everything else that is a part of your life, freedom is the result of decisions that you make. How could it be otherwise?

Did you want to be free before you became aware that freedom is possible? Until an idea actually enters awareness, there is no possibility of its attainment. The mind asleep and dreaming that it is awake, does not realize it is in a condition of bondage. Until you are ready to honestly consider the true state of your life and mind, you will be in a state of denial. As long as denial rules your awareness, keeping unconscious all that you do not wish to face, true freedom will not be possible. Freedom is your natural condition as the Self.

To be in the natural state is of itself effortless. You need make no effort to be what you are and always have been. Yet you have lost the awareness of what you are in Truth, and have replaced it with a substitute identity whose purpose is to keep Truth away. As your present self is the result of effort, and much energy and effort are expended to defend and maintain it, the undoing of it will also require effort and dedication. No effort is required to be what you truly are, but effort is required to undo all that obstructs your natural awareness of what you are. When all obstacles are removed, the Self will shine forth as you.

The search for Truth is never a search for what was never lost, for how can you lose that which is your very life and Being? Rather it is the search for, the bringing to awareness, of all that clouds and dims your holy mind, that it may be corrected and the mind purified. When all obstacles have been removed, the Truth will reveal Itself as you, and you will realize It has never been lost.

The starting point for the process of undoing the false identity, must be the recognition that something is missing in your life, and the idea that perhaps there is another way to live. Until this question is raised, the mind is not ready to start down the road to Truth. If you are satisfied with where you are or afraid to change, you will defend and perpetuate the status quo as long as you are able. And you will follow the ego's guidance faithfully until it leads you to your death. What enables this sad and meaningless travesty of life to continue, is the denial of the pain you are in. The mind of separation dissociates habitually from its fear, its pain, from the contents of the unconscious mind. Through identification with the ego, dissociation is maintained and the mind kept continually busy and distracted, never truly aware in the present.

One of the fundamental requirements of spiritual life is the return of attention to the present. This can only be done by quieting the mind, by slowing it down. Truth comes to a quiet mind that is empty and open to receive It. The mind that is constantly busy chasing the succession of shadows passing across its surface, or absorbed and fascinated by the world of outer perception, has no interest in what is truly real nor has it made a place within to which Truth can return. Truth can be experienced only in the present moment for only the present is real. Although time may seem real to you, it too is but imagination. The past is over and gone. It can only be thought about in the present, and the future is the play of imagination, nothing more.

Bringing attention and awareness back to the present, is the action of a mind that has recognized the only purpose of life that is true and meaningful. No other purpose is worth pursuing. You may seek many things, pursue the many goals the world seems to offer you, but never will you find anything of lasting value. Nowhere will you find the peace, happiness, and fulfillment that you really need in the experiences of this world. Only Truth will restore you to life, and bring the freedom that was yours before you chose separation and death.

What would it take to demonstrate to you the meaningless-ness and ultimate futility of all pursuits that lead only to death in the end? Surely by now you have reached some understanding of the conditions of life here, their constant changeability, the shifting sands of circumstances, and the lack of anything that deserves your lasting trust. The world is not bereft of proof that happiness cannot be found within it. Is anyone you know truly happy? Have you found anything that gives you lasting happiness? Yes, there are amusements, stimulations, and distractions of all kinds, that can keep you busy indefinitely. Yet do not all these activities and their effects on you turn out to be empty and unfulfilling in the end? Don't you go from one to another, never finding lasting satisfaction of any kind? Does the restlessness of your mind ever cease and leave you in peace? We know the answers to these questions, don't we? You have more than enough evidence from your own experience to convince a rational mind that change is needed; a change of outlook, change in understanding, change in the way you think and believe and act.

The world you see has grown old and tired. Those who think they live in it, who call it their home, are sad and fearful, bereft of hope. All who are called to the Light must accept the responsibility of healing the world, one mind at a time. When you are healed, is the world's healing included. As has been so often stated, when I am healed I am not healed alone. To accept healing for yourself is to accept it for the world and everyone and everything in it. Nothing is separate from you, despite appearances. Even in the dream, mind is One, uninterrupted by time and difference.

Let your Love for your brothers pervade all that you think, do, and say. When Love rules your mind and directs your life, you will bring the blessings and Grace of God to all you know or meet or see. God's Grace is given to those who have chosen Love in the midst of darkness, forgiveness in a world of conflict. His Grace is available to all, but It cannot be received by a mind dedicated to attack. Love opens the door that Grace may enter. Grace accompanies Love as surely as sorrow accompanies hatred.

God's Grace is all encompassing; It cannot be put into words. By Grace you live, by Grace you are released. By Grace you give, by Grace you will release. All that is given by God must be shared, that It extend to the whole world and beyond. The Grace and the Love of God is the greatest Gift that can be given or received.

CHAPTER FIFTEEN

Lessons

We will conclude this supplementary teaching with a series of practical exercises whose purpose is to train and focus the mind. Each exercise is a lesson on an important theme or idea whose aim is to help bring about deeper understanding and, if possible, direct experience of the Truth which the idea represents.

There are twelve lessons given, each with very specific instructions on how, when, how long, and how often to do them. It is suggested that each lesson be done daily for one week. A total of twelve weeks of practice is thus required to receive their full benefit. It is recommended that you stay with the one lesson a week for twelve weeks guidelines, each done daily without missing any days if possible. Both the weeks' duration of practice for each lesson, and the completion of all twelve in order, are needed to achieve the maximum positive effect.

Those readers who are students and teachers of *A Course in Miracles* will recognize the similarity of these lessons to the lessons in the workbook of the Course, and they share the same goal: to help bring about direct spiritual experience that will ultimately return your mind to the Self, the Christ, that is What and Who you are.

Let yourself be guided as to whether you do these lessons or not. As has been previously stated, the lessons, like this teaching as a whole, are intended to support and supplement *A Course in Miracles*. For those who are not practitioners of the Course, the lessons can be a good introduction to some of the ideas presented in the Course, and may inspire you to take up the study and practice of *A Course in Miracles*. May all who read these pages and do these lessons, if so guided, find the spiritual help that is always waiting and available to those who truly desire it.

LESSON 1

Forgiveness Will Set Me Free

Sure it is that the world does not understand real forgiveness or its results. To the worldly mind, forgiveness is a gift from you to your brother, often unmerited, given out of the goodness of your heart. Yet deep down there remains the memory of the grievance, and the bitterness that is a part of it.

Real forgiveness arises from a very different understanding; always it is based on the recognition that your brother deserves it, no matter what the 'crime'. To truly forgive, you must accept that whatever the appearance, your brother is not guilty, for in a dream no one is really doing anything to anyone. In your dream last night in which you were perhaps threatened or attacked, made to suffer loss, did that really happen? Did you suffer loss or injury? If the figure in your dream was someone you know, when you awoke, did you blame him for what was done while you were dreaming?

The world you see in the 'waking' state, is just as much a dream as your nightly dreams. As in sleeping dreams, all you see around you is the projected imagery of your own mind. You assign yourself a role as you do with everything that appears, and whatever happens is what you have asked for. In dreams, no one is guilty, for nothing that seems to happen is real.

Simply put, this is why neither you nor your brothers are guilty. You are not bodies nor are you what the body appears to do and say in dreams. All are worthy of complete and total forgiveness. Only through this understanding and acceptance, by putting this into practice always, will your mind be healed of its belief in your guilt.

The terrible stain of guilt hidden deep in your mind, keeps you a prisoner of fear for guilt demands punishment. You must project the guilt and the need for punishment onto the world around you, for the pressure and discomfort within is unbearable. Through this constant projection do you relieve temporarily the inner pain, but never do you actually release or heal it entirely. Like a swollen wound that is periodically drained to relieve the pain it is causing, yet is the wound never healed for its cause is left untreated.

The only cure for what ails you is to renounce guilt entirely in all its forms, wherever it appears, no matter the circumstances. Deny that anyone is ever guilty. Forgive yourself and everyone and everything; only then will Love return to reclaim your mind and set you free from fear and guilt.

This exercise, like the ones that follow, will have two parts. The first part should be done twice a day, morning and evening. It can be done one or two more times each day if you feel comfortable, but do not overdo it. If there is a sense of strain or tension, you are overdoing it.

As soon as you can after waking in the morning, sit quietly where you will not be disturbed. Repeat the idea for the day several times silently to yourself with eyes closed. Completely relaxing your body, let all tension go. Follow this by relaxing your mind also; let the sense of inner awareness be calm and untroubled. Let go all thoughts of the future or the past, letting the mind be silent. Then, without straining, without a sense of struggle, gently search your mind for examples of unforgiveness. Any slights or hurts remembered, anyone you do not like, or any situation that causes you anxiety or discomfort, are all good candidates. For each one that arises to awareness, pause for a few moments and feel your unforgiveness. It may be slight irritation, anxiety, or even strong anger or rage. It does not matter. If there is any upset or negative feeling, there is unforgiveness. To each example of unforgiveness say:

In this situation regarding_____, forgiveness will set me free.

Fill in the blank with the person's name or the situation you are forgiving. Remember you are not only forgiving your brothers, you are forgiving the world and all situations, events, and circumstances that upset you. Where there is upset, no matter the cause, forgiveness is needed.

If the practice is going well, you should feel a sense of release, of relief at the conclusion of the exercise. Start with three to five minutes, no more. As the week progresses, you can increase the length to eight to ten minutes if you feel comfortable. If you seem to run out of examples, sit quietly and repeat the lesson for the day slowly to yourself. When examples occur that need forgiving, go back to the exercise. Remember to do it slowly, with no sense of hurry or strain. It is particularly helpful, if you can, to feel the upset that needs forgiving for a few moments, then repeat the lesson and move on. Repeat this exercise again in the evening. Always begin by reading the entire lesson including the exercise instructions.

During the day, remember the lesson frequently, several times an hour if possible. Close your eyes and say it silently to yourself. Be sure to use it in this form immediately if anything upsets you:

Forgiveness will set me free from this.

LESSON 2

Judgment Will Bring Me Only Pain

Today's idea, if truly understood and accepted, will free you from the awful burden of judgment you have laid upon yourself. You think that to judge another is your right. That it will bring you benefit, and help you set the world right by offering correction where it is needed. The world does not need correction, being the effect of your own thinking. Correction does not deal with effects; it must be applied to their cause.

Judgment is a weapon you use against your brother. What you do not realize is that this weapon is really directed at yourself. You think you can judge your brother without harming yourself, that you will escape the effect of your own condemnation, for to judge is to condemn. Do not forget the principle of salvation: whatever you give, you give yourself. Always this is true regardless of person, situation, or circumstance. This can also be stated thus: Whatever I do, I do to myself. All doing, no matter the apparent object of action, has its desired effect on myself though that may not have been its intent. There is no evading the effects of any action I may take.

As to judge is to condemn, and to condemn is to attack, all judgment, though meant to be an attack on my brother, is an attack on myself. The purpose of attack is to inflict harm; I will receive the pain that was my intention to inflict on my brother. If you were aware of this, truly believed and accepted it as fact, you would give up judgment altogether. No one would persist in doing what clearly causes him great pain.

There is an additional price to be paid for careless judgment. Being an attack on another, it cannot but increase my sense of being guilty. The guilt in my mind must be healed if I am to return to Truth. Every judgment I make is an attack on Truth, an attempt to delay salvation, and a needless prolonging of pain and suffering. Clearly I gain nothing from judgment despite my belief to the contrary, and through the projection of judgment, I lose everything of real value including peace of mind.

Judgment is the function of the Holy Spirit Who alone has the knowledge to judge truly. His judgment on the Son of God does not change. God's Son is forever guiltless, innocent, and loving, and deserving of his Father's Love. Turn all judgment over to Him and cease this attempt to usurp a function not your own. It was the attempt to usurp a function not your own that led to a world of illusion and all the misery it contains. Lay down this sharpened sword you hold against your own throat.

Today we will attempt to do just that. Two or three exercise periods of ten minutes each are suggested. As usual, it is best to do one in the morning, one in the evening, and one in between if you are so motivated. You can shorten this time if you find yourself feeling uncomfortable.

Sit quietly to begin with eyes closed and body relaxed. Repeat today's idea silently several times. Then calmly and without strain, search your mind for situations, people, and behavior where you are accustomed to judge. If you look honestly, you should have no difficulty finding examples of judgment. Look calmly at each example, briefly reviewing your reasons for judging, then say to yourself:

> Judgment will bring me only pain.
> It is not my function to judge.

Then move on to the next. After some minutes of this, stop and sit quietly for a few moments. Say the idea for today silently two or three times. Then go on gently searching your mind. Conclude the exercise by again repeating today's idea slowly two or three times.

As you go through your day, try to remember today's lesson frequently, several times an hour at least. Do your best not to go a long period of time without repeating today's idea. This regular remembering has a very beneficial effect on your mind and strengthens your commitment to Truth. If you find yourself in judgment of anyone or anything, stop immediately and remind yourself:

Judgment will bring me only pain.

LESSON 3

All That I See Is In My Mind

Upon first glance, this statement surely seems to be but madness. In the forgetting of the role you play in making and maintaining the world, it does appear as if there is something there before you, apart from you, beyond your control and functioning according to its own laws quite independently of your existence. Experience brings conviction, whether it be of the Truth or illusion.

Do not rest content with the belief in the reality of experience in separation. What you experience here is what you have chosen to be your reality; your experience then 'proves' it real. Everything you see represents your belief in and commitment to separation. All apparently different forms and forces are but variations on the one belief in separation. You choose what you want to believe, then send perception out to witness to its reality. It is but the play of imagination, fueled by desire, nothing more.

Today we will try a different approach. We will let reality be what it is, and use perception to discover what is true. All perception is illusion, even the unified perception of the vision of Christ. Yet does Christ's vision show you the reflection of Truth in the world of dreams. Thus is perception brought so close to knowledge that knowledge can flow across the little gap between them, and restore your mind to Truth.

Your mind is not in your body, your body is in your mind as is everything you see and experience. The world you see is the projected imagery of your mind, nothing more. It does not exist independent of your mind; it cannot for it is your invention. Today we will try to have the experience of the non-separateness of all things. We will try to take an important step that will begin to show us the Unity that is our Mind and Being.

Today's exercise require three practice periods of six to eight minutes each, one in the morning, one in the evening, and one in between when it is convenient. Begin by sitting quietly with eyes closed, in front of a window if possible. Repeat today's lesson silently to yourself once or twice. When you are ready, open your eyes and slowly look around the room. As your glance naturally falls upon a certain object, say slowly to yourself:

> This chair is in my mind.
> This book is in my mind.
> This wall is in my mind.

Look around unhurriedly and avoid deliberately picking out what you would see. Do not choose anything in particular and do not exclude anything. After you have looked around the room for a little while, close your eyes and repeat today's lesson. Then open your eyes, look out the window and repeat the exercise, looking slowly around.

> This person is in my mind.
> This tree is in my mind.
> This house is in my mind.
> This fence is in my mind.

And so on. Again, no deliberate choosing; just repeat to yourself that whatever object you see is in your mind and do not deliberately choose or exclude anything. After looking at a number of objects, close your eyes and slowly repeat today's lesson several times. To conclude, sit quietly and let your thoughts bring to mind persons or events. To each one say:

> This person_____ is in my mind.
> This situation involving_____ is in my mind.

Be sure to name them. Finally, open your eyes and say the lesson one or two times slowly followed by this reminder: Nothing that I see is separate from me.

During the rest of your day, each hour, remembering as often as you can, close your eyes and repeat the lesson slowly. Then open your eyes, slowly look around and repeat it again if the situation allows. If you can, do both parts of this exercise. If you cannot, merely do it with closed eyes or open eyes, one or the other. Set your intent to remember. Tell yourself you are doing something very important and beneficial. Try to remember. Please try. We are attempting to open your mind to the fact that it is not contained by the body or limited in any way. Your mind is everywhere.

LESSON 4

I Am The One Self

The idea of One Self that is the Self of all, does not make sense in a world where everything that appears seems to be a form, an image, separate from other forms and complete in itself. Each one thus appears to be a separate self; there seems to be an almost unlimited number of selves, each separate and different from all others. Such is the world of illusion, in which those who would be separate from their Creator and their Self, come for a little while to pretend they are what they are not until they tire of their childish game and turn their minds toward Truth.

There is One Self that is the Self of all; It is not affected by the apparent confusion of those who would forget. Yet the awareness of It has been lost to the sleeping mind. Is there a greater tragedy than this? To lose the awareness of what you are, Its Love, Its peace, and wander alone in a strange and barren land, populated by many isolated figures, each as lost and alone as you. If you could but realize the enormity of your loss, you would rush back to the Self.

The One Self is what you are. In It, you are joined with God and everything created. Even now you are still the One Self, joined with everything you see or think of. As the Self, you are Spirit, Mind, Love, and Light. Nothing in your experience here can ever take the place of your One Self. Happiness cannot be found in separation from the Self. The Christ is happiness and joy. You need not seek for them outside yourself. Only by returning to the awareness of the Self will happiness and joy be restored to you.

The exercises for this lesson will be a little different from what we have attempted so far. All that you need is already deep within you. We will attempt to reach That which is our only Self. In That lies our salvation. When once you actually experience your One Self, doubt will vanish and certainty will take its place. Do not allow doubt to hinder your progress along the way. Doubt is one of the weapons that ego uses against the Truth; it will not prevail against your single purpose.

For the longer practice periods, begin as usual by sitting quietly with eyes closed after taking a minute or two to deeply relax mind and body. Two practice periods are recommended of about ten minutes each, one in the morning, one in the evening. Begin by saying silently to yourself:

I am the One Self.
My Self is always with me.
Today I would reach my One Self.

Then let your awareness turn deeply within. Let it sink past all the thoughts, the steady stream of unnecessary noise that usually fills your awareness. Sink deeply into your mind below the steady chatter of superficial consciousness. Let your attention, your sense of self awareness, gently sink until you feel a sense of stillness and depth. Rest quietly there. Let your mind be open, receptive, not doing anything, simply resting as awareness itself. If thoughts come, do not pay attention to them. Let them come and go like shadows, passing across the surface of mind. Rest quietly beneath and beyond them, and let the One Self reveal Itself. If you should become distracted by thoughts moving across the mind, simply let them go, relax again and return to resting in simple awareness. You need do nothing; simply be present, open, rest and receive. The Holy Spirit will do the rest.

If you are doing the exercise well, you may feel a deep sense of stillness, of silence. You may feel a depth, a place in your mind that is completely empty, yet filled with strength and Presence. Or you may simply feel a sense of peace. Even if you do not feel anything in particular, this exercise is still very beneficial, and you may be sure you are receiving the benefits. When your practice period is over, quietly come back, gently open your eyes and repeat today's lesson once more. Sit quietly for a minute or so before you get up and go about the business of the day.

The shorter practice periods should be frequent throughout the day. Remember as often as you can; you will gain much thereby. If you can, close your eyes and repeat today's idea, and spend a minute or so in silence. If that is not possible, just repeat the idea silently to yourself.

LESSON 5

My Brother And I Are One

In the world in which you see yourself, your brothers appear to be separate from you. Like you, they seem to be bodies that walk and talk and move about, each with his own thoughts, goals, and aspirations, that are for him alone. Joining, except in the most superficial way, is clearly impossible in such a condition. The mind that believes in separation thinks it is part of the body, and is unable to see that in itself, it is something entirely other than a body. So long accustomed to identifying with what you are not, to being limited to a particular location occupied by a body, you do not know the limitlessness and freedom that are yours.

Your Mind extends everywhere and contains everything. Though your brother appears to be separate from you and you from him, this is but a choice you make, not a fact. Your mind and his are continuous, unseparated by the bodies that your eyes see. If you would have him be separate, that will be your experience. If you would recognize the Truth and overlook what the body's eyes see, your mind will be freed of its false containment and will extend everywhere. By learning to see with the mind as it truly is, you will understand that nothing separates you from your brother; he is in you and you are in him. You and your brother are One, joined in the One Self that is God's Holy Creation. Nothing separates you, even in the dream, unless you want it to be so.

Today we try to turn these words into experience, for it is through experience that conviction comes. The Oneness that is you and your brother, is not so difficult to reach if you are willing. One longer practice period of about ten minutes is required for this lesson, preferably at the beginning of your day. If that is not possible, any suitable time will do.

Begin by sitting quietly with eyes closed. After relaxing body and mind, repeat today's idea silently to yourself three or four times. If you notice any resistance in your mind to repeating today's idea, stop and go on to the next phase of the exercise. With no sense of strain and no attempt to search for anyone in particular, sitting quietly and attentively, let the name or image of someone in your life rise to awareness. Hold this brother gently in your mind and say silently to yourself:

My brother_____ and I are One.

Fill in the blank with the name of the person you are addressing. Repeat this idea once or twice, then let the mind go blank until the next person appears in your awareness. If no one occurs to you, sit quietly and repeat today's idea once or twice, then wait. If you feel resistance to including a particular brother in your Oneness, stop for a moment, take a deep breath, relax and try again. If resistance still arises, stop, relax, and go on to the next person.

Anyone whom you would exclude is someone you do not want to forgive and thus extend your Love to. It is particularly helpful in these cases to release the resistance if you can, and include them in the exercise. If you cannot, do not fight with yourself but move on. You can try again the following day if you are willing. It is very important to do this exercise in a relaxed and unhurried manner; do not struggle or force yourself. Conclude by repeating today's idea slowly several times.

In the shorter practice periods which should be done frequently throughout the day in all kinds of situations and circumstances, two variations are suggested: take a minute and merely repeat today's idea slowly and silently to yourself once or twice with eyes closed, then wait in silence for a short time before you open your eyes and go about your day. Alternate this if you will when feasible, by looking at a brother who is in your vicinity and saying silently to yourself:

My brother _____ and I are One.

If you don't know the name, just use the original idea. Then smile and move on.

We are attempting with this exercise to take a giant step towards the day when you will indeed directly experience the Oneness you and your brother share. You may even, during the practice periods or in between, have a glimpse or a short experience of no separation, of Oneness. Be very grateful if this occurs, for it means you are drawing near to the goal of awakening.

LESSON 6

To Hear God's Voice I Must Listen

To be told that to hear something I must listen, seems too obvious to need be stated. Yet it is the obvious that is obscured and covered over by the complexity that burdens and clouds your mind. How often do you really listen to anything that is said to you? Too often is listening marred by inattention, by a distracted and wandering mind. The untrained mind has very little control over itself. Much time is spent lost in the wandering and constantly changing movement of thought that is unceasingly active. To listen well, no matter to whom, requires that attention be stable, that you be self aware.

To listen inwardly is a different kind of listening, just as being aware inwardly is a different use of awareness. It requires a quietness of mind, a stability and openness that must be learned. To actually be willing to hear the Voice for God requires keen interest, sensitivity of mind, and the intention, even if partial, to receive guidance. This implies a measure of trust, and the recognition that help is needed. The motivation to hear God's Voice must come from you. You must make that decision, just as you decided long ago to listen to the voice of separation, the ego, and you have been faithful to that decision ever since.

To learn to listen to the Holy Spirit, and be willing to receive His communication and act on it, is an important and fundamental step on the road to freedom. Today we begin to practice taking that step. No one can take it for us; it is our decision alone.

Begin today's exercise by sitting quietly for a minute or two with eyes closed, completely relaxing the body and letting the mind become quiet. Two formal practice periods are required, morning and evening as usual, of about ten to twelve minutes each. When you feel relaxed and receptive, begin by repeating today's idea quietly to yourself two or three times. Allowing yourself to relax deeply in body and mind, rest your sense of attention in awareness itself, completely open and receptive. Let your awareness sink deep into the stillness that lies beneath all the surface chatter, the unceasing busyness of the mind. Rest in the stillness and without strain or effort, listen inwardly. What is needed is a still and quiet mind, sensitive to the movements within it. If you feel your mind wandering, becoming busy with extraneous thoughts, relax again and repeat today's idea once or twice, then return to the exercise.

If you are doing this well, you may feel a sense of contact with something deep in your mind, or a subtle feeling may arise that may translate itself into thoughts you can hear. If you are very receptive and ready, you may hear a gentle, still, small voice. Listen to it carefully. You may continue this exercise longer if you feel moved to do so and have the time. Conclude by repeating the lesson for today.

To hear God's Voice I must listen.

For the shorter practice periods, as often as you can remember, close your eyes and repeat the lesson silently to yourself. Then wait quietly for a minute, or whatever amount of time you have, for God's Voice to speak to you. You cannot remember this idea too often. What you are trying to do is very important and very holy. You are trying to open the communication channel to God's Answer to the separation and every problem you may perceive in your life. You will succeed if you try sincerely with an open heart and mind, and persevere till communication is attained. The Holy Spirit is always communicating with you, ever ready to help. You must simply open the channel at your end. The Holy Spirit is in your mind, and nothing is more natural than this communication.

LESSON 7

The Love Of God Is What I Am

Sure it is that I am Love, created by Love to be Itself. God is the Source of all Love; there is no Love but God's Love. Through the extension of His Love I was created, and through the extension of Love, I create. God created me to extend His Creation. Love is the motivating force through which everything that is real is created. Nothing exists that does not have Love as its Source. Love is what I am, what I have been, and what I will always be. In that, I have no choice.

Yet in the world I have invented to take the place of Truth, Love is absent, banished by my choice of fear, and appearing only in sickly forms limited by my unwillingness to give. Fear has become the great motivator driving behavior and determining the conditions of human life. How can that which I have invented as substitute for what God created, assume Love's role and drive It from my mind? Only in dreams could this be so; if dreams are my reality in separation, then fear is real and Love is absent.

The dream world of separation was made real in my imagination through the choice of fear and the rejection of Love. To reverse this error, I must reject fear and return to the Love in which I was created. Today it is my intent to begin to feel the Love hidden deep within me, and to choose that Love over the fear that darkens my mind and makes happiness impossible.

For today's lesson, three exercise periods are recommended, one in the morning soon after waking, one in the evening shortly before retiring, and one in between at anytime that is convenient. Each should last approximately eight to ten minutes; you can take longer if you are comfortable and feel so motivated.

Begin as usual by deeply relaxing mind and body while sitting comfortably in a quiet, undisturbed place. With eyes closed, repeat today's idea silently to yourself two or three times. Then, in a calm, unhurried manner, search your mind for situations in which you have acted unlovingly. The form of unlove does not matter, just the fact that love was absent is enough to warrant correction. Briefly review each situation in your mind but do not linger too long on any one example. Say slowly and quietly to yourself:

> In this situation involving _____, I chose fear,
> but I would choose Love instead.
> The Love of God is what I am.

Fill in the blank with a brief description. Then go on to the next example. Sometime during this exercise, pause and let your awareness sink deep within. Gently try to feel the peace and Love of God within you. If you feel something, something that seems real, stay with that feeling until it fades. Then go on as before. Conclude the exercise by repeating today's idea quietly to yourself several times.

Today's lesson should be remembered frequently as you go about your day. If you can, close your eyes and stay with it for a minute or less. Let this idea permeate your mind and fill you up. If you are in a situation where this cannot be done, merely repeat the idea slowly and silently to yourself. Try to feel the truth of it. You are Love, created in the image of God. You are merely trying to experience the Truth within you, the Truth that is you.

LESSON 8

I Am The One Light

Within you is the One Light that illuminates the universe. There is nothing this Light cannot do. It can heal all pain and sickness, erase all sorrow, and end all suffering. The Light within you can lift you up to Heaven; It is the same Light that shines there.

In this world, you do not see this Light for It is denied entry. Like Love, the Light must be denied in a world of separation built on fear. Fear excludes the Light as surely as it excludes Love. The Light, like Love, is One and all-inclusive, a part of all that God created. Yet what is One and given to all cannot enter where giving is partial and limited.

To a world shrouded in darkness, the Light comes to shine away all that is unreal. All who live in separation long to see this Light. It still lives in everyone as a tiny point of Light unseen beneath the heavy veil of ignorance that covers it. Your brothers look to you to show them the Light of Heaven. They have forgotten It long ago. You must bring the Light to all those lost in the darkness of despair and misery. But first you must reawaken It in yourself, until It shines so brightly that all sin and ignorance dissolve in Its Presence.

In the real universe that lies far beyond all illusion, all is Light, for only the creations of Light are real. This Light can be reflected here in the minds of all who love Truth, and would give all assistance possible to their brothers. You are a Light bearer, you who have chosen to serve your Father's Great Plan. But first you must awaken to the Light within you, that your mind be healed of the darkness of sin and guilt. As your mind is purified, the Light within shines more and more brightly, until It goes before you, illuminating the path you must walk. From your mind can this Light be rekindled in other minds, spreading from one to another in a long line of transmission, until the whole world stands revealed in the One Light.

Today we take a giant step in this direction as we turn our attention to the Light within us. It cannot be difficult to reach that which has always been a part of us since we were created. We need only try with firm determination and the certainty given us by the Holy Spirit.

Two practice periods are recommended for today of about ten minutes each, though you may do more if so inclined as the week unfolds. It is best to do one in the morning before you start the activities of the day, and one in the evening after you conclude the days' activities.

In a quiet place free from distractions and disturbances, say the lesson to yourself three or four times silently with eyes closed. Try to say it slowly and with conviction. The Light is in your mind and today we will try to reach It directly. Relax your body and mind completely. Turn your attention within, and let your awareness extend itself deep within, past the constant activity of thought, past all worldly concerns, deep, deep within. Let it rest in the deep silence that prevails in the depths of your mind. Rest there in a state of quiet attention; let thoughts come and go, without giving them your attention. If you remain quiet, resting your attention in awareness itself, the stream of passing thoughts will slow down and will not distract you.

Have no expectations or ideas of what to experience. Just rest in awareness; quiet, attentive, and open. If you are ready, you may actually see a Light with your inner vision. It may be brief or It may last a short while. It may even be very bright, like an inner sun. You may feel something like a force, a movement, a vibration, like a kind of energy. This experience may be very subtle, or may feel very bright, or you may feel nothing but a sense of peace or deep relaxation. Whatever you experience is good. End the exercise by silently repeating the lesson again three or four times.

Throughout the day, repeat the lesson frequently to yourself. Try not to let long periods of time go by without remembering. Frequent repetitions are more helpful than you realize. Close your eyes, say the lesson slowly to yourself once or twice, then go on with your day. Remember, the One Light shines within you as you.

LESSON 9

Only God Is

The lesson for today is liable to bring up resistance in one form or another. There is nothing more threatening to the ego than today's idea. The ego's purpose is to replace God; thereby it thinks it secures and maintains its existence. The absurdity of this belief, that a cowering and frightened little idea of existence, can by arrogance and bluster replace the Creator of the universe, is apparent to any sane mind.

However, the mind lost in separation is not sane. Crippled by fear and distorted by false purposes, it believes and adheres to the most fantastic ideas with which it has replaced Truth. Foremost is the belief that something not created by God, Who is the Source of all that is real, can exist. This belief is closely tied to the idea that I am responsible for my own creation. If I create myself then I am complete, and need answer to no one nor follow laws I did not make. This is what you believe when you usurp authority that is not yours. All the madness of this world then follows. Selfishness, greed, judgment, guilt, sin, attack; all these and more proceed from the insane idea that you created yourself, and are justified and entitled to do whatever you please without concern for others. All the laws invented to regulate human behavior, are attempts to control the chaos resulting from this authority confusion.

Truth is not affected by chaos and confusion, nor has God been dethroned from His role as Creator of all that is. You who live, move, and have your Being in God, cannot be apart from Him except in dreams of madness. Everything that is, cannot be apart from Him. Ideas leave not their source; everything created is a Thought in the Mind of God, and still remains where it has always been.

Today's idea is why the world you invented is but idle dreaming. It is why fear and separation, sin and guilt, pain and suffering, do not exist. They were not created by God and invested with His Being, therefore they are not real. Only what God has created exists, and what is not created by God does not exist. Only what lives in Him, in Truth, is. Therefore we say: Only God (Truth) is.

For the practice of today's idea, one longer practice period of about fifteen minutes is recommended. If it is going well, you can extend it a little longer. If you encounter resistance or discomfort, shorten it accordingly. Begin by sitting comfortably with eyes closed. Put a little smile on your face and say:

Only God is.
Only Truth is.

Repeat this slowly to yourself three times. Then sit quietly and let thoughts relating to your life, its conditions and problems, pass through your mind. State each condition or problem briefly in this form: This _____ does not exist in God, therefore it does not exist at all. A suitable list of thoughts might be:

This house does not exist in God.
This problem with _____ does not exist in God.
My conflict over _____ does not exist in God.
My fear about _____ does not exist in God.
This sickness_____ does not exist in God.

Do not limit your thoughts to what may be considered negative. Include neutral or even positive references.

My new car does not exist in God.
This snowstorm does not exist in God.
My coming trip to _____ does not exist in God.
This sidewalk does not exist in God.

Be sure to follow each example with:

Therefore it does not exist at all.

After several examples have been considered, repeat today's idea. Then move on.

Spend half of today's practice period with this exercise, then stop and sit quietly. Repeat today's idea and let your mind be still. See if you can feel a sense of vastness, or of Light unlimited. Perhaps you will feel peace, or a deep sense of relaxation. In any case, sit quietly and let Truth come. If your mind begins to wander, repeat today's idea once or twice, then return to stillness.

For the shorter practice periods which should be done once or twice an hour, close your eyes and repeat the idea for today. Then spend a minute or so in silence, letting Truth be. If you are not in a situation where this can be done, simply repeat today's lesson slowly once or twice, eyes open or closed. That is enough. Open your mind and heart to Truth today. Let your Father's Voice speak to you.

LESSON 10

I Live In God

To the mind lost in the darkness of illusion, today's idea makes no sense. In fact, to the mind of ignorance, asleep to the reality of its own Being, this is madness, a thought not even worthy of serious consideration. In the midst of an experience of life characterized by fear, misery, and chaos, subject to pain, suffering, and death, any thought of God does indeed seem superfluous. The mind of separation does not realize it has banished God from its world, and fears and hates its Creator. How otherwise could the world you see have arisen unless God was absent from the mind that invented it?

Today we attempt to bring God back to the world that thought it could expel Him, and expunge even His memory. God is not mocked. He is still everywhere and in everything forever. He cannot be absent from your world because He is in your mind and you still abide in His. Actively kept from your awareness however, He cannot be experienced nor can you receive His help until you change your mind.

The Holy Spirit's goal is just this change of mind, that you be made ready and willing for your Father's return. The mind must be purified and emptied of all that obstructs the awareness of God's Presence. The fear of God that lies deep in your mind, must be brought to the Light of awareness and released, that the way be clear for the reunion of the Father and the Son.

We will take a big step today towards the time of that reunion. What is important for the success of this exercise is the awareness that you are attempting something very holy. You are attempting to reach your Father, the Creator of all that is, and welcome Him back to your awareness. We will not let old ideas of fear or unworthiness interfere with our single purpose. We will remember that we are His Creation, a part of Him that can never be separated. Our holiness mirrors His, all that we are is His gift, and we have no life but what we share with Him. God is not far away from us; He can be reached if the mind is clear and quiet and the heart sincere.

For today's longer practice period, fifteen to twenty minutes is recommended. Make sure you are in a place that is very quiet, where you will not be disturbed. Remember who you are and your real relationship with your Creator. Put aside all worries, considerations, plans; let all extraneous thoughts go. Sit comfortably with eyes closed, body relaxed, and breathing slow and even. Repeat today's idea slowly and gently to yourself several times. Let your mind be completely open and receptive. Gently turn your attention inward and let it rest in the core of your Being, in the heart of you. In the silence and stillness of Being, rest quietly without effort. Let be what would be. If you are disturbed by extraneous thoughts, repeat today's idea slowly several times, then return to silence. You need do nothing, just allow what needs to happen to occur. If you are doing today's exercise well and are ready, you may feel a sense of deep peace, or happiness, perhaps even a feeling of subtle presence. In any case, no matter what happens, today's exercise sincerely done, will help pave the way for the return of the awareness of God's Presence.

For the shorter practice periods which should be done several times an hour or more, close your eyes and repeat today's idea slowly and with feeling. Try to get a sense that this is not just an idea, this is true, a fact of your existence. Spend a minute with eyes closed, feeling the Truth of what you are. If you cannot, due to circumstances or time constraints, just repeat to yourself quietly:

I live in God.
And I am glad that is so.

LESSON 11

What Do I Really Want

This is the question that is seldom asked in a way that illuminates the mind that asks it. The mind of separation seldom asks itself questions that would induce serious consideration of motives or the values on which they are based. Typically, you see something that attracts you be it a person, situation, activity, or thing, and you react to that attraction. There may be some consideration of the goal in a superficial way, but your response to attraction, to desire, is automatic and self justifying. Seldom is it seriously examined or understood.

Why do I want it is never asked. To do so would require a serious examination of values, and what they are designed to hide. The sleeping mind does not want to disturb its comfortable slumber. The many wants and desires you have, have very little to do with what you really need. And what you really need is what you really want.

Today we will attempt to uncover what you really need. When that question is answered, you will know what you really want. In truth, to want and to need are the same. To bring them together as one will make salvation possible. All the things you think you want are but a smoke screen to keep what you really need from your awareness. Their result is the continuation of a life based on illusion, chasing shadows with the ego as your guide.

For today, one longer practice session is recommended, preferably at the start of your day. If that is not possible, whenever you can find the time will do. Start this exercise of fifteen to twenty minutes by sitting quietly with eyes closed. When you feel relaxed and ready, repeat today's idea to yourself, then watch as your mind responds with a long list of things that have no meaning. Let all your desires, all your wanting of what you think you do not have, of what you think you need, be revealed. Do not censor or resist, but let all wanting, regardless of its nature, present itself to you nakedly. You may, for example, experience thoughts such as these:

> I want a new _____ .
> I want a better relationship with _____ .
> I want to achieve _____ .

Fill in the blank appropriately. It does not matter what the nature of the desire, let it come up. After each example, ask yourself this question:

> Is this what I really want?

You may find as the exercise progresses that this question will make you uneasy, for it is asking you to look deeply at what you value and give importance to. You are questioning part of the foundation of your life, that which gives it meaning and purpose. If uneasiness occurs, stop the questioning process and sit quietly for a minute, then resume the exercise. If discomfort persists, discontinue and sit quietly, eyes closed, for the remainder of the exercise period, watching your thoughts and letting them go one by one. If uneasiness does not persist, continue with the exercise. When no more examples are forthcoming, ask yourself once again:

What do I really want?

This time, try to go beyond the more superficial level of answers and let your mind reveal itself. Listen carefully to what you hear. Your deepest yearning is for peace, happiness, and Wholeness. You want to love and be loved, not partially but completely. Deep within, you long to be reunited with your Father. You long to know once again His Love for you and your Love for Him. Do not be concerned if you are unable to receive these deeper answers to your question. By doing this lesson, you are taking a significant step in their direction. The real answer to your question will be given you, perhaps now, perhaps later. It is the answer you really want, the only answer you truly need.

For the shorter exercise periods which should be done throughout the day, once an hour at least, close your eyes and ask once again:

What do I really want?

Then spend a minute or two in silence waiting for the answer. It will come.

LESSON 12

God Is My Only Need

No one living in this world realizes there is only one need just as you do not realize there is only one problem. Fulfilling your only need is the solution to your only problem. The Truth Itself is very simple. It is the ego, the mind of separation, that is complicated and convoluted. The many problems arising from complexity and confusion cannot be solved on the level on which they manifest. They can only be resolved on the level from which they originate. The mind is the origin of all problems. Its belief in separation gives rise to all the problems you think you have. As long as the belief in the reality of illusions persists, your life will be marked by a constant parade of problems that call for a response. As soon as one situation is resolved, another will arise to take its place. And so it will go, on and on until you are ready to recognize the single nature of what appears as many. The one problem you have is separation from God, your only Source, and thus separation from the Truth of what you are. If the one problem is thus one of lack, then the answer is to fill that lack.

To return to God is your only need. In Truth, you have never left your home in your Father, yet in a world of dreams it does seem as if He is absent from your experience. Your experience then becomes one of lack and loss, and the constant struggle to find and keep what you seemingly lack, and prevent the loss of what you think you need. In this condition, peace and happiness will elude you, and fear will be your constant companion in one form or another.

There is one solution to all that ails you; it is the one thing you really need. God is your only need. When you return to the full awareness of His Presence in you, the direct knowledge of your real relationship with Him, the world and all its problems will vanish, and you will be again as you have always been.

Today, with the exercise we do, we will take a step towards conscious reunion with our Father. Our longer practice period of fifteen to twenty minutes can be done at any time during the day when convenient, although using it to begin the day is best. While sitting quietly with eyes closed, repeat today's lesson slowly and clearly to yourself several times:

God is my only need.

Sit quietly and let the truth of this statement dawn on your mind. Let your mind go deep, beneath the surface consciousness, beyond the flow of thoughts and images that dominate it. Let it sink into the depths where peace and stillness prevail, where the memory of your Father waits but for the opportunity to return to your awareness and set you free.

In the shorter practice periods which should be done throughout the day, several times an hour if you remember, close your eyes briefly and repeat the lesson silently to yourself:

God is my only need.

Try for a few moments to feel the truth of this. Let it penetrate your mind.

Epilogue

Thank you my brother for your efforts on behalf of us all and your dedication to our single purpose. Let every step on the journey home be guided by the Holy Spirit, and do not worry if at times you seem to falter or grow weary. The journey may seem long and arduous, the goal far off and beyond your vision; all will come right in the end. You need only do your part each day to the best of your ability, ask for help, and trust in the help you are given. Everything you need in any way will be available when you need it.

Do not forget Who goes with you every step of the way and remember, when doubt and fear may arise, their meaningless source and illusory nature. Nothing will or can prevent you from returning to your Source and True Condition as the One Self. Your Father waits for you and all the angels will rejoice as you walk through the Gates of Heaven and disappear into the Heart of God.

CPSIA information can be obtained
at www.ICGtesting.com
Printed in the USA
LVOW10s0025230418
574487LV00025B/852/P